Frustrated Fellowship

Frustrated Fellowship

The Black Baptist Quest
for Social Power

by

James Melvin Washington

M·E·R·C·E·R

ISBN 0-86554-191-4 (cloth)
ISBN 0-86554-192-2 (paper)

The paper used in this publication meets
the minimum requirements of American National Standard
for Information Sciences—Permanence of Paper
for Printed Library Materials, ANSI Z39.48-1984.

Library of Congress Cataloging-in-Publication Data

Washington, James Melvin
Frustrated fellowship

   Bibliography: p. 209.
   Includes index.
   1. Afro-American Baptists—History. I. Title.
BX6443.W37   1986   286'.08996073   85-31955
ISBN 0-86554-191-4 (alk. paper)
ISBN 0-86554-192-2 (pbk. : alk. paper)

Contents

Dedication

To

The Reverend William Townsend Crutcher, D.D.

*Pastor of the Mount Olive Baptist Church
of Knoxville, Tennessee, for fifty years*

*Chairman of the Publishing Board
of the National Baptist Convention, U.S.A., Inc.*

Civil Rights Leader

My Dearly Beloved Father in the Ministry

and to

The Reverend Gardner Calvin Taylor, D.D.

*Pastor of the Concord Baptist Church of Christ
Brooklyn, New York, for thirty-seven years*

*Former President
of the Progressive National Baptist Convention*

Legendary Pulpiteer

Fighter for Justice and Freedom

My Dearly Beloved Friend and Pastor

Nota bene: Jesus prayed, ''I do not pray for these only, but also for those who believe in me through their word, that they may all be one; even as thou, Father, art in me, and I in thee, that they also may be in us, so that the world may believe that thou hast sent me. The glory which thou hast given me I have given to them, that they may be one even as we are one.'' (John 17: 20-22, RSV)

Abbreviations

ABFMS American Baptist Free Mission Society (integrated)
ABHMS American Baptist Home Mission Society (white)
ABMC American Baptist Missionary Convention (black)
ABMU American Baptist Missionary Union (Northern white
 foreign mission agency)
ABPS American Baptist Publication Society (white)
ANBC American National Baptist Convention (black)
BFMC Baptist Foreign Mission Convention (black)
BGA Baptist General Association of Western States
 and Territories (black)
CABMC Consolidated American Baptist Missionary Convention (black)
LCFMC Lott Carey Foreign Mission Convention (black)
NBC National Baptist Convention (black)
NBCI National Baptist Convention, U. S. A., Inc. (black)
NBEC National Baptist Educational Convention (black)
NBCU National Baptist Convention of America,
 Unincorporated (black)
NHFMS National Home and Foreign Missionary Society (black)
NPBC National Primitive Baptist Convention (black)
NwSBC Northwestern and Southern Baptist Convention (black)
PNBC Progressive National Baptist Convention (black)
SBC Southern Baptist Convention (white)

Nota Bene: Parentheses indicate what racial group controlled the affairs of the organization.

Preface

The culture shock engendered by New World slavery brought pain and psychic disorientation.[1] Whenever the ancient absurdity of the slave experience invaded their personal histories, the Africans became early modern "stalkers after meaning." The experience of captivity disrupted the ritual and mythic patterns of the religions of their homeland. And in that very disorientation their slavery provided the opportunity—indeed the necessity—of a new religious synthesis. The call to repentance and the promise of mercy set forth by the preachers of the Great Awakening and successive waves of evangelical fervor took hold of the distressed souls of some of the slaves. This fresh emphasis on spiritual renewal helped these slaves to gain a new sense of self-worth.[2]

---

[1]I do not share the conviction of some scholars, such as Stanley M. Elkins (*Slavery: A Problem in American Institutional and Intellectual Life*, 3rd ed., rev. [Chicago: University of Chicago Press, 1976]) who argue that slavery created a culture of dependence on the masters. John Blassingame argues a more balanced view: "[T]he slave had many referents for self-esteem, for instance, other than his master. In religion, a slave exercised his own independence of conscience." Religion also helped preserve the mental health of the slaves. See John W. Blassingame, *The Slave Community: Plantation Life in the Antebellum South*, rev. and enl. (New York: Oxford University Press, 1979) 310-11.

[2]The origins of slave religion from the standpoint of cultural anthropology have been ably examined by Albert J. Raboteau in his *Slave Religion: The Invisible Institution in the Antebellum South* (New York: Oxford University Press, 1978). Blassingame, *Slave Community*, offers the most helpful discussion of the psychological value of slave religion. Eugene D. Genovese (*Roll, Jordan, Roll: The World the Slaves Made* [New York: Pantheon Books, 1974] 202-84) proposes the boldest interpretation of the slaves' social and psychological condition and the evangelical response to it. Donald G. Mathews (*Religion in the Old South* [Chicago: University of Chicago Press, 1977] 136-236), on the other hand, offers an analysis that is more detailed and far better informed by a knowledge of Southern *religious* history. The work of John B. Boles (*Black Southerners, 1619-1869* [Lexington KY: University Press of Kentucky, 1984]) is a fine historical introduction to the general life and culture of antebellum black Southerners.

This process was not orderly nor did it lead to what Stanley Elkins calls "infantilization."[3] The contrary is true. Slave children and adults had to think hard and quickly in order to survive the often intentional, yet sometimes unwitting, attempt to destroy their African cultural heritage. To argue that this heritage either stayed intact or was totally destroyed is thoroughly to misconstrue the dialectics of cultural contact.[4]

On the other hand, with the exception of some slave preachers, the appropriation of the new evangelical faith rarely signaled any important change in the status, needs, or outward burdens of the slave. Very gradually in the eighteenth century an increasing number of slave owners came to believe that the converted slave was a "better" slave. While that question cannot be taken up here, there is evidence that the evangelical movement among slaves tried with minimal success to be a channel of acculturation and social control. The congregations gathered by slave preachers were important centers of communal and psychic solace. They could do little to alter the status of the enslaved communicant. By contrast the independent congregations of the urban free black Northern and Southern communities played a much larger role in initially shaping the social status of their constituents.

The emergence of both free black preachers and independent black Baptist congregations in the 1780s was a momentous achievement for the African slave community in America. It was the closest thing to revolutionary expression available to them. Perhaps William Ernest Hocking was correct in his belief that "mystic experience," like that of the slaves, "must complete itself in prophetic consciousness."[5] Those white ritualists of

---

[3]Elkins, *Slavery,* 86-87, 111-12, 130-32, and 308-309.

[4]Much of the debate over the processes of cultural contact depends on the work of Robert E. Park, who drew his basic concept of marginality from a misunderstanding of Georg Simmel's famous essay, "The Stranger." See Donald N. Levine, "Simmel at a Distance: On the History and Systematics of the Stranger" in William A. Shack and Elliott P. Skinner, eds., *Strangers in African Societies* (Berkeley: University of California Press, 1979) 21-36; Robert Ezra Park, *Race and Culture: Essays in the Sociology of Contemporary Man* (1950; reprint, New York: Free Press, 1964); and E. Franklin Frazier, *Race and Culture Contacts in the Modern World* (Boston: Beacon Press, 1957).

[5]William Ernest Hocking, *The Meaning of God in Human Experience* (1912; reprint, New Haven: Yale University Press, 1924) 511.

"consensus"[6] who supported the American Revolution certainly believed this. Nonetheless, while the American, French, and Haitian revolutions received both actual and more often tacit religious support, the slaves benefited only gradually from the creation of a new egalitarian impulse. Something far more subtle and cunning lay in store for African-Americans.

They became religious "subversive genealogists"[7] devoted to a cosmology of deep moral and religious redemption, and committed as well to resisting the slave regime. What was at stake for them was not only their eventual material freedom, but resurrection from what Orlando Patterson calls "natal alienation" or "social death."[8] White society tried to erase slave memories of Africa, reduce slaves to the status of dependent children, and often tried to argue that they had no souls. These efforts did not succeed. The slaves' resistance to "thingification" was passionate and persistent. We see this poignant human drama disclosed with verve and power in the black struggle for religious freedom.

Indeed, several scholars[9] assert that the freedom motif is the central motif of all dimensions of the history of Africans in the Western Hemisphere. As Edward L. Wheeler correctly argues, this is certainly a central theme in the history of the black Baptist movement.[10] Freedom is also a major motif in other phases of American history as well. I agree with Hegel that the idea of freedom is the modus vivendi of history itself.[11] Never-

---

[6]Sacvan Bercovitch, *The American Jeremiad* (Madison: University of Wisconsin Press, 1978) 132-75.

[7]See Judith N. Shklar, "Subversive Genealogies" in Clifford Geertz, ed., *Myth, Symbol, and Culture* (New York: W. W. Norton, 1971) 129-54.

[8]Orlando Patterson, *Slavery and Social Death: A Comparative Study* (Cambridge MA: Harvard University Press, 1982).

[9]The larger story using the paradigm of freedom, at least for the antebellum period, is eloquently narrated by Vincent Harding in *There Is a River: The Black Struggle for Freedom in America* (New York: Vintage Books, 1983).

[10]Edward L. Wheeler, "Beyond One Man: A General Survey of Black Baptist Church History," *Review and Expositor* 70,3 (Summer 1973): 309-19.

[11]According to Hegel, "The History of the world is none other than the progress of the consciousness of freedom; a progress whose development according to the necessity if its nature, it is our business to investigate." See Georg Wilhelm Friedrich Hegel, *The Philosophy of History*, trans. J. Sibree (1899; reprint, New York: Dover Publications, 1956) 19.

theless, most scholars of religion in America fail to relate this general impulse to struggles involving church politics. The status quo, often called the "mainline"[12] churches, receives the limelight. Those who dissent from the status quo are called "dissenters" and "protesters," and are usually seen through paternalistic lenses. Thus the black church movement is often characterized as a protest movement, part of a great tradition of dissent in American history.[13] Those who endure such deviants are dubbed "tolerant;" those who do not indulge them are called, of course, "intolerant." The history of religious liberty is often called the history of religious toleration.[14] Ironically, this old insider/outsider[15] dichotomy often helps to perpetuate religious classism because it assumes that those who have wealth and power are somehow immune to barbarity. They are the norm for civilized behavior. All others are delightful deviants, freaks, or protesters.

The spirit of African-American Protestantism certainly involved protest. But more than this was at risk. As Robert McAfee Brown has argued, "no faith, Protestantism least of all, lives by its denials. The denials, unless they are simply neurotic, are by-products of the affirmations."[16] The founders of the black church movement were strong believers in religious freedom. They led black folk in affirming what they believed to be the natural, God-given right to freedom. But this was not a notion of freedom without responsibility. Souls had to be saved, brothers and sisters in bondage had to be liberated, churches had to be organized and built. In the early

----

[12]For example, see Martin E. Marty, *A Nation of Behavers* (Chicago: University of Chicago Press, 1976) 52-79.

[13]Edwin S. Gaustad, *Dissent in American Religion* (Chicago and London: University of Chicago Press, 1973) 32-35.

[14]Roland H. Bainton, *The Travail of Religious Liberty* (New York: Harper and Brothers, 1951) 229-52.

[15]The classic essay on this theme is Robert K. Merton, "Insiders and Outsiders: A Chapter in the Sociology of Knowledge," *American Journal of Sociology* 78,1 (July 1972): 9-47. *American Historical Review* Forum recently featured a debate about the methodological issues this theme raises for historians. See R. Laurence Moore, "Insiders and Outsiders in American Historical Narrative and American History," *American Historical Review* 87 (1982): 390-412. Edwin S. Gaustad and Gene Wise comment on this article and Moore replies on pages 413-23.

[16]Robert McAfee Brown, *The Spirit of Protestantism* (New York: Oxford University Press, 1961) 5.

stages, this often involved covenanting with white churches to form what one able scholar calls "biracial congregations."[17] But it also entailed worshiping more freely in clandestine gatherings like the early Christians who met in the catacombs of Rome.

Baptists played a major role in this struggle. But too much focus upon institutional vehicles for this struggle has often eclipsed its equally important "countercultural" character. Baptists and Methodists of this period helped to produce a distinct political religious culture. Rhys Isaac marshals solid evidence to argue that "the social world of the Baptists seems so striking a negative image of gentry-dominated milieus that it must be considered to have been shaped to a large extent in reaction to the dominant culture."[18] Isaac does not extend this judgment to the slaves. He agrees with Mechal Sobel[19] that their distinctiveness was largely cultural. But scholars overlook the symbolic politics of slave religious practices. If the lower class whites who populated the early Baptist movement in the South were essentially counter-cultural, certainly African-American slaves were more authentically counter-cultural than lower class whites who were on a different social and economic level, but were not culturally distinct. I agree that powerful cultural distinctives were operating among black slaves. But these distinctives were not devoid of political content.

The political cosmology of their own internal social world and that of their oppressors both thoroughly shaped the cultural milieu of the slaves. The powerful political ambience of the slave quarters cannot be separated from the various religious polities that gradually became available to the slaves after the Separate Baptists and Methodists invaded the South from 1760 onward. Religious options were also political, and vice versa. In other words, the popular theological discourse available to the slaves was also a

---

[17]Kenneth K. Bailey, "Protestantism and Afro-Americans in the Old South: Another Look," *Journal of Southern History* 41 (November 1975): 451-72.

[18]Rhys Isaac, *The Transformation of Virginia, 1740-1790* (Chapel Hill: University of North Carolina Press, 1982) 163-64.

[19]Mechal Sobel, *Trabelin' On: The Slave Journey To An Afro-Baptist Faith* (Westport CT: Greenwood, 1979). Excellent studies of the cultural distinctiveness of slave culture and the issue of African retentions should also be consulted: Sidney W. Mintz and Richard Price, *An Anthropological Approach to the Afro-American Past: A Caribbean Perspective* (Philadelphia: Institute for the Study of Human Issues, 1976); Monica Schuler, "Afro-American Slave Culture," *Historical Reflections/Reflexions Historiques* 6,1 (Summer 1979): 121-37.

political discourse. The faith content of this discourse[20] was peculiarly African-American because it was situational. The religious discourse and rituals of slaves were quite African. How could it be otherwise? It strikes me as rather evasive to argue that the primary difference between the idioms of black and lower class white worship is found in the "absence in Afro-American life of a sharp line between the religious and secular."[21] The critical difference was not this dichotomy. The critical difference was in the total situation. The *Sitz im Leben* of the slaves demanded that they become some kind of community. But this was indeed a frustrating enterprise, like making ancient Egyptian bricks without straw.

Despite the difficulties I find in the prodigious scholarship of Rhys Isaac, he offers a most important contribution to this discussion by correctly arguing that religious worship shaped a political culture. Religious dramaturgy,[22] which the church calls "liturgy," carries both "cultic" and "political" connotations.[23] Liturgy is the theological term for what anthropologists call "ritual." Even in this scholarly camp, there seems to be broad agreement that liturgies or rituals are "political tactics by which, in the absence of more direct political tactics, both performers and observers may gauge each other's future intentions and attempt to manipulate and monitor current public opinion."[24] The "public" referred to here does not have to be the general public. Indeed, it is more often than not those who

------

[20]For a more complete discussion of the faith content of the theological discourse of slaves, as well as other issues related to African-American spirituality, see the extensive introduction in James Melvin Washington, ed., *Afro-American Protestant Spirituality* (Ramsey NJ: Paulist Press, 1986).

[21]Isaac, *Transformation*, 307.

[22]This highly suggestive concept receives a powerful application in Abner Cohen (*The Politics of Elite Culture: Explorations in the Dramaturgy of Power in Modern African Society* [Berkeley: University of California Press, 1981] 144-215), a brilliant taxonomy of the Creole elite in Sierra Leone. See also Tracy B. Strong, "Dramaturgical Discourse and Political Enactments: Toward an Artistic Foundation for Political Space," in Richard Harvey Brown and Stanford M. Lyman, eds., *Structure, Consciousness, and History* (Cambridge: Cambridge University Press, 1978) 237-60.

[23]See Paul Lehmann's discussion of this relation in his *Ethics in a Christian Context* (New York: Harper and Row, 1963) 102-103.

[24]Karen Ericksen Paige and Jeffrey M. Paige, *The Politics of Reproductive Ritual* (Berkeley: University of California Press, 1981) 48. See also Theodore W. Jennings, "On Ritual Knowledge," *Journal of Religion* 62,2 (April 1982): 111-27.

inhabit one's social world. Those slaves who found themselves in a genuinely "liminal"[25] situation were trapped inside a social world that both absolved and deflected the values of the larger society. I offer my reading of these developments in chapter 1.

Chapter 2 discusses the relation between abolitionism and the formation of the first black Baptist associations. Chapters 3, 4, and 5 deal with the church politics, race relations, and the relation between religious and secular politics during Reconstruction. Chapters 6 and 7 deal with the consequences of the ascendancy of the separatist spirit among African-American Baptists. I conclude with an Epilogue that reflects on the meaning of the quest for social power in the twentieth century. I discuss questions and resources that greatly assisted in the production of this book in the Bibliographical Essay. I hope it will also be helpful to others who would like to do research and writing in this area.

This work began as a Yale dissertation, and has been revised for this publication. I conceived it when I visited the Sunday School Publishing Board of the National Baptist Convention, U. S. A., Inc. in the summer of 1962 while on a Youth Retreat at the American Baptist Theological Seminary in Nashville, Tennessee. There is a large display in the main hallway of this old building which features the one hundred ministers who donated the first $100 toward the construction of this building in the 1920s. In addition to answering my call to the ministry, I also was inspired by the oral histories of the heroes of this gigantic movement, the largest organization in Afro-America. I later tried to find information about them. I discovered that they were not in the history books. A nagging curiosity about them, as well as a profound introduction to the study of religion at the University of Tennessee in Knoxville under David Dungan, Gerald Larson, David Linge, Ralph Norman, and Charles Reynolds, and to the study of American church history at Harvard Divinity School under William R. Hutchison and Charles Conrad Wright, led me to Yale University.

I learned quickly that librarians are among those peculiar and wonderful blessings that God has bestowed on the determined scholar. I owe a special debt of gratitude for the immense understanding and assistance given to me, expecially in light of my many idiosyncrasies, by Dr. Maria Gross-

---

[25]Victor Turner, *The Ritual Process: Structure and Anti-Structure* (Ithaca NY: Cornell University Press, 1969) 94-130.

man of Harvard Divinity School, Dr. Stephen Peterson of Yale Divinity School, the Reverend Dr. Robert M. Malloy of Union Theological Seminary, New York, the Reverend Edward Starr and Dr. William H. Brackney of the American Baptist Historical Society, and Dr. Lynn E. May of the Historical Commission of the Southern Baptist Convention.

My personal debts are enormous. But at the top of the list is the gracious and exceptionally competent advice given me by Professor Sydney Eckman Ahlstrom, my much beloved doctoral adviser, who died on 3 July 1984. His encyclopedic knowledge of American religious history, massive intellect, and powerful yet quite charming wit are greatly missed by all of us who care about the history of religion in America.

Several esteemed colleagues gave criticism and advice beyond the call of duty. They include John W. Blassingame, James H. Cone, William B. Gravely, Robert T. Handy, Samuel S. Hill, Albert J. Raboteau, Edwin S. Redkey, Lester B. Scherer, and many others too numerous to mention. I owe a special debt to Professor C. Vann Woodward who guided me in the production of the core paper for this work in his graduate seminar on the New South. That paper now appears in this work, greatly revised, as chapters 6 and 7. These able professional scholars tried their best to offer good advice. Any faults in this work are mine alone and not theirs.

Financial assistance in the form of research grants and fellowships from Harvard Divinity School, the National Woodrow Wilson Fellowship, the Fund for Theological Education, Yale Divinity School, Union Theological Seminary, New York, and the Historical Commission of the Southern Baptist Convention reminds me of the depth of human compassion. A special word of thanks in this regard must go to President Donald W. Shriver, Jr., Dean Milton McCormick Gatch, Jr., and faculty colleagues at the great Union Theological Seminary in the City of New York who believed in me during some very trying days and sealed that belief with several generous grants from Union's Faculty Research Fund. I cannot express the meaning of the deep personal and intellectual friendships I enjoy with Professor Cornel West of Yale Divinity School, Professor James A. Forbes, Jr., of Union, the Reverend Mr. Obie Wright, Jr., Monsieur Nathaniel Everett Ellis, Dr. Genna Rae McNeil, numerous colleagues belonging to the Northeastern Seminar for the Study of Black Religion, and the Society for the Study of Black Religion. Sharon Abner typed the dissertation version, and Brian and Constance D'Agostino faithfully typed this version on computer diskettes. My Kaypro 4 helped me do the rest. Technophobia is not one of my fears.

I must add that the *title* for this book is borrowed from a lecture by the late Reverend Dr. Sandy F. Ray, the famous pastor of the Cornerstone Baptist Church of Brooklyn, New York, at Yale Divinity School, just a few months before his death in 1981. He spoke in moving terms about the joys of being the pastor of a people that had known slavery, the evils of racism, and economic injustice. He referred to the national life of black Baptists as a ''frustrated fellowship'' whose unfocused collective power is one of the great tragedies of African-American religious history.

My deepest gratitude and love goes to Patricia, my spouse who lovingly endures a single-minded scholar and bibliophile as he pursues his calling. Her support is a monument to the preciousness of covenants made in the embrace of faith, hope, and love. My daughter Ayanna provided sunshine on cloudy days and a daily supply of joy. The strength and precious love of my mother, Annie Beatrice Washington, has been a model of courage and endurance. My father, James William Washington, who now sleeps, questioned the usefulness of this pursuit. I believe he now understands.

Part I

Roots
of a Charismatic
Pedagogy

The Formation
of the Chattel Church:
The Baptist Phase

The history of Black Baptists is intimately interwoven with the general history of Baptists in the United States. Baptists are correctly viewed as a series of voluntary associations in pursuit of the fulfillment of certain missionary goals. But pursuit of these goals has often been frustrated because Baptists have had difficulty reaching consensus on the proper polity needed to achieve those goals outside the local congregation. Major scholars such as Winthrop S. Hudson and Robert T. Handy have devoted a considerable portion of their professional lives to attempts to unravel the tangled history of this struggle to create a viable polity.[1] The mission of most Baptist causes has usually been quite clear, but effective collective organization beyond the local congregation has often eluded this branch of American Christianity. This has been an important continuing struggle. Before narrating how Black Baptists both claim partnership in this drama and deviate from it, some clarity about the relation between polity and power on the one hand, and the theological conviction of social movements on the other, seems in order.

Talcott Parsons's way of relating polity and power is quite useful in this context. He argues that "the goal or function of a polity I conceive to

---

[1]See Winthrop S. Hudson, *Baptists in Transition: Individualism and Christian Responsibility*, foreword by Robert T. Handy (Valley Forge PA: Judson Press, 1979).

be . . . attainment of *collective* goals.'' He then relates polity to power:
''The 'product' of the polity as a system is power, which I would like to
define as the generalized capacity of a social system to get things done in
the interest of collective goals.''[2] The power that results from collective
covenants is what I call ''social power.'' Understanding the doctrinal links
of any organization or movement, be it secular or religious, helps us to understand the nature, shape, and frustrations of collective social power. If
a group has no common purpose, it is inchoate, diffused, powerless. But
if it does have a common purpose or mission, it has power. According to
George Lundberg and his collaborators, ''To the extent that a voluntary
association has a 'mission,' it can be referred to as a *social movement.*''[3]

Given these definitions, let me assert at the outset that the collective
mission of black Baptists both merges and diverges from the general Baptist quest for social power. I turn now to the task of relating this aspect of
the story in order to examine the personal covenants that black Baptists
made with God and the major corporate covenants they made with each
other. Tracing the sources, contours, and reasons why black Baptists
yearned for these social bonds helps us see how they used their social power.
The black Baptist story, however, is not a segregated series of happenings.
It is part of the history of Christianity itself. So we begin at the beginning.

Baptist Beginnings

Some Baptists maintain that there has been a continuous succession of
Baptist congregations since the time of John the Baptist, Jesus, and the
Apostles. Other Baptists cite the continental Anabaptists of the sixteenth
century as the major progenitors of the Baptist movement. Despite these
disagreements, most scholars now locate the origins of the Baptist movement among certain seventeenth-century British Puritans, who differed
from other Puritans regarding two doctrinal points. They believed in baptism by immersion rather than by sprinkling, and in baptizing adult believers rather than infants. Baptists believed that these practices followed
necessarily from their own Puritan interpretation of the New Testament,

---

[2]Talcott Parsons, *Structure and Process in Modern Societies* (New York: Free Press, 1960) 181.

[3]George A. Lundberg, Clarence C. Schrag, Otto N. Larsen, and William R. Catton, Jr., *Sociology,* 4th ed. (New York: Harper and Row, 1968) 631.

by which the true church is "a body of believers who have been regenerated and sanctified."[4] After the development of these views among a group of estranged Puritans in the Netherlands, the Baptist remnant of these expatriates returned to England under the leadership of Thomas Helwys and established a congregation in London in 1611 or 1612. Another congregation with similar views was formed by Henry Jacob in 1616, but refused to leave the Church of England. And a third was organized by John Spilsbury in 1638.

Meanwhile, about this same time, Baptists appeared in America. A few bravely raised their heads in Massachusetts Bay. Henry Dunster, the first president of Harvard, was among their number and suffered the consequences when he was dismissed from his position. Because of this hostile religious environment, only a few Baptist congregations arose in the Bay colony. The real locus of Baptist strength in seventeenth-century America was in neighboring Rhode Island. The universalist views of the "General" Baptists, who believed that Christ died for all and not only for an elect, were pervasive in seventeenth-century Rhode Island. But the "Particular" Baptists, who believed that Christ died for an elect few, represented the major Baptist theological party in eighteenth-century British America. This more rigid theological conviction guaranteed that a dependable Providence would provide psychic and even material security needed in a rapidly changing society.

Particular Baptists became especially strong in the Middle Colonies. This growth was largely directed by the efficient missionary work of the Philadelphia Association, formed in 1707. This famous association of congregations grew so rapidly that by 1767 two subsidiary associations, the Warren in New England and the Ketocton in Virginia, had to be formed. Although much of this Particular Baptist growth resulted from the labors of their own missionaries, the largest influx came as a result of the "Great Awakening," a mass religious revival that swept through the colonies between 1730 and up to (and beyond) the end of the French and Indian War in 1763.

In New England the Awakening produced the Separate Baptists. Numerous "New Light" (or revivalistic) Congregational churches became

---

[4]Albert Henry Newman, *A History of the Baptist Churches in the United States* (New York: Christian Literature, 1894) 3.

Baptist. These Baptists may be characterized as revivalistic hyper-Partic-
ulars; in their wanderings they radically changed the religious demography
of the South. They added more fuel to the revivalistic fires of "The Great
Awakening in the South" that had already been ignited by Presbyterians
in Virginia during the 1750s.[5] Some of these "New Light" or Separate
Baptists, led by Shubal Stearns and Daniel Marshall, migrated to Virginia
in 1755. Soon afterward Stearns led a group to North Carolina, and Marshall around 1772 led another to Georgia. The Georgia group settled near
Kiokee Creek, a tributary of the Savannah River.

Undaunted by the successes of the fiery Separates, representatives of
the Particular Baptist tradition of the Philadelphia Association maintained
and extended their version of the faith. They called themselves Regular
Baptists as a rebuke to the Separate group, which they deemed "irregular"
if not disorderly in the way it formed and governed churches. Matthew
Moore, living in Burke County, Georgia, near Marshall's mushrooming
band, was one of several Regular pastors who responded to the Separate
challenge by stepping up their own revival activity. Moore was pastor of
the Buckhead Creek Church, which was probably formed shortly after
George Liele, the first formally ordained black Baptist minister, was converted sometime in 1772.

Between 1772 and 1782 six Baptist congregations were organized in
Georgia. They included Kiokee (1772); Edmund Botsford's congregation
on Brier Creek (1773); Buckhead Creek (sometime in 1773 or 1774); Red's
Creek (1774); Little Brier Creek (1777); and Fishing Creek (1782). These
churches were located near Augusta in St. George's Parish, later called
Burke County. The Separate and Regular Baptist split that was present in
other colonies was not a significant factor in Georgia. The skilled diplo-
macy of Daniel Marshall, founder of the Kiokee Church, was largely responsible for this development. His alliance with his friend Edmund
Botsford certainly added that personal touch necessary to heal old wounds.
Botsford was a missionary for the Charleston Association, the oldest Reg-

---

[5]Three books provide the most helpful interpretations of these developments: Clarence
C. Goen, *Revivalism and Separatism in New England, 1740-1800: Strict Congregationalists and Separate Baptists in the Great Awakening* (New Haven: Yale University Press,
1962); John B. Boles, *The Great Revival, 1787-1805* (Lexington, KY: University of Kentucky Press, 1972); and Rhys Isaac, *The Transformation of Virginia, 1740-1790* (Chapel
Hill: University of North Carolina Press, 1982).

ular (or Particular) Baptist deliberative body in the South, before he was called to the Brier Creek Church. Both preachers were also loyal to the cause of American independence from Britain. Matthew Moore and some of his parishioners were, on the contrary, British sympathizers. Their views contributed to the eventual demise of the Buckhead congregation. The Buckhead Creek Church became extinct during or after the Revolutionary War when Moore had to leave the country because of his loyalist sentiments.[6]

Both Moore and Abraham Marshall, along with other Regulars and Separates, had a hand in the beginning of black Baptist churches.

The Rise of Independent Black Baptist Congregations

Masters sometimes permitted slaves to attend these renewed revival services. When slaves accepted the evangelical faith, it was more for existential than for doctrinal reasons. They found this new movement ethically and spiritually attractive. Evangelical preachers, by preaching damnation for the unregenerate, offered slaves a vision of God's inexorable justice, either now or in the future.[7] Furthermore, by permitting demonstrative religious expression, these revivals fostered a union between the native religions of slaves and the mighty current of religious enthusiasm flowing through the white population. This evangelical ethos provided a new veneer behind which slaves could retain important fragments of their old faiths. And it provided a new source of psychic energy to help them meet the harsh challenge of the New World.

---

[6]The Index Publishing Company, *History of the Baptist Denomination in Georgia: With Biographical Compendium and Portrait Gallery of Baptist Ministers and Other Georgia Baptists* (Atlanta: James P. Harrison, 1881) 23, 47; Reba Carolyn Strickland, *Religion and State in Georgia in the Eighteenth Century* (New York: Columbia University Press, 1939) 148, 180.

[7]For an elaboration of this perspective, see James M. Washington, "The Origins of Black Evangelicalism and the Ethical Function of Evangelical Cosmology," *Union Seminary Quarterly Review* 32 (Winter 1977): 104-16; See also Washington, "Spettri storici della teologia nera: riflessioni di uno studioso di storia ecclesiastica," in Rosino Gibellini, ed., *Teologia Nera* (Brescia, Italy: Queriniana, 1978) 103-29. This quest for divine justice is also assumed in Vincent Harding, "Religion and Resistance Among Antebellum Negroes, 1800-1860," in August Meier and Elliot Rudwick, eds., *The Making of Black America: Essays in Negro Life and History* (New York: Atheneum, 1969) 1:179-97. The connection between making political judgments and speculations about divine justice among black slaves is suggestively but briefly discussed in Eugene D. Genovese, *Roll, Jordan, Roll: The World the Slaves Made* (New York: Pantheon Books, 1974) 250-51.

The story of independent black Baptist congregations begins in Virginia and Georgia, where some slaves who had answered the revivalists' call for repentance during the Southern phase of the revivals of the 1750s covenanted to form their own churches.[8] They believed that spiritual bondage was a greater affliction than material bondage, and that freedom from one might lead to freedom from the other. They knew their churches were chattel arrangements. But they stubbornly trusted in the promises of the Bible that God is a liberator.[9]

Only a few slaves in these two British colonies or anywhere else in the New World freely joined churches before the 1770s. But the preaching of the new wave of revivalists who emerged during the political revolutionary mood of the 1770s emboldened them to believe that maybe a few white people would assist them in establishing their own congregations. This re-

---

[8]Unfortunately Gayraud S. Wilmore identifies with a culturally biased definition of the church when he argues that "whatever those first gatherings of slaves for religious purposes outside the supervision of whites may have been like, it is inaccurate to think of the religious institutions that made their first appearance among blacks as 'churches' in the sense of the European or American model." See his *Black Religion and Black Radicalism: An Interpretation of the Religious History of Afro-American People,* 2nd ed., rev. and enl. (Maryknoll NY: Orbis Books, 1983) 5. This view would exclude many early Christian churches as well. Nevertheless, Wilmore himself notes that such notable black scholars as W. E. B. DuBois share this view. See DuBois's *The Negro Church* (Atlanta: Atlanta University Press, 1903) 5. Joseph R. Washington offered the most emphatic statement of this position, now considerably modified, in his article, "Are Negro Churches Christian?" *Theology Today* 20 (April 1963): 76-86, more fully elaborated in his book, *Black Religion* (Boston: Beacon Press, 1964). Charles H. Long characterizes this sort of history as "a kind of theological history of the Black Churches" that my own work—as well as that of other historians such as Evelyn Brooks, Randall K. Burkett, Dennis Dickerson, Richard Newman, Albert J. Raboteau, Edwin S. Redkey, Milton Sernett, David Swift, and David Wills, who all belong to the Northeastern Seminar for the Study of Black Religion—tries to deepen and expand. See Long's "Assessment and New Departures for A Study of Black Religion in the United States of America" in Charles Shelby Rooks, ed., *Black Religious Scholarship, Reflection and Promise: Addresses at the Tenth Annual Meeting of the Society for the Study of Black Religion* (Chicago: n.p., 1981) 6.

[9]The recent Black Theology movement led by James H. Cone systematized this persistent theme in the history of African-American folk thought. See Cone's *God of the Oppressed* (New York: Seabury Press, 1975). See also the brilliant attempt to deepen this movement's philosophical and cultural base in Cornel West, *Prophesy Deliverance! An Afro-American Revolutionary Christianity* (Philadelphia: Westminster Press, 1982). An invaluable resource for the history of this movement is Gayraud S. Wilmore and James H. Cone, eds., *Black Theology: A Documentary History, 1966-1979* (Maryknoll NY: Orbis Books, 1979).

quired developing their own indigenous leadership, or at least relying on bold white Christians willing to offer political protection in addition to spiritual nurture.

George Liele became one of the first slaves to be deeply affected by the missionary zeal of these new revivals. He was the slave of Henry Sharpe, a deacon in Matthew Moore's Buckhead Creek Baptist Church, and was converted under Moore's preaching in 1772. After his conversion, he began to share his newly found faith with other slaves "on the same plantation with himself, by reading hymns among them, encouraging them to sing, and sometimes by explaining the most striking parts to them."[10] The Buckhead Creek Church ordained Liele in accord with the general practice of Baptists to invest congregations with such authority. They ordained Liele to perform missionary labors among slaves on other plantations in the surrounding area.

Liele's evangelistic work produced two preachers: David George, an older friend who had known Liele as a child when the two were slaves in Virginia, and Jesse Galphin. Both converts were slaves of George Galphin who ran an Indian trading post at his place called "Silver Bluff," which overlooked the Savannah River from its South Carolina bank.[11] Liele encouraged David George to assume the pastoral leadership of the tiny slave congregation that had gathered among Galphin's slaves. But before the reluctant David George could get settled into his new position, this congregation had to disband as the British seized Galphin's trading post in the early stages of the Revolutionary War. Several of Galphin's slaves accompanied David George to Yamacraw, a suburb of Savannah. This group later left with several other loyalist slaves, whom the British shipped to Nova Scotia in 1783. By 1792 a sizable number of this group settled in Sierra Leone under the leadership of David George and Boston King, a black Methodist preacher.[12]

---

[10]John Rippon, *The Baptist Annual Register* (1790-1793): 333.

[11]Dorothy K. MacDowell, "George Galphin: Nabob of the Backwoods," *South Carolina History Illustrated* (1970): 51-56.

[12]The entire story of these black loyalists has been told recently by Ellen Gibson Wilson (*The Loyal Blacks* [New York: G. P. Putnam's Sons, 1976]) and by James W. St. G. Walker (*The Black Loyalists: The Search for a Promised Land in Nova Scotia and Sierra Leone, 1783-1870* [New York: Holmes and Meier, 1976]).

Other members of the Silver Bluff Church crossed the river into Augusta where Jesse Galphin formed another independent African Baptist Church. George Liele also benefited from the British evacuation. After several fortuitous events, including his own manumission, Liele and a number of other former slaves migrated to Jamaica as the British evacuated Savannah in 1783. But because his ship had to dock temporarily due to a storm, Liele made his way back to Savannah where he stayed with friends until the storm cleared. While there he baptized some slaves who five years later were among the original members of the first Baptist church in Savannah. [13]

Andrew Bryan, a slave, emerged as the leader of this group. He received much encouragement from his master, Jonathan Bryan, Esq., a noted American patriot and a ''New Light'' Presbyterian. [14] Besides this devout master's encouragement, New Light influence on this congregation was evident in the irregular way in which it was established. Partly responding to local persecution, this little band sought the help of Jesse Galphin of Augusta to identify with the Baptist denomination. Galphin had become a trusted friend of Abraham Marshall, the son of Daniel Marshall of Kiokee and the patriarch of New Light Separate Baptists in the area. Marshall with the help of Galphin ''acted the part of a bishop,'' ordaining Bryan and constituting Bryan's group as a Baptist congregation. [15] This procedure was ir-

---

[13]James M. Simms, *The First Colored Baptist Church in North America* (Philadelphia: J. B. Lippincott, 1888; reprint, New York: Negro Universities Press, 1969) 15.

[14]Frank B. Screvens, ''The Georgia Bryans and Screvens, 1685-1861,'' *Georgia Historical Quarterly* (December 1956): 325-48; Reba Strickland, *Religion and State in Georgia,* 103-104; Ronald G. Killion and Charles T. Waller, *Georgia and the Revolution* (Atlanta: Cherokee Publishing, 1975). Jonathan Bryan was converted under the preaching of George Whitefield. George Whitefield (*George Whitefield's Journals* [London: n.p., 1905] 439, 447-48, 501-504) offers an account of the conversion experiences of Jonathan Bryan, his wife, and his brother. See also [Anne Dutton], *A Letter to the Negroes Lately Converted to Christ in America: And Particularly to those, Lately Called Out of Darkness, into God's Marvelous Light, at Mr. Jonathan Bryan's in South Carolina: Or a Welcome to the Believing Negroes, into the Household of God* (London: Printed by J. Hart, 1743) 26; Stephen J. Stein, ''A Note on Anne Dutton, Eighteenth-Century Evangelical,'' *Church History* 44 (December 1975): 485-91. For a careful recent historical analysis of the impact of slavery on colonial culture in Georgia, see Betty Wood, *Slavery in Colonial Georgia, 1730-1775* (Athens: University of Georgia Press, 1984) 110-68.

[15]David Benedict, *Fifty Years Among the Baptists* (New York: Sheldon; Charleston: Southern Baptist Publication Society, 1860) 54; and David Benedict, *A General History of the Baptist Denomination in America and Other Parts of the World* (New York: Lewis Colby, 1848) 727.

regular because usually one church or more participated in the formation of new congregations. Neither the Separates nor the Africans felt bound by tradition at that time, but they both changed their minds later.

On learning about the irregular nature of its formation, Bryan inquired about the denominational legitimacy of his congregation. In 1790 he asked the Georgia Baptist Association, formed in 1784, whether or not his ordination was valid since Marshall ordained him and constituted his church without even calling a council of ministers. This inquiry obviously embarrassed Marshall since he was the moderator of the Association for that year. The Association chose to view Marshall's actions as an excusable "extraordinary case." To prove its sincerity, the Association admitted the First African Church into its fellowship. First African remained in this fellowship until 1802 when it withdrew in order to become one of the three founding churches of the Savannah Association. The newly formed white First Baptist Church of Savannah, a small nearby white church at Newington, and the First African Baptist Church of Savannah organized this association on 3 April 1803.

First African became so large that on 26 December 1802 "several hundred were dismissed, and constituted another society" with a membership of 200 under the leadership of Henry Cunningham. A week later the Savannah Association also recognized the Ogechee African Baptist Church, located near the Ogechee River, with a membership of 250. First African of Savannah still had a membership of 400 after permitting the Second and Ogechee African Churches to organize. Thus by 1803 the black Baptists of the Savannah area, having started with fifty members fifteen years earlier, had 850 members. There were eighty-three white Baptists in the area.[16]

The Struggle in Virginia

Black Baptists elsewhere in the South also participated in the rapid growth of legal biracial congregations,[17] and were sometimes invited to attend association meetings. This was especially the case in Virginia.

---

[16]Henry Holcomb, *The First Fruits in A Series of Letters* (Philadelphia: Printed for the Author by Ann Cochran, 1812) 83; and Holcomb, ed., *The Georgia Analytical Repository* (1802): 75-78. See Boles, *The Great Revival,* for a very useful discussion of the thought of this important early Baptist leader.

[17]For an intriguing article on this phenomenon, see Kenneth K. Bailey, "Protestantism and Afro-Americans in the Old South: Another Look," *Journal of Southern History* 41 (November 1975): 451-72.

Given the oppressed status of blacks within the emergent American society, black participation in this new evangelical resurgence was somewhat limited insofar as the creation of religious organizations is concerned. But insofar as personal opportunities for religious conversions were concerned, the sheer numbers of blacks who converted to Christianity testify that many of them believed that the inequities of limited participation were far outweighed by the felicities of communion with the Holy Spirit. The novelty of this religious and social phenomenon is impressive. Carter Godwin Woodson has characterized the Second Great Awakening as "the dawning of a new day"[18] for blacks who wanted to become Christians, and indeed it was. But there is really no adequate way to determine the number of blacks who converted to the Baptist version of the Christian faith during this period.

Looking at this general Baptist growth in this period, we can gain some perspective on these independent black congregations. In 1795 there were in the United States about eighty thousand Baptists, black and white, of whom more than eighteen thousand were blacks living south of Maryland. Charles Colcock Jones, the famous Presbyterian plantation missionary, estimated that in 1813 there were forty thousand black members of Baptist churches. Thus in 1795 and 1812-13 blacks made up something under a quarter of the Baptist population.[19] If that ratio held through the antebellum period, there were about 170,000 blacks among the 720,000 Baptists in 1844.

By 1812, according to Sydney Ahlstrom, "the entire denomination registered 172,972 members in 2,194 churches with 1,605 ministers, having doubled in the previous decade." Among the denominations only the Methodists exceeded the Baptist growth and no other group came close to those two front-runners, who grew at nearly double the rate of the general population.[20] Virginia illustrates the effects of these developments. More-

---

[18]Carter G. Woodson, *The History of the Negro Church* (1921; reprint, Washington DC: Associated Publishers, 1970).

[19]Charles Colcock Jones, *The Religious Instruction of the Negroes in the United States* (Savannah GA: n.p., 1842) 52-58.

[20]Newman, *A History of the Baptist Churches,* 332; Ahlstrom, *A Religious History of the American People,* 443; Charles Colcock Jones, *The Religious Instruction of the Ne-*

over, fugitive or freed slaves from this state, among them Richard De-Baptiste, William P. Newman, Anthony J. Binga, and many others, were more often than not in the forefront of various black Baptist efforts to liberate the slaves and build a black Baptist denomination. In the midst of white uncertainty about how much, if any, ecclesiastical power to share with fellow black congregants, blacks still acquired invaluable organizational skills that many used to advance their own church movements.

Since there were laws in all the slave states regulating the movement of blacks, the social status of black church members determined the degree of participation in the decision-making process of the congregation as well as whether or not they could have full, partial, or no participation in the life of the congregation. As early as 1794, the Portsmouth Association in Virginia had to answer this query posed by one of its constituent congregations: "Is it agreeable to the word of God, and that decency which ought to be observed in the church of Christ, to send a free black man a delegate to the association?" The Association responded, "We see nothing in the word of God, nor any thing contrary to the rules of decency, to prohibit a church sending as a delegate, any male member they shall choose."[21] But this was a rather inconclusive response. While it was certainly true that the Great Revival of 1787-1805 bore witness, as evident in the liberal attitudes of the Portsmouth and Savannah Associations, to a greater degree of black participation in associational gatherings, this view barely saw the light of day.

Despite the tortuous pangs of conscience some whites endured over the issue of whether or not slavery was a sin, an important expansion of the Baptist movement among free and enslaved blacks occurred in Virginia, which had the largest black population in the South during this period. Virginia gradually lost this distinction as the Southern frontier moved southward and westward to the states of Georgia, Alabama, Mississippi, and Florida.

---

groes, 53; William Warren Sweet, *The Story of Religion in America* (New York: Harper and Brothers, 1950) 420; William Warren Sweet, *Religion in the Development of American Culture, 1765-1840* (New York: Charles Scribner's Sons, 1952) 279; and Edwin S. Gaustad, *Historical Atlas of Religion in America* (New York: Harper and Row, 1962) 10-13, a quite useful discussion of the demographic history of American religion.

[21]Portsmouth Association *Minutes,* 1794, 6.

Ironically, while the influence of the Separate Baptists on the formation of African Baptist congregations was strongly felt in Georgia, their impact in Virginia, where they were quite numerous, was negligible. The main leadership came directly from the free black population, which was much larger in Virginia than in Georgia. Free blacks such as Gowan Pamphlet, Jacob Bishop, Daniel Jackson, Abram Brown, and John Benn were prominent figures in the organization of these early independent congregations. Otherwise the pattern was similar. Blacks who had experienced conversion would begin to hold meetings and then would form themselves into congregations that were later recognized by white Baptist associations. Many of these associations arose during the 1780s and 1790s at the close of the War of Independence and the beginning of the Second Great Awakening in 1787. Several black congregations that had actually been meeting for some time previously locate this period as the date of their founding since this was when white associations began to recognize them.[22]

For instance the stubborn and fiery free black preacher Gowan Pamphlet organized a black Baptist church at Williamsburg, Virginia, in 1781 and became its pastor. The Church had actually been meeting since 1776. By 1791 this church was admitted into the white Dover Baptist Association. A short-lived church in King and Queen County was formed during 1782 under a preacher called "Toney." In 1788, the same year that blacks formed First African Baptist Church of Savannah, they also organized what is now known as the Gillfield Baptist Church of Petersburg in Prince George County as a racially mixed congregation. When this congregation moved to Petersburg sometime before 1809, the black group separated in order to form the independent Sandy Beach Church, which was admitted into the Portsmouth Association in 1810. During this same period both free and enslaved Africans also formed the Harrison Street Baptist Church of Peters-

---

[22]Luther Porter Jackson, "Religious Development of the Negro in Virginia From 1760 to 1860," *Journal of Negro History* 16 (April 1931): 188. Mechal Sobel disagrees with this estimate, and suggests different dates for the founding of these congregations as well as others in *Trabelin' On,* 257-356. This fine appendix is a substantial initial compilation, but is only a beginning. Dates for several congregations are incorrect, and many more are missing. Sobel's point, however, needs to be emphasized. That is, the development of black congregations probably began much earlier than the founding of the Silver Bluff Church in 1773. She correctly cites the founding of a slave congregation on the plantation of William Byrd III in 1758. This church was called the African Baptist or Bluestone Church; ibid., 296.

burg, as well as Bank Street Church in Norfolk and Elam Baptist Church in Charles City shortly after 1800.

Separate and biracial congregations like these are too numerous to discuss individually. But what is consistent is that whenever and wherever free blacks and slaves found an opportunity to organize themselves into "legitimate" congregations they did so. These black Baptists, as well as other black Christians, formed social bonds and clandestine networks that crossed lines of social status and eventually exceeded regional boundaries. One former slave recalled after the Civil War how much the gatherings of the faithful meant to him. The Reverend Richard DeBaptiste, onetime president of the black Consolidated American Baptist Missionary Convention, wrote a letter to the *American Baptist* that captures the pathos of the black Baptist sense of pride and pain, as well as how much they valued their communal memories.

> I can remember the names of many of the veterans in the cause of Christ of those [antebellum] days, who were the companions of my father [Deacon William DeBaptiste of Virginia] in Christian labors and heavenly joys. The *Youngs*, the *Walkers*, the *Shepards*, the *Amsteads*, and such a host of others, it would be too tedious to name them. I have seen them weep together in their afflictions and sorrows, and I have seen them rejoice together over the sweet theme of a Savior's love. I have listened by night to their earnest and solemn conferences at their committee meetings in my father's own house, concerning the interests of that cause which their hearts loved so dearly. And at their separation I have watched in my father's countenance for the signs of emotion, which were not always joyful, but sometimes overcast with evidences of sorrow. Then I saw through a glass darkly, but now by experience I understand what all those things mean. The earnest-hearted servants of God of those days have finished their work, they have been where they *"Meet beyond the river, Where the surges cease to role, Where in all the blest forever, Sorrow ne'er shall press the soul."*
> But upon us has fallen the work they have left. And *"greater work"* than that which fell to their lot to perform now devolves upon us to do.[23]

Despite the good intentions of some white brothers and sisters in the faith, the persistence of slavery as an institution in a *Herrenvolk* democracy en-

---

[23]*The American Baptist* (27 May 1870).

couraged blacks to develop and maintain primarily clandestine social networks.[24]

Nota Bene:
Black Slavery and the White Baptist Conscience

Baptists vacillated about whether or not to commit themselves to the
emerging antislavery crusade. Many believed so adamantly in individual
liberty of conscience[25] that they thought it odious to infringe on all the rights
enjoyed by white males, such as the ownership of property. Both Northern
and Southern white Baptists debated about where and whether to draw a
line between religious conscience and social responsibility. Many simply
did not believe that there was much of a conflict between the two.

Isaac Backus's views, for instance, reflected this dilemma. Backus
personally disliked slavery, but had a greater affection for the right of the
individual to own property. As a delegate from Middleborough, Massachusetts, to the Boston state convention that met in 1788 to consider rati-
fying the new United States Constitution, he argued in favor of maintaining
the status quo. He had not reached the tentative judgment of several Southern Separate Baptists that slavery is a sin. On the contrary, Backus argued,

> No man abhors that wicked practice more than I do, and would gladly make
> use of all lawful means towards the abolishing of slavery in all parts of the
> land. But let us consider where we are and what we are doing. In the ar-
> ticles of confederation no provision was made to hinder the importing of
> slaves into any of these states; but a door is now open hereafter to do it, as
> they please . . . . slavery grows more and more odious through the world;
> and as an honorable gentleman said [here] some days ago, ''Though we

---

[24]I agree with John Boles that more studies of biracial congregations are needed. But I
disagree with his contention that Albert J. Raboteau's *Slave Religion* ''exaggerates the underground nature of slave worship''; see Boles, *Black Southerners,* 234. White Protestants
published most of the records that accent biracial churches, while those that support Raboteau's position primarily constitute what Blassingame calls ''slave testimony''; see John
W. Blassingame, ed., *Slave Testimony: Two Centuries of Letters, Speeches, Interviews,
and Autobiographies* (Baton Rouge: Louisiana University Press, 1977). I am not dissuaded
by the argument that many of these sources were edited by white abolitionists. No one can
absolutely guarantee the veracity of any text.

[25]See William G. McLoughlin, *New England Dissent, 1630-1833: The Baptists and the
Separation of Church and State* (Cambridge MA: Harvard University Press, 1971) 2:763-
69.

cannot say that slavery is struck with apoplexy, yet we may hope it will
die with a consumption.''[26]

Other religious groups faced the same dilemma. But there was a small band
whose struggle in this early period foreshadowed a later debate during the
1830s and 1840s regarding whether or not slavery is a sin.

Given the earnestness of the ''Quaker Ethic'' and its influence on national and international antislavery efforts, Baptist antislavery convictions
were declared most loudly in areas where Baptists and Quakers coexisted
with at least a minimal degree of mutual toleration. The heavy commitment to intense spirituality on the part of separate Baptists in the South made
this area more open to the equivalent moralistic spirituality of the Quakers.
This was especially true in Virginia where ''Quakers from the north were
migrating south, adding numbers to Virginia Quakers. So the Virginia
Yearly Meeting was subsequently held chiefly in Charles City, Surry,
Southampton, and Dinwiddie Counties to 1830.''[27]

Baptists and Quakers shared a common commitment to the ''sectar-
ian'' view of the church, but a slightly different understanding of the process of conversion. Commenting on the development of British Quakerism,
Richard Vann argues that the Quakers sought a mystical ''communion with
God so deep that it might be called 'continuous conversion.' And they rejected the the Baptist or Independent claim to find assurance of salvation
in a single influx of grace which could be precisely dated and described for
the edification and discernment of other Christians.''[28]

Baptists who identified with the antislavery Quakers—who were known
as ''Friends of Humanity''—included David Barrow (who freed his slaves
in 1784), John Leland, James Lemen, Councillor Robert Carter of Nomini
Hall, and Jacob Grigg. By the 1790s these converts had made strong declarations against slavery. But they were only echoes in a region where

---

[26]Quoted in William G. McLoughlin, *Isaac Backus and the American Pietistic Tradition* (Boston: Little, Brown, 1967) 199.

[27]Miles Mark Fisher, ''Friends of Humanity: A Quaker Anti-Slavery Influence,'' *Church
History* 4,3 (September 1935): 190; David Brion Davis, *The Problem of Slavery in the Age
of Revolution, 1770-1823* (Ithaca NY: Cornell University Press, 1975) 196-254.

[28]Richard T. Vann, *The Social Development of English Quakerism, 1655-1755* (Cambridge MA: Harvard University Press, 1969) 32-33.

ownership of chattel slaves was counted as one of the cherished rights of "free men." [29]

Although Baptists were slow to join the cause of emancipation, they were zealous in their efforts to emancipate souls from the bondage of sin. The Baptists, like most evangelicals, seldom offered their own love to enslaved and free Americans. They offered God's love. They believed and preached that "for as many as are led by the Spirit of God, they are the sons of God" (Romans 8:14 KJV). The clearer exponents of antislavery did not make their best pronouncements on the grounds that blacks were inherently equal to whites. They challenged the prevailing argument that slavery rather than religion is the most effective means of social control.

The question of the validity of "hereditary slavery" was constantly up for debate during the last two decades of the eighteenth century. This question was especially alive among the Baptists. The Ketocton Association, whose openness was largely responsible for the unification of the Regular and Separate Baptists in Virginia, raised the question in 1787 about "the lawfulness of hereditary slavery," According to Robert Semple, a contemporary historian of these early Virginia Baptists,

> They determined that hereditary slavery was a breach of the divine law. They then appointed a committee to bring in a plan of gradual emancipation, which acted accordingly. They were treading upon delicate ground. It excited considerable tumult in the churches, and according in their letters to the next Association they remonstrated so decidedly that the Association resolved to take no further steps in the business. [30]

John Leland introduced another resolution in 1789 before a different Virginia Baptist body, the meeting of the General Committee. But this

---

[29]W. Harrison Daniel, "Virginia Baptists and the Negro in the Early Republic," *Virginia Magazine of History and Biography* 80,1 (January 1972): 60-69; L. F. Greene, ed., *The Writings of John Leland* (New York, 1845) 95; Louis Morton, *Robert Carter of Nomini Hall: A Virginia Planter of the Eighteenth Century* (Williamsburg: Colonial Williamsburg, 1941); Howard Grimshaw Hartzell, "Jacob Grigg—Missionary and Minister," *The Chronicle: A Baptist Historical Quarterly* 6 (1943): 83-90, 130-43. The most recent and the finest summary of this early evangelical antislavery crusade is James D. Essig, *The Bonds of Wickedness: American Evangelicals Against Slavery, 1770-1808* (Philadelphia: Temple University Press, 1982) especially 140-65.

[30]Robert B. Semple, *A History of the Rise and Progress of the Baptists in Virginia*, rev. G. W. Beale (Richmond: Pitt and Dickinson, 1894) 392.

committee, like all Baptist associations in theory (with the significant exception of the Philadelphia Association), only had authority to function as an advisory body. Without the power to excommunicate, which was unthinkable to such Baptists, social questions of a controversial nature had to be avoided. Although Leland's nonbinding resolution was accepted, it could not be enforced. That did not matter, however. The Committee did not direct it at the churches anyway. It was pastoral advice to the newly constituted government.

> Resolved, That slavery is a violent deprivation of the rights of nature and inconsistent with a republican government, and therefore recommend it to our brethren to make use of every legal measure to extirpate this horrid evil from the land; and pray Almighty God that our honorable Legislature may have it in their power to proclaim the great Jubilee, consistent with the principles of good policy.[31]

This statement reflected an interest in the political problem attending the presence of slavery in a land with a "republican government." Oddly enough, however, it did not deal with the theological ramifications of holding Christians in bondage. Such a fragile body could not easily take bold positions that would cause internal disruption.

But there was another reason for avoiding theological and ethical debate. These Baptists had very little faith in the merits of rational discussion. They emphasized the inward rather than the outward or verbal expression of Christian conscience, conscientiousness, and consciousness. Leland himself, ever a fervent defender of religious liberty, believed in an individualistic understanding of "Conscience."

> Conscience is a court of judicature, erected in every breast, to take cognizance of every action in the home department, but has nothing to do with another man's conduct. My best judgement tells me that my neighbor does wrong, but my conscience has nothing to say to it. Were I to do as he does, my conscience would arrest and condemn me, but guilt is not transferable. Every one must give account of himself.[32]

---

[31]Ibid., 105.

[32]Quoted in Edwin S. Gaustad, "The Backus-Leland Tradition" in Winthrop S. Hudson, ed., *Baptist Concepts of the Church: A Survey of the Historical and Theological Issues which Have Produced Changes in Church Order* (Chicago: Judson Press, 1959) 111.

This peculiar social ethic fell prey to the needs of "Christian" masters to rationalize their enslavement of black persons, especially professing black Christians. But this same idea of the conscience as the God-given tribunal that mediates between sinners and their Lord, with its theological, ethical, and psychosocial overtones, also affirmed the right of black persons to hear the drumbeats of a denied past and to feel the rhythms of a promised, consecrated future. While conscience-bearing ecclesiology influenced the development of black congregationalism among the Baptists, a similar impulse emerged among the American Methodists—that other fiery branch of evangelicalism—when the Bethel African Methodist Episcopal Church was founded in 1792 under the leadership of Richard Allen.

Ironically, the formation of black churches gained greater momentum in the South than in the North. This phenomenon is often explained by the presence of a larger black populace in the South. It is also explained by the benefits of social "control" that masters derived from allowing blacks to profess religious beliefs openly and to practice religious worship. But neither explanation tells us how blacks viewed their newly acquired religion, nor does it provide an internal view of the origins of a separatist ideology among these black Christians.

Glancing Ahead

While the developments of both clandestine and biracial congregations flowered in the South, a separate independent black Baptist church movement was being formed by free blacks in the Northeastern states. Thomas Paul and his brothers Benjamin and Nathaniel were the first leaders. The renewal of revivals in New Hampshire aroused them. They subsequently traveled throughout New England preaching the gospel among small, scattered black communities.

In 1805 Thomas organized Joy Street Church in Boston, and in 1808 he organized the Abyssinian Baptist Church in New York City.[33] These churches were later enlarged by numerous free black immigrants, mostly

---

[33]J. Marcus Mitchell, "The Paul Family," *Old Time New England* 63 (Winter 1973): 73-77; John Dowling, "Sketches of New York Baptists: Rev. Thomas Paul and the Colored Baptist Churches," *The Baptist Memorial and Monthly Chronicle* 8 (September 1849): 295-301; George A. Levesque, "Inherent Reformers—Inherited Orthodoxy: Black Baptists in Boston, 1800-1873," *Journal of Negro History* 40 (October 1975): 491-519; William G. McLoughlin, *New England Dissent*, 1:1157.

from Maryland and Virginia. In 1809 Henry Cunningham, pastor of the Second African Baptist Church of Savannah, organized the black members of the white First Baptist Church of Philadelphia into the First African Baptist Church. He did this while seeking financial aid for his Savannah church from the influential and wealthy Philadelphia Baptist Association.[34] Other black Baptist congregations arose rapidly throughout the antebellum period.[35]

Among the burgeoning numbers of black Baptists, the independent churches formed a tiny percentage. Indeed, in the prewar decades, the fears of white Southerners sharply limited the expansion and activity of independent black congregations and of free black ministers. Most Southern black Baptists worshiped either in racially mixed churches under white ministers or in black-led secret conventicles (the "invisible institution") or both. The leaders who gained experience and charismatic power in these gatherings did not acquire any semblance of ecclesiastical power until after the Civil War. But they did forge a powerful religious tradition whose cultural legacy has greatly enriched American culture, and helped reconstitute African culture in a new guise.

At this stage their resistance to slavocracy was primarily symbolic. That is not to say that symbolism is vacuous and impotent. I agree with Pierre Bourdieu that every social group creates and nurtures "cultural competence." But groups with minimal social power, such as the Algerian peasants of Kabylia, in Bordieu's case illustration, cannot transform the socioeconomic potential of their mostly inherited "cultural competence" into "cultural capital" until such competence is "inserted into the objective relations between the system of economic production and the system

---

[34]Cunningham was a close friend and a one-time parishioner of Henry Holcombe, pastor of the white First Baptist Church of Savannah. Holcombe had close ties with the Philadelphia Association. He later served as pastor of Philadelphia's historic First Baptist Church. See Simms, *The First Colored Baptist Church*, 56-59. See also Charles H. Brooks, *Official History of the First African Baptist Church, Philadelphia, Pa.* (Philadelphia: n.p., 1923) for Cunningham's administration.

[35]The story of the development of black Baptist congregations deserves more attention than I am able to give in this study. My overall focus centers more on the story of alliances of congregations in the form of associations, state conventions, and national organizations rather than on the fascinating story of the development of separate local congregations. Other scholars such as Professor William B. Gravely of the University of Denver are working diligently to fill this gap.

producing the producers (which is itself constituted by the relation between the school system and the family)."[36] I would add religious institutions as well. Acquiring the social skills of collective organization enabled black religious workers to insert themselves subtly but effectively in a major part of the larger system of cultural production that produced producers of cultural capital for the religious world. This was a very subtle development. Its reality became more evident in a later period. Yet this was precisely the major development among the slaves during the antebellum period. John Blassingame, Albert J. Raboteau, Eugene Genovese, and others have provided rich analyses of the content and development of this kind of "cultural capital." But the political reality of black oppression is implicated even in the contours of the amazing ingenuity and creativity of the slaves.

The major black resistance to this oppression came from blacks in the Northeast and Midwest, most of whom, ironically, came from Virginia. Once they tasted freedom, they determined never to return to the perverse trusteeship of the slave regime.

---

[36]Pierre Bourdieu, *Outline of a Theory of Practice,* trans, Richard Nice (Cambridge: Cambridge University Press, 1977) 183-86.

2

Abolitionism and the Quest for a Prophetic Polity

In chapter 1, I discussed the important gestation period for both the Baptists and the American republic. This chapter partly overlaps the previous one. Between 1788 and 1834, black Baptists formed their first consciously black Baptist congregations and supported the rise of the major black Baptist leaders who formed regional associations. These leaders argued for the formation of these associations ostensibly for the purpose of engaging in missionary work beyond the local congregation. But more was at stake than the fulfillment of the missionary dream to save the world for Christ. Between 1788 and 1831, black Baptist congregations acquired a peculiar and precarious religious freedom. This development owed much to the general struggle within the new American republic to insure freedom of worship by outlawing all forms of official religion.

But white slave masters slowed the movement's growth considerably after Nat Turner, an enslaved black Baptist preacher, led his revolt in 1831. Turner substantiated the paranoia of white slave masters who feared black preachers would become revolutionary prophets. In addition to this, the black "Native Baptist War" was being waged against Jamaican plantations at about the same time. That campaign led to the liberation of British slaves in the West Indies. With such occurrences in both the United States and Jamaica, white officials concluded black preachers were a menace to society. African-American preachers were thus denied any right to engage freely in interstate proselytizing. Consequently, only the most "white" mulattoes among them like Sampson White and John H. Raymond could travel back and forth across the Mason-Dixon line without being detected. Despite such restrictions, black preachers valiantly persisted in trying to acquire and exercise religious freedom.

Black claims to religious freedom were peculiar and precarious precisely because most blacks were slaves. Yet, many slaves considered religious freedom to be a natural right, and they exercised it with skillful cunning. Esther Boulwares Winney, a Kentucky slave who was allowed to join the Elkhorn Baptist Church, illustrates this skill. Once she was converted, she let her antislavery sentiments be known.

> The 2nd. Saturday in January after divine Worship brought against Sister Esther Boulwares Winney. . . for saying she once thought it her duty to serve her Master & Mistress but since the Lord converted her, she had never believed that any Christian kept Negroes or Slaves—2nd. For saying she believed there was Thousands of white people Wallowing in Hell for their treatment to Negroes—and she did not care if there was as many more— Refer'd to next Meeting.[1]

It is unclear from extant records what the church decided to do. But the very existence of Christian slaves presented a difficult moral problem for white Christians who held them and who worshiped with them. Indeed the Christian slaves themselves often took the opportunity to prick the conscience of their white brothers and sisters in the faith.

Slavocracy and Christendom coexisted uncomfortably well. They were, after all, the institutional expressions of a nascent desire for freedom. But, in the case of the ideology of the slave masters, freedom was understood as freedom for the few. This aristocratic impulse never received universal approval among theologians. It challenged some very basic New Testament anthropological assumptions.[2] But a new breed of lay and clerical Christian ideologues forged what today we call a "Protestant Ethic." This new brand of tribalism spun doctrines of social and economic freedom for

---

[1]Records of the folks of Elkhorn Baptist Church, Kentucky, 1800-1820 in William Warren Sweet, *Religion on the American Frontier: The Baptists, 1783-1830, A Collection of Source Material* (Chicago: University of Chicago Press, 1931) 329.

[2]The best discussion of the theological debate over slavery is H. Shelton Smith, *In His Image, But . . . .: Racism in Southern Religion, 1780-1910* (Durham NC: Duke University Press, 1972), and a profound discussion of the social and political consequences of the debate can be found in C. C. Goen, *Broken Churches, Broken Nation: Denominational Schisms and the Coming of the American Civil War* (Macon GA: Mercer University Press, 1985).

the many but denied it to blacks. This ideology of the emerging bourgeoisie allowed the desire for upward mobility to be translated into a providential schema. Providence and progress became virtually synonymous.

The notion of ''religious liberty'' often meant greater freedom for middle-class Christians to form close alliances with the state. This alliance was built on an emerging definition of the division of labor between religion and civil government. John Locke saw this very clearly: ''A good life,'' he wrote,

> in which consists not the least part of religion and true piety, concerns also the civil government: and in it lies the safety both of men's souls, and of the commonwealth. Moral actions belong therefore to the jurisdiction both of the outward and inward court. Both of the civil and domestic governor. I mean, both of the magistrate and conscience. Here therefore is great danger, lest one of these jurisdictions entrench upon the other, and discord arise between the keeper of the public peace and the overseers of souls.[3]

But this proposal did not work well for African slaves and free blacks, the chief outcasts of the New World.

Black people found the best opportunities for independent organizational development in the North, where only about ten percent of them lived. But having noted that the independent black Baptists were numerically small and geographically restricted, I should observe their significance in other terms. For one thing the sectional identification is misleading. The Northern black churches had an authentically intersectional leadership and constituency. Many of the ''Northern'' leaders were transplanted Southerners, either fugitive slaves or free immigrants, pressed northward by growing hostility in the South. Furthermore, these people maintained their Southern connections. Letters and other documents reveal the degree to which many of them felt a debt and a duty to southern relatives and friends. In addition to their commitment to Christian missions, these personal ties explain their preoccupation with the Southern mission after emancipation. And although the Northern black churches were no more ''political'' organizations than white evangelical churches were, they usually had a strong moral concern for abolition.

---

[3]John Locke, ''A Letter Concerning Toleration,'' in Maurice Cranston, ed., *Locke on Politics, Religion, and Education* (New York: Macmillan, 1965) 134.

Many Northern black Baptists, poor and despised though they generally were, deemed it a measure of their Christian faith to assist fugitive slaves and otherwise strike at the slave regime. They were not deterred by the general public's seeming indifference to the plight of the slaves. Indeed the public often regarded abolitionists as nothing less than political subversives, and many people viewed religious abolitionists as divisive hotheads. Romantic abolitionists, who believed the churches to be bastions of cowardly compromise, often misunderstood the refusal of many abolitionist church leaders to make a distinction between sacred and public responsibility. They saw issues such as slavery as an offense against what was often called "the moral government of God." They were seeking a more excellent and enduring form of social reform that included what they called "soul liberty" as well as material freedom. As Samuel H. Davis, black Baptist minister and president of the 1843 National Negro Convention stated, "We must learn to act in harmony with the principles of God's moral government, or permanent prosperity can never be ours."[4] Black leaders like Frederick Douglass and Samuel Davis, who had abandoned this outlook, castigated fellow black Christians for holding this position.

Regardless of what tactic black religious leaders pursued, most of them despised slavery. Nathaniel Paul was one among many prominent black Baptist ministers who combined pastoral activities, such as organizing churches, with abolitionist activities. He reflected a pervasive black Baptist hatred for slavery when he argued that Providence is on the side of the oppressed.

> The captive must be liberated, the oppressed go free, and slavery must be revert back to its original chaos of darkness, and be forever annihilated from the earth. Did I believe that it would always continue, and that man to the end of time would be permitted with impunity to usurp the same undue authority over his fellow, I would disallow any allegiance or obligation I was under to my fellow creatures, or any submission that I owed to the laws of my country; I would deny the superintending power of divine providence in the affairs of this life; I would ridicule the religion of the Saviour of the world, and treat as the worst of men the ministers of the everlasting gospel; I would consider my Bible as a book of false and de-

---

[4]See the 1843 *Minutes of the National Convention of Colored Citizens*, in Howard Holman Bell, ed., *Minutes of the Proceedings of the National Negro Conventions, 1830-1864* (New York: Arno Press, 1969).

lusive fables; I would at once confess myself an atheist, and deny the existence of a holy God.[5]

This antislavery concern played a major role in the formation of black regional religious organizations. Finally, the antebellum black Baptists formed associations and conventions that were extended and duplicated in the South after emancipation. The early independent black Baptists were thus the pioneers of the denominational cooperative organizations that are the subject of this study.

Baptist Antislavery
and the Early Black Baptist Associations

The new need for slave labor after 1793 left little room for the mostly agrarian South to discuss the morality of slavery or the theological issue it raised regarding the nature of the slave's soul. Nevertheless, whenever the opportunity availed itself, most Southern free black preachers proclaimed that "God is no respecter of persons" (Acts 10:34). I agree with Donald Mathews that this "was one of the most popular biblical passages in black Christianity, cropping up as it did in sermons, conversations, reminiscences, and confrontations with white people."[6] Between 1784 and 1800, a few white Baptist ministers also challenged the slave regime publicly, first by confessing their own complicity and then by liberating their own slaves. This movement was most evident in the Tidewater region of Virginia where most of the early urban black churches were located.[7]

Substantial migrations of intense antislavery Quakers from the North to Charles City, Surry, Southhampton, and Dinwiddie Counties during the 1780s influenced the rise of antislavery views in this area. Baptist leaders who identified with these antislavery Quakers were known as "Friends of Humanity." They included David Barrow, who freed his slaves in 1784, John Leland, James Lemen, and Councillor Robert Carter of Nomini Hall.

---

[5]Nathaniel H. Paul, *An Address, Delivered on the Celebration of the Abolition of Slavery, in the State of New York, July 5, 1827* (Albany NY: John B. Van Steenburgh, 1827) 16-17; reprint, Dorothy Porter, comp., *Negro Protest Pamphlets* (New York: Arno Press, 1969).

[6]Donald G. Mathews, *Religion in the Old South* (Chicago: University of Chicago Press, 1977) 219.

[7]Luther P. Jackson, "Religious Development of the Negro in Virginia from 1760-1860," *Journal of Negro History* 16 (1931): 188.

Of this group Barrow and Lemen were largely responsible for encouraging the growth of antislavery Baptist associations in the Midwest, where they later migrated.[8]

Lemen moved to Illinois in 1787 and Barrow to Kentucky in 1797. They established antislavery churches out of which came several antislavery "Friends of Humanity" associations. Blacks organized the "Colored Baptist Association and Friends to Humanity of Illinois," the third oldest black Baptist Association, in 1839 with Lemen's assistance. But that puts us a little ahead of our story.

In general black Baptist associations arose with much the same aims as white Baptist associations: cooperative endeavor in such activities as domestic missions, mutual aid, and education. But there was a major difference: whereas very few white associations had an active interest in antislavery, all of the black associations did. Between 1834 and 1841 the first black Baptist associations were formed; two in Ohio, one in Illinois and one combining churches in Southern Michigan and Canada West.

The Providence Association. In 1834 Robert Townsend of Meigs County, Ohio, formed the Providence Baptist Association, consisting of six churches in the Southeastern corner of that state. The precarious status of such a venture is suggested by the fact that there were fewer than ten thousand free blacks among Ohio's 930,000 people in 1830. The growth of black population in the Northwest Territory and the trans-Mississippi West was very slow.[9] Townsend, a black minister, was appointed by the white Ohio Baptist State Convention in 1833-1834 to work five months as a missionary in the counties of Athens, Meigs, Jackson, and Gallia, an area

---

[8]Miles Mark Fisher, "Friends of Humanity: A Quaker Anti-slavery Influence," *Church History* 4 (December 1935): 190; David Brion Davis, *The Problem of Slavery in the Age of Revolution, 1770-1823* (Ithaca: Cornell University Press, 1975) 196-254; W. Harrison Daniel, "Virginia Baptists and the Negro in the Early Republic," *Virginia Magazine of History and Biography* 80 (January 1972): 60-69; L. F. Greene, ed., *The Writings of John Leland* (New York: n.p., 1845) 95; Louis Morton, *Robert Carter of Nomini Hall: A Virginia Planter of the Eighteenth Century* (Williamsburg: Colonial Williamsburg, 1941); Howard Grimshaw Hartzell, "Jacob Grigg—Missionary and Minister," *The Chronicle* 6 (1943): 83-90, 130-43.

[9]Carter G. Woodson, *Free Negro Heads of Families in the United States in 1830: Together with a Brief Treatment of the Free Negro* (Washington DC: Association for the Study of Negro Life and History, 1925) xx; and Frederick Jackson Turner, *The United States, 1830-1850: The Nation and Its Sections* (New York: Holt, Rinehart and Winston, 1935; reprint ed., New York: W. W. Norton, 1963) 261, 275.

of 2,045 square miles. Although he gained few converts, reporting only twenty baptisms in that time, he did succeed in bringing cohesion to the free black Baptist churches scattered among the hills. He was elected the Providence Association's first moderator.[10] Elders James B. Steward, Gabriel Hargo, Jacob Ward, and Jesse Corn were also active in forming the first black Baptist association.[11]

The antislavery concerns of this group are shown by a later change of name: Providence Antislavery (Colored) Baptist Association. By 1859 the association counted fifteen member churches and had become so radical in its antislavery views that it publicly supported a black man who had defied the Fugitive Slave Law of 1850 by aiding a runaway slave. They contended that this man's "Good Samaritan" act was "a practical illustration of Christianity." They chided the sort of Christianity "which expends itself in distributing tracts, in making long prayers, in erecting splendid church edifices, and reclining upon richly cushioned seats, listening to invectives against crinoline, chewing tobacco and dancing, while it opens not its ears to the piteous groans of the bleeding slaves, as they issue from the *hell* of slavery."[12]

The Union Association. The second black association, created in 1836, consisted of churches in Cincinnati, Columbus, Chillicothe, and Brush Creek. This group was called the Association of the Regular Baptist Churches of Color in Ohio.[13] In 1837 Elders Reuben Malvin and Charles B. Satchell served respectively as moderator and clerk. In 1837 there were five member churches, of which Union Baptist of Cincinnati, Second Baptist of Columbus, and African Baptist of Chillicothe were the largest and oldest. David Nickens, pastor of Union Church and probably the first ordained black Baptist minister in Ohio, was also a leader of the association, together with Wallace Shelton, T. R. Cressy, John Liverpool, and Wil-

---

[10]The 1834 minutes are not extant, but Townsend is listed as the moderator in the 1835 minutes. See Providence Baptist Association *Minutes,* 1835, 1; and Ohio Baptist Convention *Records of Annual Meetings,* 1826-34, 35.

[11]Providence *Minutes,* 1835, 2; *The Triennial Baptist Register* 2 (1836): 250.

[12]Quoted in David Christy, *Pulpit Politics: Or, Ecclesiastical Legislation on Slavery, in Its Disturbing Influences on the American Union* (Cincinnati: Faran & McLean, 1862) 185.

[13]Association of Regular Baptist Churches of Color *Minutes,* 1837.

liam Watson.[14] Minutes of 1837 indicate a debate on whether to emphasize greater missionary endeavor or to work harder for abolition and other social reforms. They temporarily resolved this tension by concentrating on racial religious uplift among the free black community in Ohio. They passed a resolution to this effect: "Resolved, That the principal object of this Association is to support a missionary preacher of color, and to encourage all other kindred institutions, calculated to promote the moral and religious elevation of the colored race." They also desired greater unity with other black Baptist churches in other states, and therefore also "Resolved, That this Association open correspondence with churches of color, of other States, and that Br. David Nickens be appointed Corresponding Secretary in behalf of the Association."[15] This activity continued after Nickens's death in 1838.

For awhile the churches of the Union Association also retained membership in white Baptist associations. In 1840, however, most of them withdrew from white associations and changed their name to the Union Baptist Antislavery Association, showing more clearly their abolitionist priorities.[16] Nevertheless, Union Baptist of Cincinnati and Second Baptist of Columbus, which had close alliances with antislavery white churches, such as William H. Brisbane's Sixth Baptist Church of Cincinnati, also maintained their former connections.

Through the missionary labors of Wallace Shelton, Peter Farley Fossett, and especially Charles Satchell, this highly important association "spread its beneficial influence" throughout Ohio as well as in the neighboring states of Indiana and Illinois. Between 1855 and 1857 it had grown from about twenty-two churches to twenty-seven with a total membership of 1,567. By 1860 it had formed close cooperative relations with the Providence Anti-slavery Baptist Association, its Southeastern neighbor. Moreover, it provided the most significant leadership during 1864 when the

---

[14]Ibid., 3-4.

[15]Ibid., 5.

[16]Richard Hunter Clossman, "A History of the Organization and Development of the Baptist Churches in Ohio from 1789 to 1907, With Particular Reference to the Ohio Baptist Convention" (Ph.D. dissertation, Ohio State University, 1971) 205.

regional black Baptist body called the Northwestern and Southern Baptist Convention was formed.[17]

The Wood River Association. In 1839 the third black Baptist association was formed in St. Clair County in Southwestern Illinois. Originally named the Colored Baptist Association and Friends to Humanity, it was usually called the Wood River Association. It included three churches in St. Clair and Madison Counties under the care of a free black preacher named John Livingston. The oldest was Mount Sinai Church (sometimes called Mount Zion) founded in the 1820s by Livingston with the help of James Lemen, founder of the white Illinois Union Baptist Association and Friends of Humanity.[18]

Although Livingston was the first moderator of the black association, the impetus for forming it came from Alfred H. Richardson, who became the association's first clerk. Richardson was a free black from Tennessee, who arrived in Upper Alton in 1837. He and his wife encountered some sort of discrimination in the white Baptist church, which destroyed his hope that a free state would treat free Negroes differently.

> I was comfortably seated, the singing was all that could be desired, but an incident occurred at this juncture not necessary to relate here, that no doubt had considerable to do with the organization of the Alton church and the birth of the Association. It caused me to reflect on the difference that should be between a slave state and a free state. Being in a free state why not have a church of our own? Going home from church I remarked to some friends that I was not going to that church anymore.[19]

---

[17]Short biographical sketches of Fossett and Shelton are in Theodore S. Boone, *From George Lisle to L. K. Williams: Short Visits to the Tombs of Negro Baptists*, rev. (Detroit: A. P. Publishing, 1941) 28, 62; also see David Benedict, *A General History of the Baptist Denomination in America and Other Parts of the World* (New York: Lewis Colby, 1848) 890; Christy, *Pulpit Politics*, 184; and Union Baptist Antislavery Association *Minutes*, 1860, 2.

[18]Joseph B. Lemen, "The Baptist Churches of St. Clair County" in *History of St. Clair County, Illinois, 1686-1881* (Philadelphia: Brink and McDonough, 1881[?]) 172; Miles Mark Fisher, "Negro Churches in Illinois: A Fragmentary History With Emphasis on Chicago," *Journal of the Illinois State Historical Society* 51 (Autumn 1963): 553.

[19]"Address of A. H. Richardson, First Clerk of Wood River Association," The Wood River Association *Minutes*, 1888, 58.

Richardson subsequently discovered that there were six of his free black neighbors who had letters from their former churches in the South, and who were willing to form an all-black congregation in Upper Alton. They knew that John Livingston was the only ordained black Baptist minister in the whole state of Illinois, and therefore asked him to come to Alton to advise them. On his arrival, ''Bro. John was opposed at first on account of our small number and smaller means, but told us to pray over it.'' When Livingston returned a few weeks later, he found that they were still willing to form a congregation. He was asked to be pastor, and Richardson was asked to be the clerk. The clerk of a church was often more powerful than the pastor since many pastors were illiterate and the clerk was not.

Richardson proposed to write letters to Lemen and the Illinois Union Association in behalf of the three churches under Livingston's care. Richardson asked the white association to receive these churches as members and then to permit them to organize their own separate black association. The letters were presented in 1838 and all three churches were received into the Association. Richardson then asked the Association to form these black churches into a separate association of their own. Much discussion ensued, but Moderator Lemen brought it to a successful end by asking Livingston ''if he thought he could hold an Association in good order.'' According to Richardson, ''Bro. John raised from his seat and said, WITH THE HELP OF GOD I BELIEVE WE CAN.''[20] The motion passed, and in the spring of 1839 Lemen traveled to the home of Samuel Vincent in St. Clair County where he formally constituted the black association.[21]

Between 1839 and 1862 the Wood River Association grew from five to ten churches plus four mission churches as far away as Racine, Wisconsin, and Leavenworth, Kansas. Starting with sixty-four members in 1839, it had more than four hundred in 1862, a remarkable record considering the slow growth of the black community in Illinois and farther west.[22] The Association's camp meetings, held in various parts of the state, be-

---

[20]Ibid., 59.

[21]Ibid. See also The First Colored Association and Friends to Humanity *Minutes*, 1839, 2, 7.

[22]Carter G. Woodson, *A Century of Migration* (n.p., 1918; reprint ed., New York: AMS Press, 1970) 53-54.

came legendary,[23] largely because of great preaching and singing. By inviting noted preachers from such places as St. Louis and Cincinnati, Wood River spread its influences far beyond its boundaries.

Because its members were located near the Mississippi River, the Association took a special interest in working with black communities across the river. Many Midwestern black Baptists viewed Wood River as the major association for constituting churches and ordaining ministers, since many white associations were slow to meet the challenge. For that reason the Association created the Colored Baptist Home Missionary Society in 1844. In founding this society the Association contended that it was responding to requests from blacks in nearby regions.

> The cry of our dear brethren and sisters has come to us from different parts, and corresponding brethren have informed us of their destitute condition. They have said to us, will you send us a minister? We want to hear the gospel of the Son of God. We want to be constituted in churches, that we may have regular meetings. We have sinners amongst us that we desire to see brought into the fold of God.[24]

The Association heard this "cry," and declared that it felt "much interested for our race of people, who are deprived of the privilege that we enjoy in hearing the preached word of God." This society did not meet with much success initially because the Association lacked sufficient funds to underwrite the expenses of missionaries. Nevertheless missionary efforts led in 1853 to the formation of the Western Colored Baptist convention, which included several churches located west of the Mississippi. I will return later in this chapter to the Western Convention and its successor.

---

[23]George Washington Williams, *History of the Negro Race in America, From 1619 to 1880: Together With a Preliminary Consideration of the Unity of the Human Family, An Historical Sketch of Africa, and an Account of the Negro Governments of Sierra Leone and Liberia* (New York: G. P. Putnam's Sons, 1885) 485-90. For an excellent biography of George Washington Williams, a pioneer historian and notable black Baptist minister, see John Hope Franklin, *George Washington Williams: A Biography* (Chicago: University of Chicago Press, 1985) 9-11, 13-21, 35-38, 55.

[24]The Colored Baptist Home Missionary Society of the State of Illinois *Proceedings,* 1844, 3.

Meanwhile, younger, better educated ministers, such as Duke William Anderson[25] and Richard DeBaptiste, challenged the Association's single-minded attention to domestic missions. These preachers were eager to harness Baptist energies to the antislavery cause. They had no difficulty in mingling politics and religion because they saw slavery as a moral issue that must be addressed rather than simply tolerated. When they began to take the reins of the Association, they managed to get their more cautious brethren to make public abolitionist statements. The statements became increasingly more radical as the national political climate reached a boiling point during 1859 and 1860.

First, a "Covenant" expressed the deep commitment of Association members to keep themselves unspotted from the world, especially in regard to the issue of human oppression. One part of this unusual communal agreement read, "That we will discountenance all oppression of our fellow-men, and the withholding of just wages among ourselves and others, as far as our influence may extend."[26] But this commitment was not enough for some in the Association. In 1854 it passed a resolution that ostensibly committed its members to employ all their energies for the liberation of the slave: "*Resolved,* That we deeply sympathise with our enslaved brethren, and will do all that we can morally and politically, to relieve them from their thraldom." In order to show that they were taking this stand as Christians rather than racialists, they passed another resolution later in the same meeting that declared "that we still continue to declare ourselves bound by the ties of common brotherhood, to do all we can for the general good of mankind."[27]

This tension between radical abolitionism and religious reform heightened as the Civil War approached. In its annual meeting of 1859 the Association passed a resolution that placed it squarely in the abolitionist camp.

Whereas, We believe the institution of American slavery to be a sin in the

---

[25]A full biographical sketch of Duke William Anderson is found in George W. Williams, *History of the Negro Race,* 476-503. Although D. W. Anderson was a prominent black Baptist minister, he was not as prominent as Williams appears to have thought.

[26]This covenant apparently appeared for the first time in the minutes of 1853. The 1852 minutes are probably not extant, but it did not appear in the 1851 minutes. See the Wood River Colored Baptist Association *Minutes,* 1853, 16.

[27]The Wood River Colored Baptist Association *Minutes,* 1854, 6-7.

sight of God and man, therefore, *Resolved,* That we recommend to the Churches composing this Association to do their utmost to withhold their fellowship from any and every pro-slavery Church, and not to commune with them at the table of the Lord.[28]

This resolution was opposed by only one vote. But the old issue between human liberation and the liberation of the soul resurfaced when the members next took up the question of whether or not to rank the abolition of slavery above the abolition of beverage alcohol.

Whereas, Next to slavery, we believe the drinking of ardent spirits to be the greatest curse in our land, therefore,
Resolved, That we recommend to the churches of this Association to strenuously prohibit its use as a beverage, upon pain of exclusion.[29]

A heated debate—''in which the whole delegation participated''—preceded the passage of this resolution. The balloting produced a tie vote before Moderator D. G. Lett broke the tie in favor of the resolution.

The conflict in the Association between Christian consciousness and race consciousness, however, seldom became acute. The minutes testify that it rather consistently saw itself as an agent and defender of the Baptist denomination, which fostered a heavy emphasis on emulating its conception of New Testament Christianity. In 1863, for example, the major issue at the Association's annual meeting centered on an argument about the propriety of "footwashing" as an ordinance to be observed by all of its churches. The vigorous debate on this issue resounded long after the meeting. By contrast, it is interesting that a black organization said little about either the course of the war or the problem of slave contrabands. This seeming inattentiveness to social problems could mislead researchers into thinking that these free blacks were primarily preoccupied with their own survival.

As I noted earlier, these black Baptists certainly did relate Christian witness to social responsibility. They wrote letters, petitions, and articles to various religious newspapers, such as *The Christian Recorder, The American Baptist,* and even Garrison's *Liberator,* as well as numerous regional and local newspapers. Their numerous local and regional works in

---

[28]The Wood River Colored Baptist Association *Minutes,* 1859, 6.

[29]Ibid., 6-7.

local civic reform societies and black state conventions cannot be told here. But their activities in those arenas were indeed quite numerous.[30] They encouraged the war effort and continued to oppose various racist practices. In fact many of them shared letters and messages from relatives and friends in the South in an attempt to defend the righteousness of the Civil War. Their own financial impoverishment and oppression certainly commanded a great part of their attention. Nevertheless, their intense commitment to revivalistic piety still continued to encourage some to see a dichotomy between religion and politics.

The Amherstburg Association. Originally called the Baptist Association for Colored People, this group was formed in October 1841 in the home of John Liberty in Amherstburg, Canada West. This association brought together some of the churches spread across what is now Southern Ontario from St. Catherine's near the Niagara River westward to Windsor across from Detroit, Michigan. Such places included Amherstburg, Chatham, Dresden, and the experimental black colonies of Wilberforce and Dawn. These congregations were usually located close to the American border in the hope of "an eventual return." A few Methodist and Congregational churches also sprang up among the black emigrants; but "There was no Negro community of any significance where there was not also a Baptist church."[31]

The Amherstburg Association also included five Michigan churches: Second Baptist of Detroit, which was the most important one, and congregations in Marshall, Battle Creek, Ann Arbor, and Ypsilanti. In fact the circular letter announcing the creation of the Association was issued by the

---

[30]For example, numerous references to many of the leaders mentioned here can be found in Philip S. Foner and George E. Walker, eds., *Proceedings of the Black State Conventions, 1840-1865,* 2 vols. (Philadelphia: Temple University Press, 1979, 1980).

[31]James K. Lewis, "Religious Nature of the Early Negro Migration to Canada and the Amherstburg Baptist Association," *Ontario History* 58 (June 1966): 120-21. Also see James K. Lewis, *Religious Life of Fugitive Slaves and Rise of Coloured Baptist Churches, 1820-1865, in What is now known as Ontario* (1865; reprint, New York: Arno Press, 1980); Dorothy Shadd Shreve, compiler, *Pathfinders of Liberty and Truth: A Century with the Amherstburg Regular Missionary Baptist Association* (Buxton, Ontario: n.p., 1940); and more recently Dorothy Shadd Shreve, *The AfriCanadian Church: A Stabilizer* (Jordan Station, Ontario: Paideia Press, 1983). A general excellent historical introduction to black Canadians can be found in Robin W. Winks, *The Blacks in Canada: A History* (Montreal and New Haven: McGill-Queen's University Press and Yale University Press, 1971).

influential Second Baptist Church of Detroit, founded in 1835. Among the members of Second Baptist Church were George French and Madison Lightfoot, who with their wives were highly regarded for their courageous rescue of a fugitive slave couple in 1833. Such was their reputation in both Detroit and Canada West that they were respectively first moderator and first clerk when the association was organized in 1841. From 1841 until 1856 the group maintained Israel Campbell as its first itinerant missionary. Campbell, a fugitive slave from Tennessee and an effective evangelist, was partly responsible for the Association's growth to ten churches by 1856. He later returned to the emancipated Southern black community to rekindle the fires there.[32]

The Amherstburg Association never lost sight of its abolitionist missionary concerns. In fact many of its leaders, such as William C. Monroe, who later became an Episcopal priest and an emigrant to Liberia, William P. Newman, Isaac Rice, Anthony Binga, Sr., H. H. Hawkins, William Troy, Washington William Christian, and Samuel H. Davis, were major leaders in the black abolitionist movement in Canada. In 1843 Samuel Davis gave an antislavery speech before the National Colored Convention in Buffalo that was at least as radical as Henry Highland Garnet's famous "Address to the Slaves" delivered at the same gathering. He spoke for black Baptists as well when he boldly outlined his blueprint for effective black opposition to slavery.

> Shall we, then, longer submit in silence to our accumulated wrongs? Forbid it, heaven! that we should longer stand in silence, "hugging the delusive phantom of hope," when every gale that sweeps from the South, bears on its wings, to our ears, the dismal sound of slavery's clanking chains, now rivetted on three millions of our brethren, and we ourselves are aliens and outcasts in our native land.

---

[32]Lewis, "Religious Nature," 117-32; Nathaniel Leach and Edith D. Gamble, *One Hundred Fortieth Birthday Celebration Eyewitness History* [of the] *Second Baptist Church of Detroit, 1836-1976* (Detroit: n.p., 1976) 3-4; David M. Katzman, *Before the Ghetto: Black Detroit in the Nineteenth Century* (Urbana: University of Illinois Press, 1973) 19-20; Arthur H. Pace, "The Negro in Detroit" in the Detroit Baptist Association *Minutes*, 1926, 106-12; Silas Farmer, *History of Detroit and Wayne County and Early Michigan: as Chronological Cyclopedia of Past and Present* (N.p.p.: n.p., 1890; reprint, Detroit: Gale Research, 1969) 607; and Robin W. Winks, *The Blacks in Canada: A History*, 339-48.

Later he concluded that "no other hope is left us, but in our own exertions, and an 'appeal to the God of armies!' "[33]

By 1849 the Amherstburg Association, still guided by such passionate abolitionist fervor, resolved to become the Canadian auxiliary of the radical American Baptist Free Mission Society, the major Baptist abolitionist group in the United States. While this move grew out of the majority's deep yearning to do all they could for black emancipation, a minority resented the idea that the Free Mission society wanted them to be its "auxiliary." Led by Samuel Davis, pastor of the Second Baptist Church of Detroit, and William P. Newman, editor of the *Provincial Freeman* and agent for the Free Mission Society at Dawn, this minority withdrew to form the "Canadian Anti-Slavery Baptist Association" in 1850. Seven years later the two groups reunited in time to provide important leadership in the formation of the Northwestern and Southern Baptist Convention in 1864.[34]

The Two Antebellum Black Baptist Conventions

The distinction between associations and conventions in the antebellum years appears rather arbitrary now, but was not so then. In Baptist polity the church is the congregation. Any supracongregational affiliation is by vote of the congregation and can be revoked at any time. The terms "association" and "convention" imply the voluntary, consultative nature of these organizations. Later Baptist usage reserved the term "convention" for statewide and national bodies, so that "association" denoted an organization smaller than a convention. But before the war, as we have seen, an association through its missionaries could have statewide or interstate influence. A convention might begin exactly as an association did with an agreement among three or four churches. A convention might also be a single-purpose organization, devoted to missions or education.

Despite this ambiguity of terms, however, both the American Baptist Missionary Convention and the Northwestern and Southern Baptist Convention sought and gained wide regional influence. They overcame humble beginnings to become conventions in something like the later sense.

---

[33]National Convention of Colored Citizens (1843) *Minutes,* in Bell, *Minutes of the National Negro Conventions.*

[34]James K. Lewis, "Religious Nature of the Early Negro Migration," 126-29.

After the Civil War they merged to form a national organization, which eventually led to the founding of the National Baptist convention in 1895.

The American Baptist Missionary Convention, organized in August 1840 at Abyssinian Baptist Church in New York City, was the first of its kind among black Baptists. Consisting originally of the Abyssinian and Zion churches of New York and Union Church of Philadelphia, the new convention was led by Sampson White, Abyssinian's pastor and a free black immigrant from Virginia. Western blacks, including the prominent St. Louis pastor John Berry Meachum, lent their encouragement. The constituent churches retained membership in predominantly white associations but formed the Convention without white assistance.

Indeed disagreement with white Baptists largely accounted for the founding of the black convention. The blacks had for some time desired more missions to Africa and an unequivocal Baptist stand against slavery. The abolition issue came to a head in April 1840 with the gathering in New York of the American Baptist Antislavery Convention, the first Baptist abolitionist convention of national scope. This meeting in turn was arranged by the main Baptist national organization, the General Missionary Convention of the Baptist Denomination in the United States for Foreign Missions, often called the Triennial Convention. Antislavery members of the Triennial Convention wanted to bar slaveholders from being Baptist missionaries. They achieved this policy change in a series of shrewd maneuvers, including engineering the Antislavery Convention of 1840. But blacks wanted from the Convention a more comprehensive and public antislavery policy rather than a mere housecleaning. They were also annoyed that they were blocked from significant influence in the Antislavery Convention and that the Triennial Convention discouraged strong antislavery voices in an effort to keep its Southern members. Most white Southerners withdrew anyway, and in 1845 formed the Southern Baptist Convention, effectively dividing the denomination along sectional lines.[35]

Any person could join the new black convention by sending one dollar. Church auxiliaries, mission societies, associations, and churches had to pay three dollars to become members. The fee could be sent by mail, allowing blacks in slave states to identify with the Convention. At one meeting

[35]Robert A. Baker, *The Southern Baptist Convention and Its People, 1607-1972* (Nashville: Broadman Press, 1974) 167-77.

membership fees came from twenty-eight persons in Virginia, one in South Carolina, and one in Louisiana. While the Convention was committed to African missions, most of its evangelistic efforts were domestic. It established a fund for the care of widows of deceased ministers, it supplied vacant churches with ministers when so requested, and it supported missionaries in establishing new churches. It also stressed the importance of ministerial education in addition to piety. It encouraged cooperation with Bible, Sunday School, and tract societies and discouraged the use of intoxicating beverages.

Most of these commitments were standard Baptist concerns, but on the issue of slavery the Missionary convention differed strongly with other Baptists. Not until 1853, however, did it make a public pronouncement against slavery. Its resolution defined why it was committed to the abolition of slavery. Characteristically its members saw the Christian religion as the panacea for all social ills.

> Believing an efficient gospel church to be the only sovereign and effective remedy for the many complicated evils which are the result of sin, therefore—
> *Resolved,* That we, the members of the Convention, will put forth our united efforts for the abolition of Slavery, the annihilation of the A. C. [American Colonization] Society, the removal of Intemperance and all other kindred evils, endeavoring thereby to promote the salvation of the world—God being our helper.[36]

There were members of this convention, however, who felt that the brethren were placing too much faith in political action. Some of them, such as Elder Jeremiah Asher, believed that no amount of political activity could remedy the sickness of white racism. Asher said, ''I find it far better for me to practice self-denial in these matters, than to be contending for right with a set of creatures who are lost to all true sense of right; it seems to me to be casting pearls before swine.''[37] Asher, who was born free in the state of Connecticut, had an amazingly consistent commitment to the creation of a black Christian civilization in Africa as well. He said, ''The

---

[36]The American Baptist Missionary Convention *Report,* 1853, 9.

[37]*Incidents in the Life of Rev. Jeremiah Asher* (n.p., 1850; reprint, Freeport: Books for Libraries, 1971) 71.

gospel must first be preached to the untutored [African] heathen, in order to prepare the way for civilization—and we believe the only effectual remedy for the traffic in human flesh on the shores of Africa."[38] His belief in missionary abolitionism was shared by other members of the American Baptist Missionary Convention who also wanted to create a black Christian civilization, preferably in the United States but ideally in Africa. Yet many of them saw no contradiction between missionary abolitionism and political abolitionism. Such outspoken abolitionist ministers as Leonard Grimes, William Spellman, Sampson White, and Theodore Doughty Miller were also the major leaders of this movement to establish a national black Baptist denomination.

In 1858 these men, led by Sampson White, insisted that the churches belonging to the convention sever all connections with white Baptist associations. They agreed that "in view of the wicked prejudice and proscription which exists among our white brethren, we, the churches composing this Convention, withdraw our connexion with the different associations, and form one among ourselves."[39] The next year White succeeded in getting the convention to make its strongest statement against slavery, and persuaded it to refuse fellowship to those ministers who held slaves.

White presented three resolutions before the 1859 session of the convention: "*Resolved,* That slavery is against the progress of the gospel at home and abroad. *Resolved,* That we use all laudable means to abrogate it. *Resolved,* That no slaveholding minister be invited into the pulpits of any of our churches."[40] A lengthy discussion ensued. Opposition to the resolutions came from ministers committed to serving churches in slave

---

[38]ABMC *Report,* 1859, 16-17.

[39]ABMC *Report,* 1858, 13.

[40]ABMC *Report,* 1859, 13. The issue of disfellowshipping tested the theological universalism of some of the most ardent black abolitionists. Those who favored disfellowshipping either did so for strategic reasons or were Calvinists who believed that only the elect should worship together. Of course they all agreed that the practice of slavery was a sinful abomination. But some of their members, like some members of the African Methodist Episcopal Church, practiced holding slaves as a means of enabling slaves to earn enough money to purchase freedom. Scholars often overlook this peculiar praxis. A very useful discussion of the issue of the role of disfellowshipping among abolitionists can be found in John R. McKivigan, *The War Against Proslavery Religion: Abolitionism and the Northern Churches, 1830-1865* (Ithaca: Cornell University Press, 1984) 18-35, 93-110.

states, such as Moses C. Clayton of Baltimore, Nelson G. Merry of Nashville, and William Evans, Samuel Madden, and William E. Walker, all three from Virginia. At least one convention member, Meachum of St. Louis, had been a slave owner, but he was not involved in the present debate, having died in 1854.[41] Not even such firm opposition, however, could avert the radicalizing effect of the events of 1859, especially John Brown's raid at Harper's Ferry. The resolution passed.

Disagreement and debate about these issues should not be viewed, however, as a tacit endorsement of slavery. John McKivigan correctly argues that "black organizations such as the American Baptist Missionary Convention can be regarded as having adopted most of the functions of antislavery comeouter sects."[42] These sects believed fervently, as did the black groups, that compromise with the slave regime was tantamount to making a pact with the devil.

Nor did the antislavery debate obscure the missionary concern implied in the convention's name. By 1858 it succeeded in sending William John Barnett to Waterloo, Sierra Leone, the British colony where Barnett had been born. The Convention supported the Waterloo station until its merger in 1866 with a western convention. By the time of its silver anniversary in 1865 the American Baptist Missionary Convention had grown to include forty-eight churches, twelve auxiliary societies, and sixty-five ministers. Although it was mainly an Eastern organization, its Western members included Meachum and Charles Satchell. Satchell had moved west from Ohio

---

[41]Meachum has been the subject of several biographical sketches: John Richard Anderson, *A Sermon on the Life, Character, and Death of Rev. John B. Meachum, Late Pastor of the First African Baptist Church, Saint Louis, Mo.* (Saint Louis: Charles' Job Printing Office, 1854); N. Webster Moore, "John Berry Meachum, Saint Louis Pioneer, Black Abolitionist, Educator, and Preacher," Missouri Historical Society *Bulletin* 29 (January 1973): 96-103; "Rev. John Berry Meachum" in William Cathcart, ed., *The Baptist Encyclopedia* (Philadelphia: Louis Everts, 1883) 775. "Some Undistinguished Negroes," *Journal of Negro History* 6 (January 1921): 115-16 is a misleading article about Meachum as a slave owner. Meachum was a committed capitalist who, although he objected to the slave system, did not have ethical difficulties with practicing a form of gradual emancipation. See his *An Address to All the Colored Citizens of the United States* (Philadelphia: King and Baird, 1846) 26-27, in which he calls upon free blacks to buy land and farms. He said, "I am led to believe that it [farming] is the greatest office in the United States."

[42]McKivigan, *The War Against Proslavery Religion,* 108.

by 1858, and had organized churches in Silver City, Nevada, and in San Francisco and Sacramento, California.[43]

Before turning to the Western convention, we should look briefly at the American Baptist Free Mission Society, a small, predominantly white abolitionist body that was important in the history of black Baptist cooperative organizations. It included such black ministers as Wallace Shelton and Sampson White as early members. For a time it appeared that this group might merge with a black convention to become a national "anticaste" convention. The Society also played an important role in focusing Baptist opinion favorable to Radical Reconstruction.

Formed in Boston in May 1843 under the original name of American and Foreign Mission Society, the Free Mission Society consisted of those who, like the blacks in the American Baptist Missionary Convention, were opposed to the Triennial Convention's caution on the abolition issue. Early ministerial leaders of this movement included Albert L. Post, Cyrus P. Grosvenor, and William Henry Brisbane. In addition to being strongly abolitionist, these Baptists were also anti-Masonic, a posture that later prevented their merger with black Baptists on a national level. They were also opposed to centralization and oath-taking and were staunch nativists. A short while after its founding, the society took a strong stand against the practice of soliciting life memberships from individuals, a growing practice among voluntary societies of the period. Although the reasons for its opposition are not entirely clear, its members regarded the principle as second in importance only to their abolitionist principles. By supporting mission stations in Canada and Haiti, this society was able to claim a visible role in African missions. But both of these mission stations were barely successful before the demise of the Free Mission Society in 1872 when it turned over this part of its foreign mission work to the black Baptists.[44]

---

[43]Elmer R. Rusco, *Good Time Coming?: Black Nevadans in the Nineteenth Century* (Westport CT: Greenwood Press, 1975) 174. At 191 n7 Rusco erroneously reports that Satchell was "one of five 'leading clergymen in the colored Baptist churches' in Ohio" during the 1880s. Satchell died in 1872; see Consolidated American Baptist Missionary Convention *Report,* 1872, 27.

[44]American Baptist Free Mission Society, *Minutes,* 1848, 40; ABFMS *Minutes,* 1849, 11; Carthcart, ed., *Baptist Encyclopedia,* 415; A. T. Foss and E. Mathews, compilers, *Facts for Baptist Churches* (Utica NY: American Baptist Free Mission Society, 1850) 384-403;

I turn finally to the second of the black conventions that persisted into the postbellum era. Although the major leaders of the Northwestern and Southern Baptist Convention were also members of the Free Mission Society, the former group was all black from its beginning in 1864. Its forerunner was the Western Colored Baptist Convention, organized for trans-Mississippi church extension under the auspices of the Wood River Association in St. Louis in 1853, as mentioned earlier. It met regularly between 1853 and 1859, when it extended its program to include the formal training of ministers. Between 1859 and 1864 there were no meetings because of the Civil War. But in 1863 the Wood River Association resolved to reorganize the Western Convention.

Rejuvenated and renamed in St. Louis in June 1864, the convention included twenty-six churches from Illinois, Indiana, Ohio, Missouri, Tennessee, Louisiana, Mississippi, and Arkansas. William P. Newman, fresh from a four-year missionary tour in Haiti and Jamaica, was named president of the new convention; Richard DeBaptiste became corresponding secretary; and William Troy, formerly of Canada West, became the general agent, whose duty was to rally support and raise funds for the missionary objectives of the convention.

The major difference between this convention and its forerunner was the new commitment to missions among the "freed brethren in the valley of the lower Mississippi" and "in the states of Tennessee, Arkansas and Missouri." The Western Convention was limited to the more northerly banks of the Mississippi and the free states and territories west of St. Louis. The Emancipation Proclamation promised the opening of the South as a mission field, and the new commitment was implied by the new name, Northwestern and Southern Baptist Convention.

Unlike the older American Baptist Missionary Convention, the Northwestern Convention more readily incorporated an antislavery and "anti-caste" provision into its constitution. Article 3 of the convention's constitution did not sidestep the issue: "This Convention shall be com-

---

Edmund F. Merriam, *A History of American Baptist Missions* (Philadelphia: American Baptist Publication Society, 1900) 91-94; and Kenneth Richard Short, "The Widening Gap: The Story of the Abolition within the Ranks of the Baptist Denomination, 1830 to 1850" (Seminar Paper, Colgate Rochester Divinity School, 1958). Freewill Baptists were also deeply committed to abolitionism. They organized the "Freewill Baptist Anti-Slavery Society" in the New Hampshire Yearly Meeting of 1843. See J. M. Brewster, et al., *The Centennial Record of Freewill Baptists, 1780-1880* (Dover NH, 1881).

posed of delegates from churches and associations of Regular Baptists, of anti-slavery principles, who recognize the equality of man, and the brotherhood of the race.'' This antislavery posture doubtless reflects the influence of the former members of the Amherstburg and Canadian antislavery associations, as well as views of leaders of the Providence and Union antislavery Baptist associations. But the presence of the phrase, ''the brotherhood of the race,'' in Article 3 presaged the rise of a new black religious nationalism that this convention helped to foster among black Baptists during the 1860s.[45]

In order to understand the postwar development of black Baptist cooperation and union, however, we must first look at the relations between white and black Baptist leaders as they confronted the opportunities and problems of Reconstruction and the Southern mission field.

---

[45]Northwestern and Southern Baptist Convention *Minutes*, 1866, 3; Western Colored Baptist Convention *Minutes*, 1853, in Wood River Colored Baptist Association *Minutes*, 1854, 10-12; and Miles Mark Fisher, *A Short History of the Baptist Denomination* (Nashville: Sunday School Publishing Board of the National Baptist Convention, USA, Inc., 1933) 107-108.

Part II

The Polity
and Politics
of a New
Religious Culture

3

The Politics
of Religious
Reconstruction,
1864-1866

Willie Lee Rose offers this summary of the chaotic state of post-Civil War America: "The long war was over. Now the nation, still divided in spirit, plunged into a decade of political and social turmoil. Northern victory had preserved the Union and had ended slavery; the constitutional right of states to secede would never be argued again. But all else was confusion."[1] Yet decisions had to be made even in the wake of national catastrophe. The pressure of this social crisis greatly affected how American institutions—especially Protestant churches—responded to the most serious problem of all, the plight of destitute slaves.

The war dealt the fatal blow that shattered the institutional structures of Southern church life. But the churches were forewarned by events occurring more than a decade before the war. Many Christians became convinced then that if the slavery issue were left unresolved a hard-won solidarity among evangelical Protestants would be sacrificed. The fragile voluntaristic structure of Southern religious institutions was especially

---

[1]John Blum, Edmund S. Morgan, Willie Lee Rose, et al., *The National Experience: A History of the United States to 1877,* 4th ed. (New York: Harcourt Brace Jovanovich, 1977) 1:357.

vulnerable. It had taken shape slowly since 1607, and could have endured almost anything except the profound ethical and theological issues raised by the slavery controversy. The North was no stranger to this problem either. Beginning with the Presbyterians in 1837, the entire American ecclesiastical fabric was rent asunder by the challenges of theological modernity and political abolitionism. Southern Methodists formed a denomination in May 1845. By December Southern Baptists had incorporated themselves as a chartered denomination under the statutes of the state of Georgia. Several radical abolitionist offshoots of these major bodies, such as the Wesleyan Methodists and the Free Mission Baptists, had already formed denominations. The spiritual posterity of the magisterial Reformers, such as the Lutherans and the Anglicans, managed to retain their rather loose confederacies. Despite the Protestant cast of the theological debates, Catholics also entered the fray and and later fought on both sides of the battle fields. The hierarchy walked a delicate tightrope between moral condemnation of slavery and pastoral care for proslavers.

The political events of the 1850s transformed this serious ecclesiastical malady into a malignant and lingering case of pneumonia within the American Body of Christ. The Fugitive Slave Law of 1850 even dismissed the relevance of Deuteronomy 23:15—"Thou shalt not deliver unto his master the servant which escaped from his master unto thee." Many of the spiritual descendants of Bible-believing Puritans lamented that God's New Israel was becoming a haven for those who would desecrate the Word of God.

Such apocalyptic views of American history gained in popularity as more and more events seemed to them to approximate biblical parallels. Harriet Beecher Stowe, the undaunted spouse of a professor of Old Testament, published her influential novel, *Uncle Tom's Cabin,* in 1852. She drew a powerful picture of the slave as a Christlike Suffering Servant whose very blood was being drained by the vampires of slavocracy. By 1857 Chief Justice Roger Brooke Taney unwittingly fanned already flaming announcements of an impending Apocalypse by offering legal support to those who suspected that Africans were not part of the human race. In a famous *obiter dictum* aimed at John Sanford's slave, Dred Scott, Taney reminded all who sought to bestow citizenship on the Negro through the judicial process that Negroes were mere chattel property, "beings of an inferior order" who had "no rights a white man was bound to respect."

Behind an ominous spiderweb of tangled, momentous events, John Brown was waging his own "Private War," which became visible in the fall of 1859 at Harper's Ferry, Virginia. Apocalyptic seers now had their martyr. During the same season of historic anxiety, James William Charles Pennington, a fugitive slave and a Brooklyn Presbyterian clergyman, published a sermon that painted a heavenly scene that left little doubt the Apocalypse peered over the horizon: "Every department of God's moral government is desecrated. . . . The souls of thousands of murdered slaves are now making their own pleas before God; all heaven is filled with feeling, and God will surely soon visit the earth."[2] The tocsin of such sacramental readings of American history rang loudly and clearly. It tolled deafening and macabre decibels when Fort Sumter was fired upon in December 1860. Four months later Abraham Lincoln prophesied to his native Southland, "In your hands, my dissatisfied fellow-countrymen, and not in mine, is the momentous issue of civil war." The die was cast. Armageddon had arrived.[3]

The war lasted longer than either side had anticipated. But in the meantime, on 1 January 1863, President Lincoln signed the Emancipation Proclamation in the name of expediency and belated justice. This Executive Order did not solve either the future problem of Southern white reparation and economic restitution nor the problem of reparations for the injustices suffered by the slaves. Resolution would depend on the nature of the restructuring that lay ahead. A gun shot at Ford's Theatre unburdened the Chief Executive. But the nation could not so simply unhitch the yoke of social responsibility, especially for its former slaves.

The white Protestant denominations, accustomed to the blessings Scripture promised to the charitable, bore an impressive share of the burden. Yet their yoke was uneasy and the burden was heavy. Only the inflationary coffers of the Northern government had the potential to meet the mammoth economic demands that lay ahead. The private sector also had

---

[2]J. W. C. Pennington, "The Great Conflict Requires Great Faith," *The Anglo-African Magazine* 1,11 (November 1859): 343-45.

[3]For Northern views of the war, see James Moorhead, *Yankee Apocalypse: Yankee Protestants and the Civil War, 1860-1869* (New Haven: Yale University Press, 1978) and William A. Clebsch, "Christian Interpretations of the Civil War," *Church History* 30 (June 1961): 212-22. Charles Reagan Wilson discusses the Southern side of American public religion during this period in his *Baptized in Blood: The Religion of the Lost Cause, 1865-1920* (Athens GA: University of Georgia Press, 1980). For the role of American Protestants in the processes that led to civil war, see C. C. Goen, *Broken Churches, Broken Nation* (Macon GA: Mercer University Press, 1985).

vast wealth. But neither had wills strong enough to destroy the poisonous fangs of the cunning serpent called "oppression." They were in the grips of laissez-faire economic views and an ideology of rugged individualism that frowned on giving too much aid to the downtrodden. They were afraid of fostering laziness.

Leaders of the huge black constituency, consisting of more than one-tenth of the population, realized that there was much that blacks could do for themselves. Thus they too began to reorganize for the task of restructuring Southern culture. Their churches, especially those in the North, prepared themselves for the labor ahead. A large portion of this constituency among Protestants was Baptist. For them, as well as their compatriots in other denominations, the old arrangements, both North and South, had become obsolete and unacceptable.[4] These black Christians believed that

---

[4]Clarence Walker, *Rock in a Weary Land: The African Methodist Episcopal Church During the Civil War and Reconstruction* (Baton Rouge: Louisiana State University Press, 1982). In addition to this solid study, see note 30 for references to William B. Gravely's fine work on race relations among Methodists during this momentous period. Bishop William Jacob Walls, *The African Methodist Episcopal Zion Church: Reality of the Black Church* (Charlotte NC: A. M. E. Zion Publishing House, 1974) 185-202 is a useful introduction, but leaves many questions unanswered. Developments among Black Presbyterians are ably discussed by Andrew E. Murray, *Presbyterians and the Negro—A History* (Philadelphia: Presbyterian Historical Society, 1966) 103-202, as well as Gayraud S. Wilmore, *Black Presbyterians: The Heritage and the Hope* (Philadelphia: Geneva Press, 1983). Fine summaries of recent scholarship on black Congregationalists are found in Percel O. Alston, "The Afro-Christian Connection" and Clara Merritt DeBoer, "Blacks and the American Missionary Association" in Barbara Brown Zikmund, ed., *Hidden Histories in the United Church of Christ* (New York: United Church Press, 1984). A. Knighton Stanley, *The Children Is Crying: Congregationalism Among Black People* (New York: Pilgrim Press, 1979) is a helpful introduction. The finest study of race relations among Congregationalists during Reconstruction, however, is an article by Joel Williamson, "Why the American Missionary Association Failed in the South," *Southern Studies* (Spring 1979): 51-73. The critical role of the American Missionary Association, a basically Congregationalist enterprise that sought to be ecumenical, is examined in three important studies: Richard Bryant Drake, "The American Missionary Association and the Southern Negro, 1861-1888" (Ph.D. dissertation, Emory University, 1957); Clifton Herman Johnson, "The American Missionary Association, 1846-1861: A Study of Christian Abolitionism" (Ph.D. dissertation, University of North Carolina, 1959); and Clara Merritt DeBoer, "The Role of Afro-Americans in the Origin and Work of the American Missionary Association: 1839-1877" (Ph.D. dissertation, Rutgers University, 1973). The Roman Catholic side of this story is sadly unclear. But important insights are provided by Albert J. Raboteau, *Slave Religion: The Invisible Institution in the Antebellum South* (New York: Oxford University Press, 1978)

nothing short of a national denomination could meet the domestic challenge for which they had worked and prayed so hard. Their resources were limited on many counts; yet a reorganization, born of necessity and the desire for racial fraternity, did take place. By 1863 a single black Baptist national convention of nearly 100 churches with more than 100,000 members was envisioned. By 1866 it had taken shape. These seemingly parochial events were nudged along by the lively course of the rise and fall of Radical Reconstruction. That failure nurtured Jim Crow and his bourgeois siblings, the New South and the New Negro movements.

Strategy and Tactics of the Southern Mission

In the period 1864-1866 Baptist leaders, black and white, were preoccupied with the challenge of more than four million freed slaves: how to evangelize them, educate them, and help them reorganize their religious lives. As Northern-based organizations took up this challenge, they were impeded by disagreement over at least three broad issues.

First was the question of policy with regard to white Southerners. Here the debate followed the lines of the national postwar controversy. Should the emphasis be on speedy reconciliation of Northern and Southern Baptists? Many, perhaps most, white Baptists thought so. They were opposed by the ecclesiastical equivalent of the Radical Republicans, who viewed the Southerners as a conquered people and who thought that reconciliation should occur only after appropriate punishment or reformation or both.

Then there was the question of priorities for allocation of money and personnel. Was the mission to freed slaves so important as to preclude for a time all other mission fields? Some Baptists thought so, particularly many black Baptist leaders. Others, including most whites, saw the Southern field as one of several domestic concerns that in turn had to be balanced with overseas missions. Finally there were questions of race as applied to missionaries and their executives. Should blacks be preferred as missionaries? Should white organizations funnel their funds through black organizations? Blacks were virtually unanimous in saying yes to both questions,

---

111-14, 271-75; John W. Blassingame, *Black New Orleans, 1860-1880* (Chicago: University of Chicago Press, 1973) 173-210; John T. Gillard, *The Catholic Church and the American Negro . . .* (Baltimore: St. Joseph's Society Press, 1930) 10-45; and James Hennesey, *American Catholics: A History of the Roman Catholic Community in the United States,* (New York: Oxford University Press, 1981) 161-63, 182, 193.

while whites were nearly unanimous in saying no, especially to the latter question. This racial issue also extended to the matter of protecting the religious freedom of Southern blacks. A closer look at the missionary organizations shows how these issues affected their work.

The American Baptist Home Mission Society. Founded in 1832, this predominantly white Northern society was the oldest, largest, and best financed of the Baptist groups devoted to domestic missions. It assumed an impressive share of the mission to emancipated blacks.[5] Meeting in Providence, Rhode Island, on 29 May 1862, it resolved to begin work among black refugees in the District of Columbia and "in other places" held by Union forces. On 25 June the Executive Board voted "that immediate measures be taken for the occupation by our missionaries of such Southern fields as in the Providence of God may be opened to our operations."[6] Although Union armies did not open new fields as fast as anticipated, the Society was able in the fall of 1862 to begin work in Beaufort and St. Helena, South Carolina.

But evangelizing homeless, hungry, and uneducated black refugees without giving immediate attention to their bodily needs was clearly inappropriate. The ABHMS could not meet all of these needs. So, while encouraging the government to meet bodily needs, it focused its attention on the spiritual and educational needs of the black "contrabands." Even then, however, some Baptists wondered whether the general education of blacks was consistent with the missionary purpose of the Society. This matter, raised at the Society's meeting in May 1863, was referred to the Executive Board, which resolved it by appointing teachers as "Assistants to missionaries," who were "to engage in such instruction of the colored people as will enable them to read the Bible and to become self-supporting and

---

[5]Harold Lynn McManus, "The American Baptist Home Mission Society and Freedmen Education in the South, with Special Reference to Georgia, 1862-1897" (Ph.D. dissertation, Yale University, 1953); also see Robert A. Baker, *Relations between Northern and Southern Baptists* (Fort Worth TX: Seminary Hill Press, 1948); Henry Lyman Morehouse, "A Survey of Twenty-five Years Work for the Colored People of the South," *The Baptist Home Mission Monthly* 10 (November 1888): 298-305; and Charles L. White, *A Century of Faith, Centenary Volume of the American Baptist Home Mission Society* (Philadelphia: Judson Press, 1932).

[6]Quoted in Morehouse, "A Survey of Twenty-five Years," 298.

self-directing churches.'''[7] While this satisfied the conservative missiologists within the Society, it left the ABHMS vulnerable to the charge by opposing groups that it was advocating racial separatism and caste segregation.

Detractors also claimed that the ABHMS was doing financially less than it could for Southern blacks. From one viewpoint the charge seems unreasonable. Between 1865, when it established its Freedmen's Fund, and 1872, its fortieth anniversary, the society raised $196,292.90.[8] From a different perspective, however, it is clear that the Society was beginning to spread itself too thin. It was engaged in doing mission work among Indians in the Western states and among large numbers of European immigrants arriving during the 1860s. Moreover, it could scarcely compete financially with the large capital outlay of other denominational home mission societies, such as the American Missionary Association (Congregational) and the Freedmen's Aid Society of the Methodist Church, which began with unified constituencies. On the other hand, dissenters from the policies of the Home Mission Society between 1864 and 1872 constantly threatened its budgetary expectations. In the midst of much frustration because of a deficit in their budget, ABHMS officers blamed the drop in Freedmen's Fund support—from more than $17,000 in 1867 to less than $5,000 in 1868—on the increased competition among agencies raising money for freedmen's missions.[9]

The American Baptist Free Mission Society. The ABHMS's main opponents belonged to the integrated American Baptist Free Mission Society (ABFMS), a relatively small group of radical Republicans and persistent abolitionists. Its founding in 1843 was partly in protest against the ABHMS's willingness to support missionaries who were slaveholders and to tolerate the system of individual life membership. The Free Missionists believed this latter practice offended the principle that only churches could hold membership in denominational voluntary associations.

The ABFMS opposed discrimination against blacks in denominational offices and activities. This stance offended some Northern Baptists and

---

[7]Ibid.

[8]These figures were compiled from American Baptist Home Mission Society *Reports*, 1865-1872. They only reflect the amount raised. The Society spent more than this amount.

[9]ABHMS *Report*, 1868, 9, 56.

many white Southern Baptists because they disapproved of free social intercourse between races. Several members of the ABHMS, including its popular corresponding secretary, Jay S. Backus, were reluctant to advocate the idea of black social equality, especially if it stood in the way of reunification with Southern Baptists. Many of them believed that the ABHMS had struggled too long to reconstitute the national missionary alliance of Baptists as represented in the old Triennial Convention, the first national organization of Baptists in the United States, to give up the desire to unite with the white Southern Baptists. They viewed the Free Missionists, who stood in the way of unification because of their militant stance on the race question, as "schismatic" radicals who cared more for impossible social dreams than for denominational unity.

The integrated ABFMS conducted a vigorous Southern mission of its own, and in fact was in the field before the larger ABHMS. When Union forces captured Beaufort, South Carolina, on 15 December 1861, a Free Mission agent, the Reverend C. W. Denison, preached the following Sunday in services at Hilton Head, South Carolina. From Hilton Head Denison wrote, "It was my privilege to be the first to prepare the way for the regular and systematic instruction of the emancipated masses of this part of South Carolina."[10] Many of the ABFMS missionaries were already on their future fields of labor because they served as chaplains in the military. The early ones, such as W. C. Patterson, Thomas W. Conway, T. P. Childs, and the well-known abolitionist William Henry Brisbane were involved deeply in the activities of the ABFMS before the war and wrote full accounts of their military and missionary activities for *The American Baptist*. Other Free Mission missionaries such as D. F. Cooper, Mrs. M. O. Quaiffe, C. M. Welles, and Albert L. Post occupied such fields as Beaufort, Alexandria, and Washington early in 1862.

They suffered from financial embarrassments, however, because the ABFMS had difficulty raising funds for them. It called upon its small constituency to come to the aid of the black refugees. "The question is whether, after twenty years of labor to bring about emancipation, we have the vigor to act efficiently for another twenty years in raising the emancipated to that elevation, moral, intellectual and religious, to which their new born free-

---

[10]ABFMS *Minutes*, 1862, 10.

dom entitles them.''[11] The appeal of the ABFMS apparently was successful because it raised $1,290.63 in 1863 for the ''freedmen'' compared to
the $189.25 it raised for the ''contrabands'' during 1862. Despite the
handsome increase more money was raised for the Japanese Mission under
the administration of the flamboyant missionary, Jonathan Goble. By the
next year, freedmen's fund contributions were down by two-thirds to about
$600.

The ABFMS's priorities were clearly established by 1864. The probable turning point was the Society's meeting in Mount Holly, New Jersey,
in May 1863. On that occasion the delegates were jubilant over the Emancipation Proclamation and the society's own twentieth anniversary. Proud
of the apparent success of their campaign against slavery and racism, they
reaffirmed their commitment to Afro-American social equality and reproached Baptist societies that did not embrace that principle.

> *Resolved,* That, as the African variety of man, though likely to be soon
> freed from the bondman's chain, is still threatened by pride, prejudice and
> folly, with the trammels of caste, it is the duty and solemn purpose of this
> Society to proclaim as the will of God, that the African, whether the Moor
> in the North, the Negro in the center, or the Hottentot in the South, must
> be held and treated as a *''man and a brother.''*

Apparently some persons within the ABFMS thought that perhaps the
agency's work was finished because abolition had been achieved. But a
majority felt otherwise and expressed themselves in another resolution.

> *Resolved,* That as these purposes have not yet been avowed by any
> missionary body; as the right to vote for missions, missionaries and their
> managers can still be bought with money, even by infidels and heathens;
> and as churches and church-members, as such, are not entrusted with the
> control of the ''missionary enterprise'' by any other Baptist organization,
> we, therefore, of the Free Mission Society, do, in the fear of the Lord, re-
> gard ourselves as a needed agency in his work, and we will continue, if
> God shall please, to urge our views upon our Baptist brethren, and pro-
> claim them among the heathen, till the Baptist denomination shall come
> to our platform, or till Christ shall come to reign.[12]

---

[11]Ibid., 12.

[12]ABFMS *Minutes,* 1863, 15-16.

By various arrangements the society supported missionaries, both black and white, in the Southern field. One such person was Charles Satchell, whom we noted earlier as one of the Western members of the American Baptist Missionary Convention. Taking up his station in New Orleans, he reported in the Society's paper: "My instructions were to gather up the scattered Baptists, form them into churches and associations, uniting them to the Free Mission Society."[13] Much if not all of Satchell's support came from his former church, Union Baptist in Cincinnati, whose pastor was William P. Newman. Although Satchell found that there were six black churches in New Orleans when he and his family arrived early in 1865, he still "organized a church called the Free Mission Baptist church with five members."[14]

In addition to forming this and other Free Mission black churches, Satchell followed Newman's suggestion and tried to form a statewide Black Free Mission association. "We have had in contemplation the formation of an association," Satchell reported, "but although the arrangement was made and proposed to the churches here, five months have passed and they have not taken the first step; but I have informed them that if they do not speedily act, we shall go forward and consummate its formation." Satchell attributed this delay to a lack of "the element of progress" among these black churches, and to the self-self-centeredness of the ministers: "Each minister seems to claim the right of dictating what is gospel order and what is not."[15]

The Reverend Nelson D. Saunders, black pastor of the First African Baptist Church of New Orleans and a preacher who flourished during the slave regime, led the group of established, antebellum free black Baptist ministers who opposed Satchell. Saunders long had accommodated himself and his parishioners to the oppressive social conditions of antebellum New Orleans.[16] By 1865 Saunders and other black ministers of his persuasion were able to organize their churches as the Louisiana Southern Baptist Association. The next year Satchell and other ministers—George

---

[13]*American Baptist,* 12 September 1865.

[14]Ibid.

[15]*American Baptist,* 12 April 1865.

[16]Benjamin Quarles, "Ante-Bellum Relationships Between the First African Baptist Church of New Orleans and White Agencies," *The Chronicle* 18 (January 1955): 26-36.

W. Walker, John Marks, Esau Carter, Alex Armstrong, Robert H. Steptoe, and others—organized the rival First Free Mission Association because they objected to the use of the phrase, "Southern Baptist" in the name of Saunders's group.[17]

On 9 March 1867 Satchell's association voted to make itself an auxiliary of the national Free Mission Society and to patronize its newspaper, *The American Baptist.* The following month *The Religious Herald* (Richmond, Virginia), the major newspaper of the Southern Baptist Convention, snickered at the announcement of this affiliation, which it described as "a nice little notice." It also accused Satchell's group of patronizing "a rancorous, rampant, radical, professedly religious, really political paper."[18] Replying in behalf of Satchell's group, Nathan Brown defended abolitionist Baptists as he also bragged about the triumph of Free Mission principles.

> The abolitionists never wished the slaveholders mischief, nor sought to do them harm. On the contrary they loved them just as well as their slaves, and sought their good as much; no more, no better. We opposed slavery not from hate to any body, but because it was a violation of every law of God and right of man; because it was doing mischief incalculable to both master and slave, and would undoubtedly bring down upon the guilty perpetrators and the consenting nation, the fearful judgement of a just God.

Brown then accused Southern Baptists of being jealous of black "affiliation with Northern Christians and politicians." Brown believed that Southerners, such as the editor of the *Herald,* acted "from the old motive of power [rather] than good principles" in criticizing the Louisiana black free missionists.[19]

Satchell and his colleagues were also reproached from another quarter. One of the ABHMS's newspapers, *The Examiner and Chronicle,* accused Satchell of taking an unauthorized action by publishing the notice of his board's desire to affiliate with the ABFMS. Fearing that some would interpret the action of Satchell's board as a condemnation of the Home Mis-

---

[17]William Hicks, *History of Louisiana Negro Baptists from 1804 to 1914* (Nashville: National Baptist Convention Publication Board, 1914) 27, 31-32.

[18]*Religious Herald,* 11 April 1867.

[19]*American Baptist,* 23 April 1867.

sion Society, the editors of the *Examiner* volunteered their own interpretation by asserting that the new Louisiana group "by no means wish to turn away from the Home Mission Society."[20] Satchell differed with this interpretation, and offered a statement reflecting the resentment that many black Baptists held against the Home Mission Society's pre-Civil War record of keeping slaveholders within its ranks.

> I think the people understood what they were doing, and will religiously abide their action. We had nothing to say about the Home Mission Society *pro nor con,* as I had a conversation with *Dr. Backus,* who told me that the Home Mission Society were willing to extend help to this field, *provided* we would be under their direction, but could not do anything for us while we operated with the Free Mission Society. The reason he assigned was, that they did not like to interfere with the Free Mission work.[21]

Satchell issued this statement more than two years after Newman and his congregation enabled him to pursue his missionary work while advocating the Free Mission ideology in Louisiana. Satchell was not simply voicing the opinion of his own local group, however. His friend Newman had been working on the national front to encourage the quasi-national black missionary organizations to become Free Mission and anticaste separatists who would have little to do with what they viewed as the self-centered, "caste-encouraging" work of the Home Mission Society.

Despite its appointment of Satchell and other black ministers, the Free Mission Society was unable to show until 1866 that more than one-half of its Southern missionaries were blacks. Many Free Missionists also shared the prevalent belief among white Baptists that there were not enough "prepared" black Baptist ministers to commence the large evangelistic labors among the freedmen. They disclosed their own paternalism and disregarded their own advice to Northern colaborers whom they told "the sooner they [blacks] cease to be treated as children, the sooner will they cease to be children."[22]

The Black Conventions. Looking at the reports of the white Baptist societies uncritically, one would get the impression that the black Baptists

---

[20]*Examiner and Chronicle*, 8 May 1867.

[21]*American Baptist*, 23 June 1863.

[22]ABFMS *Minutes*, 1864, 11.

themselves did little to advance the work of evangelizing unchurched black Southerners. This was not the case, however. Northern black Baptists, most of them immigrants from the South, especially from Virginia, felt a strong obligation to evangelize among their own brethren. In fact their belief in themselves as a Saving Remnant, manifest before the war, became even more pronounced after the war. Their basic agenda entailed saving freed black Southerners and especially reaching potential young ministers, who in turn would provide the personnel that they never had before the war to spread the gospel among blacks in the West Indies and Africa.

In August 1863 the black American Baptist Missionary Convention secured permission from President Lincoln himself "to go within our military lines and minister to their brethren there."[23] Accordingly, this twenty-five-year-old convention proudly recalled that it had not waited on white abolitionists to begin mission work among black Southerners. Throughout its existence, members of the Convention maintained close relations with relatives and friends in Southern states, notably in Virginia. Most of its leaders, including Leonard Grimes, Sampson White, William E. Walker, Samuel W. Madden, and William T. Dixon, were either from Virginia themselves or their parents were from Virginia. Members of this convention had a good reason for continuously reelecting Virginians to lead them; many of them also had come from Virginia and formed such important congregations as Abyssinian in New York City, Concord in Brooklyn, Joy Street and Twelfth in Boston, First African of Philadelphia, Union and Zion in Cincinnati, Olivet in Chicago, and Second Baptist in Detroit.[24]

In 1866 Leonard Grimes, pastor of Twelfth Baptist in Boston and president of the American Baptist Missionary Convention, appealed to the

---

[23]ABMC *Minutes*, 1865, 6.

[24]This information was confirmed in histories or historical sketches of these important congregations: Adam Clayton Powell, Sr., *Upon This Rock* (New York: Abyssinian Baptist Church, 1949); George A. Levesque, "Inherent Reformers—Inherited Orthodoxy: Black Baptists in Boston, 1800-1873," *The Journal of Negro History* 60 (October 1975): 291-525; Charles H. Brooks, *Official History of the First African Baptist Church, Philadelphia, Pa.* (Philadelphia: n.p., 1922); J. H. Magee, *The Night of Affliction and Morning of Recovery* (1873; reprint ed., Miami, Florida: Mnemosyne Publishing, 1969) 155-72; Miles Mark Fisher, "History of Olivet Baptist Church of Chicago" (Master's thesis, University of Chicago, 1922); also see Leach and Gamble, *One Hundred Fortieth Birthday Celebration Eyewitness History* [of the] *Second Baptist Church of Detroit, 1836-1976* (Detroit: n.p., 1976).

Home Missionary Society at its 1866 annual meeting. He reported that on a recent Southern tour he had interviewed 260 black men aspiring to be Baptist ministers.

> Most of them can read, two-thirds were licensed preachers, and a majority were old men, but thirty-six were single men between fifteen and forty years of age. We could in three months have at least 500 preparing for the ministry from Virginia alone.

Grimes's report quickly took on the quality of a vision, and from the seer came these words:

> I want the young men recently converted, the 125,000 children who are in the schools, to have educated preachers. I want an institution where the promising young men of the colored race may be educated. Other denominations were at work, but I want the Baptists to do it. The colored men have Africa on their minds. They wish to evangelize that land, and we must get 400 missionaries out of the blacks of this country for Africa. In the name of my oppressed race, I ask for some definite organization to educate the young men just emancipated. Aid us, and we will have our Newtons and Browns.[25]

Meanwhile the Reverend Richard De Baptiste of Chicago showed that the Northwestern and Southern Baptist convention, of which he was corresponding secretary, held similar views about the rights and obligations of black missionaries in the South. "One thing seems quite evident to us," DeBaptiste wrote, "and that is, no persons will prove to be so efficient as laborers among this unfortunate people as pious, intelligent, and properly qualified persons of their own race." In the same article he argued that "to help them who are trying to help themselves is Heaven's appointed way of doing this work, *we think.*"[26]

Such appeals for the support of black race pride by supporting black missionaries met with what appeared to be strong but paternal support from the mainly white societies. The ABFMS declared in 1864 that "the work of the missionary is not merely to preach and perform pastoral labors, but rather to organize and call forth the agencies of the freedmen themselves,

---

[25]ABHMS *Report,* 1866, 33-34.

[26]*American Baptist,* 4 October 1864.

so that they may learn to choose and support their own pastors, and conduct their own discipline.'' Dr. Martin B. Anderson of the University of Rochester, president-elect of the ABHMS in 1865, stated that

> It has been asked, What will you do with the negro? God does not require of us an answer to this. Our question is, What will we do *for* the negro? God will tell us, when it pleaseth him, what to *do* with the negro. Let us do *our* work, and leave the rest to God. Let us organize them into churches and Sunday schools; teach them to labor, and to make of themselves men in every sense. God will do the rest.[27]

During the 1865 meeting of the American Baptist Publication Society, its Committee on Work among Freedmen took a less theological view than Dr. Anderson, but concurred in the tendency of its sister societies to encourage black ministers. ''The ministers are of necessity raised up among themselves,'' the committee reported. ''Many of them are men of great natural power as preachers; and it should be our care that they have the means of mental expansion and higher intelligence.''[28]

The seriously disrupted Southern Baptist Convention, meeting in 1866 for the first time since the cessation of hostilities between the North and the South, also established a Committee on the Religious Instruction of the Colored People, which boldly offered a series of resolutions that were adopted by the convention. The one that most clearly expressed the convention's feelings on this subject read, ''*Resolved,* That while we are not opposed to any rightminded man aiding in this important work, it is our decided conviction, from our knowledge of the character of these people, and of the feelings of our citizens, that this work must be done mainly by ourselves.''[29]

William P. Newman, president of the Northwestern Convention, seemed undisturbed by this resolution. He sent a copy of all of these SBC resolutions to *The American Baptist,* and prefaced them with his belief that ''the Southern Baptist Convention, whose resolutions I send you herewith, seem ready to do for us, what even many of our professed friends at the

---

[27]ABHMS *Report,* 1865, 9.

[28]Ibid., 16.

[29]SBC *Proceedings,* 1866, 86.

north refused to do.''[30] Newman resorted to sarcasm here in order to shame Northern Baptists into a greater financial commitment to assist black Southerners. Newman had no intention of accepting paternalistic handouts from the Southern Baptists. Indeed, the refusal of former abolitionist black Baptist leaders to accept Southern Baptist aid later led to great discord in national meetings. Those who thrived under the biracial church arrangements of the old slave regime did not believe that acceptance of missionary aid from the Southern Baptists was tantamount to betraying their fervent belief in black solidarity. This is a debate that is still alive in black Baptist circles today. Other black denominations were also debating this same issue among themselves and with their white denominational counterparts.[31]

In his important resolution before the Northwestern Convention on 5 June 1866, which "thankfully" *accepted* the "offers" of financial aid from the Free Missionists, the Publication Society, and the Home Mission Society, Newman pointedly declined to include the name of the Southern Baptist convention, which had already met on 22-26 May in Russellville, Kentucky.[32] Newman's colleague, the Reverend Duke W. Anderson, sat on the Free Mission Society's Committee on Our Relations to Southern Baptists, which refused fellowship with the SBC partly because the latter had not disavowed a pro-Confederate creed that "the leading ministers of the Southern board" had signed. That creed declared that "the very existence of Christianity on this continent is involved in the success of the confederacy.''[33]

---

[30]See a more complete discussion of this debate among Methodists in William B. Gravely, *Gilbert Haven, Methodist Abolitionist* (Nashville: Abingdon Press, 1973); as well as his "The Social, Political and Religious Significance of the Formation of the Colored Methodist Episcopal Church," *Methodist History* 18 (October 1979); and his article titled, "James Lynch and the Black Christian Mission During Reconstruction," in David W. Wills and Richard Newman, eds., *Black Apostles at Home and Abroad: Afro-Americans and the Christian Mission from the Revolution to Reconstruction* (Boston: G. K. Hall, 1982) 161-88.

[31]*American Baptist,* 19 June 1866.

[32]NwSBC *Minutes,* 1866, 25.

[33]ABHMS *Report,* 1864, 15. For insightful historical studies of Southern nationalism in general and Southern religious nationalism in particular, see Emory M. Thomas, *The Confederate Nation: 1861-1865* (New York: Harper and Row, 1979), and Wilson, *Baptized in Blood.*

Despite the apparently benevolent manifestos issued by the white societies, suspicion and distrust existed between the two black Baptist conventions on the one hand and the Home Mission Society and the Southern Baptist Convention on the other. Southern whites were eager to dominate the mission to freed slaves or at least to forestall a large Northern missionary presence. The Home Mission Society was eager for a national Baptist reunion, and to that end wished to control the missionary labors of Northern blacks and abolitionist whites. The interests of both white groups were opposed to the agenda of the Northern black Baptist leadership. The complicated struggle that resulted is well illustrated by the issue of "abandoned" church property in the South.

Controversy Over Abandoned Southern Church Property

As the war was nearing its conclusion in several parts of the South, the church property of Baptist congregations as well as that of other denominations often was "stripped of all that was moveable." Some buildings were converted into hospitals, stables, or storehouses. This was offensive enough to the Northern Baptists who believed that they were bringing civilized life to the South as Union troops progressed there. But when Union military officers prevented Northern Baptist missionaries and chaplains from using abandoned church property for worship, the ABHMS's Executive Board became incensed. Moreover, it reported,

> Instances [were] not wanting where colored brethren [had] been shut out of, or disturbed in the use of, their own houses wherein they had worshiped for years, under the plea that the houses formerly belonged to their masters, and now to the Government, and not to them.

Accordingly the Executive Board felt obliged to bring this intrusion on First Amendment rights of blacks to the attention of "the authorities at Washington."[34]

Secretary of War Edward Stanton quickly remedied this indiscretion on the part of his subordinates by having the following order issued on 14 January 1864 to all commanding officers in the South.

> You are hereby directed to place at the disposal of the American Baptist Mission Society all houses of worship belonging to the Baptist Churches

---

[34]Ibid.

South, in which a loyal minister of said church does not now officiate. It
is a matter of great importance to the Government, in its efforts to restore
tranquility to the community and peace to the nation, that Christian ministers should, by example and precept, support and foster the loyal sentiment of the people. The American Baptist Home Mission Society enjoys
the entire confidence of this Department, and no doubt is entertained that
all ministers who may be appointed by it will be entirely loyal. You are
expected to give it all the aid, countenance, and support practicable in the
execution of its important mission.[35]

The executive board immediately accepted this new power, and appointed
the Reverend J. W. Parker of Boston, a vice-president of the New England
Freedmen's Aid Society, as its agent to take possession of this property.
Parker reported in May that there were about 5,000 Baptist meeting houses
in the seceded States, and that at least one-half of these buildings, valued
at $2,500,000, had been abandoned by Baptist Confederates. But at the
time only ''about thirty edifices'' had been ''given up to the custody of this
Society.''[36]

The ABHMS never intended to take permanent possession of the property. Its belief in the Baptist principle of local congregational autonomy
dissuaded those within the Society who had more presbyterial inclinations
from turning a caretaker role into a permanent trusteeship. The War Department allowed the Society ''to hold and use'' these properties only until
''civil authority'' could be restored. Corresponding Secretary Jay Backus
wrote that the Society's ''whole object will be accomplished if, by thus
occupying the property, they can save it from being destroyed, or passing
into other than Baptist hands, and preserve it as an inheritance for future
Baptists who may live to own and occupy it.''[37]

Two other events insured that the ABHMS would abide by its promise
to the denomination. First of all, although the Secretary of War designated
Northern denominational trustees for abandoned church properties of the
same denomination, those trustees had to restore such property ''to orig-

---

[35]Ibid.

[36]Ibid., 31. The War Department, in many of these trusteeship agreements, acted without the approval of President Lincoln. See W. W. Sweet, *The Story of Religion in America*
(New York: Harper and Brothers, 1950) 459-65.

[37]Ibid., 16.

inal owners who had received pardon of all abandoned property to which they could prove their title.'' This order was part of the new regulations established by Brevet General Oliver Otis Howard, the superintendent of the Bureau of Refugees, Freedmen, and Abandoned Lands, commonly known as the ''Freedmen's Bureau,'' which was established by an Act of Congress on 3 March 1865. This regulation itself, which favored white Southerners, ''produced great disappointment among freedmen'' who had believed they would receive much, if not most, of the abandoned lands.[38]

Meanwhile the Southern Baptist Convention's crippled but not dead Domestic and Indian Board was taking action to insure that former white trustees gained repossession of as much church property as possible. The test case related to Coliseum Place Baptist Church in New Orleans, which the Convention had briefly possessed as trustee until the federal commander turned it over to the ABHMS. In December 1865, well after the Freedmen's Bureau issued its regulations for Abandoned Lands, the Domestic Board took action. It found that if it could satisfy six demands it could repossess the Coliseum Place property.

1. Prove the Southern Baptist Convention to be an incorporated body.
2. Secure the signatures of the corporators to the application.
3. The corporators to prove their loyalty by furnishing a certified copy of their amnesty oath, or copy of their special pardon, in the event of coming under the exceptions to the amnesty proclamation.
4. Prove title to property.
5. Furnish certificate of non-alienation.
6. Show that the freedmen have no claim upon the property.

Somehow the Domestic board satisfied these requirements and in March 1866 the Adjutant General's office issued an order restoring the property to the Reverend Russell Holman, the Domestic Board's agent.[39]

The ease with which white Southerners could regain possession of church buildings insured that the Home Mission Society's role would be short-lived. In fact it lasted only a year, but in that time the ABHMS en-

---

[38]United States War Department, *Report of the Commissioner of the Bureau of Refugees, Freedmen, and Abandoned Lands,* 1 November 1866, 3.

[39]SBC *Proceedings,* 1866, 48-52; also see Walter L. Fleming, *Documentary History of Reconstruction: Political, Military, Social, Religious, Educational and Industrial, 1865 to the Present* (Cleveland OH: Arthur H. Clark, 1907) 2:215-65.

gendered a torrent of criticism against itself from other Northern Baptist societies who believed that it had compromised the Baptist principle of "separation of church and state."

Since the American Baptist Free Mission Society began its 1864 annual meeting in Perry, New York, on 25 May (the day after the American Baptist Home Mission Society finished its annual session in Philadelphia) it was the first Northern Baptist society to respond to the ABHMS's move. The Reverend Albert L. Post, president of the ABFMS, immediately established a committee on church property in the South that consisted of himself as well as R. Cheney and S. Aaron. The committee drew up resolutions that explicitly condemned the actions of the ABHMS and the Adjutant General's office, and sent them in a letter to the secretary of war.

> *Whereas,* This order was issued on the solicitation of said Society, and seems to imply an aspiration after power under the protection of the State unwarranted by the New Testament; and,
>
> *Whereas,* The great majority of many of the Southern churches are colored loyalists, yet forced to listen to traitors, or hear no preaching, and these loyalists seem to be utterly ignored both by the H. M. Society and the Secretary of War; therefore,
>
> *Resolved,* That we do hereby condemn the movement of the Home Mission Society in the above premises as unscriptural, and hostile to Baptist views from the reign of Constantine till now, because it tends inevitably to the intermingling of Church and State, the greatest blight of Christianity; and that we do sincerely regret the hasty action of the distinguished public functionary in giving his sanction to what must result in ecclesiastical tyranny.

After adopting this resolution, the ABFMS authorized its president to hand deliver this letter to Secretary of War Edward Stanton. In addition to these resolutions, the letter specifically asked the Secretary to clarify what he meant by the phrase *"place at the disposal"* in his order. The ABFMS also wanted to know if this authorization implied a permanent transference of such property to the ABHMS, and whether black loyalists would be "allowed any share in the 'disposal' of the property, and choice of their minister."[40]

---

[40]ABFMS *Minutes,* 1864, 3.

Despite these righteous protests, the ABFMS intentionally ignored the obvious fact that the government was as much at fault as the ABHMS. The Bureau's proclivity to exceed its authority caused much needless bitterness. As late as the autumn of 1865, officials of the ABFMS were still strenuously protesting the behavior of the ABHMS in regard to abandoned church property in the South. The Reverend Nathan Brown, the corresponding secretary of the ABFMS and the editor of the Society's paper *The American Baptist* (New York), emphasized that the ABHMS abetted the continual legal ouster of blacks by Southern white Baptists from churches where blacks often constituted the majority of the membership, and should have had, according to denominational polity, full control of the property. Brown believed that if the ABHMS had joined

> with the Free Mission Society in demanding that government should make over all houses of worship to the actual membership, irrespective of class distinctions, our colored brethren would not now be driven, in their poverty, to build new houses for themselves while old ones stand empty, or are, at least, reserved for a mere handful of white worshippers.[41]

Despite the sincerity of the ABFMS, some black Baptists were reluctant to join forces with it.

Since the minutes of the 1865 meetings of the Northwestern and Southern Baptist Convention and those of the American Baptist Missionary Convention have not been located, it is difficult to ascertain the official black view of the matter. However, Northwestern Convention's president, the Reverend William P. Newman, several times criticized the Home Mission Society's administration of Southern church property, which he believed favored Baptist Confederates. During the first week of October 1864, at the National Negro Convention in Syracuse, while speaking on the subject of black self-determination,

> Mr. Newman was very pointed in reference to the present action of the Baptist Home-Mission Society; which society was now holding sacredly, for the rebels who should be left, the church property in the South, just as far as they were able so to do.[42]

---

[41]*American Baptist*, 28 November 1865.

[42]National Convention of Colored Men, *Proceedings*, 1864, 26.

Almost two years after this pronouncement, Newman still was complaining about the injustice of the ABHMS's claims on abandoned Southern church property, especially since it had no official representative at the Nashville meeting of the Convention, which began on 30 June 1866.

> *Strange indeed that no agent of the Baptist Home Mission came near us.* Possibly they thought, as the *Trustees* of the Baptist church property, south, we would ask them to do to *us* as they have done to the *rebels,* with a portion of it.

Newman expressed "hope" that "they are now penitent." But even if they were not, his black missionary society "will forgive and work with them when they do the right."[43]

Baptist Interracial Rapprochement and Retreat:
The Consolidated Convention

When considering the development of black Baptist cooperative bodies, it is important to remember that the black leaders were neither always nor fully agreed on racial separatism as the best course. To be sure the attitude of the Southern Baptist Convention left so little room for black initiative that there was no possibility of cooperative relations between it and the black bodies. The ABHMS discouraged black cooperation by its eagerness to mollify white Southerners, even jeopardizing the ecclesiastical independence of Southern black Baptists.

The abolitionist principles of the ABFMS, however, though not always consistently expressed, left open the possibility of cooperation and even union with the two black conventions. Several black leaders were seriously exploring this possibility. Among them were William Troy, Charles Satchell, Richard DeBaptiste, Jesse F. Boulden, Israel Campbell, Duke W. Anderson, and Rufus Lewis Perry, but the most important was William P. Newman of Cincinnati.[44] The effort to unite black and white "anticaste" Baptists began in earnest on Newman's return to the pulpit of Union Church in Cincinnati in 1864 after thirteen years out of the country. The vision ef-

---

[43]*American Baptist,* 28 November 1865.

[44]Basic biographical information on Newman can be found in Ohio State Baptist Convention *Annual Report,* 1866, 19; ABFMS *Minutes,* 1867, 13; Robin W. Winks, *The Blacks in Canada* (Montreal and New Haven: McGill-Queen's University Press and Yale University Press, 1971) 164-65, 199-201.

fectively ended with his death two years later, although some hope remained until the dissolution of the ABFMS in 1872.

Born in Richmond, Virginia, in 1815, William P. Newman fled from slavery in the 1830s and went to Cincinnati. In 1842 he was a freshman at Oberlin College where he apparently appeared as an antislavery speaker.[45] Sometime after his arrival in Cincinnati he was licensed and ordained by the Union Baptist Church, of which he was the pastor from 1849 to 1851. Before and during this latter period he was engaged by the ABFMS to perform missionary duties in the black settlements in Canada West. After passage of the Fugitive Slave Law in 1850, he left for Chatham, Canada West, early in 1851. While in Canada, Newman served several churches, edited the militant black abolitionist newspaper, *The Provincial Freeman,* and engaged in numerous other missionary and abolitionist activities of the black Amherstburg Baptist Association and Canadian Anti-Slavery Baptist Association.

From 1859 to 1863 the ABFMS sent Newman to Haiti as its missionary to investigate the feasibility of black emigration there. Newman developed this interest in Haitian missions and emigration partly because of his persistent prejudice against Catholicism, Haiti's established religion. Newman also sided with James Theodore Holly, a black Protestant Episcopal priest who was rector of St. Luke's Church in New Haven, Connecticut, and who pressed for black emigration to Haiti at the National Emigration Convention in Cleveland in 1854 and thereafter against Martin Delaney's advocacy of black emigration to Africa.[46] Leaving Haiti in 1863 to serve a year in Jamaica, he returned to the United States in May 1864, in time for the organizational meeting of the Northwestern Convention, of which he became president the following year.[47]

It is important to note the political climate that supported Newman's efforts toward a union of black and white anticaste Baptists. There was a

---

[45]Benjamin Quarles, *Black Abolitionists* (London: Oxford University Press, 1969) 128. Newman never completed his course of study at Oberlin.

[46]James Theodore Holly and J. Dennis Harris, *Black Separatism and the Caribbean, 1860,* ed. Howard D. Bell (Ann Arbor: University of Michigan Press, 1970) 2. Floyd J. Miller (*The Search for a Black Nationality: Black Emigration and Colonization, 1787-1863* [Urbana: University of Illinois Press, 1975]) offers a superb study that discusses the context of Newman's involvement in this movement.

[47]ABFMS *Minutes,* 1864, 10.

close relationship between the white and black Free Missionists and the Radical Republicans, such as Salmon P. Chase, who tried for the Republican presidential nomination in 1864. Newman's return to the United States was partly a response to Chase's urging.[48] Of similar persuasion was Nathan Brown, white editor of *The American Baptist,* who deplored Andrew Johnson's lenient Proclamation of Amnesty and Reconstruction of May 1865.

> In reconstruction, therefore, no reform can be effected in the southern states if they have never left the Union. But reformation *must* be effected; the foundation of their institutions, both political, municipal and social *must* be broken up and *relaid,* or all our blood and treasure have been spent in vain. This can only be done by treating and holding them as a conquered people. Then all things which we can desire to do follow with logical and legitimate authority.[49]

The black American Baptist Missionary Convention adopted a lengthy resolution on Reconstruction in its August 1865 meeting in Alexandria, Virginia. Looking at the Johnson proclamation, ABMC delegates did not trust white Southerners to deal fairly with former slaves.

> The great mass of those to whom has been committed the work of reorganizing the Southern States, have heretofore defended the system of *American slavery* chiefly on the pernicious assumption, so repugnant to every principle of Christianity, or right and of truth, that the colored man was made for servitude, that a servile condition is his natural and proper condition.

The delegates especially detested the provision dealing with the reconstitution of state legislatures, which they correctly suspected would play into the hands of Southerners with ill will toward blacks.

> It may consequently be expected, that with the power of legislation affecting the interests of the colored man, entirely in their hands, they will

---

[48]National Convention of Colored Men, *Proceedings,* 1864, 26.

[49]*American Baptist,* 19 September 1865. See also John Hope Franklin, *Reconstruction After the Civil War* (Chicago: University of Chicago Press, 1961) 29, 83; it should be noted that the position of Republicans in general was somewhat more lenient than that of the Republicans of Nathan Brown's persuasion. But Brown provides a clear indication of the views of black and white Baptists who were radical Republicans.

not fail to provide, that the legislation shall, by various methods, direct or indirect, be conformed to this unchristian and inhuman maxim or rule of action. Causes do not, without the intervention of miracles, fail to produce their natural effects. Men do not gather grapes of thorns, or figs of thistles. A bitter fountain does not send forth sweet water.[50]

In this climate the ABFMS and the two black conventions drew closer together. Many delegates to the Northwestern Convention, as they gathered in St. Louis in June 1865, felt the need for allies of both races who would support the hard line toward the South. As president of the NwSBC, Newman was able to pilot through a set of resolutions calling for the unification of black and white Free Missionists.

Whereas, the principles of the American Baptist Free Mission Society are the same as those of the Convention, therefore,

Resolved that the corresponding secretary [Richard De Baptiste] be instructed to correspond with the aforesaid society for the purpose of finding out whether we cannot be more closely connected in our missionary work.[51]

The convention also passed a resolution appointing Newman as its representative to the next meeting of the ABFMS, especially since that society had sent "a delegation of brethren" to the first meeting of the convention.

At its September 1865 meeting the ABFMS's executive board voted to accept "cordially and heartily" the "proposal" of the NwSBC, so that there could be "a more intimate connection with that society in its operations for the spread of the principles common to both." They also resolved to reciprocate the gesture by sending a delegation to NwSBC's 1866 meeting in Nashville, Tennessee. Moreover, the executive board promised that the society and its missionaries would "cooperate with the missionaries and agents of the sister society." President Albert Post of the ABFMS appointed R. Hutchins, Nathan Brown, and John Duer to be a committee of

---

[50]ABMC *Minutes,* 1865, 28. For an excellent analysis of this controversy, see Eric L. McKitrick, *Andrew Johnson and Reconstruction* (Chicago: University of Chicago Press, 1960) 42-84. McKitrick does not cover black attitudes, but gives a solid analysis of the overall political situation. For a sketchy overall view of the political views of black religionists, see William Warren Sweet, "Negro Churches in the South: A Phase of Reconstruction," *Methodist Review* (May 1921): 405-18.

[51]*American Baptist,* 12 September 1865.

correspondence with the NwSBC "in regard to any further measures calculated to unite the two bodies in the same great work."[52]

Meanwhile in August the ABMC, meeting in Alexandria, Virginia, had passed a resolution proposed by Nelson G. Merry.

> Whereas, The American Baptist Free Mission Society has done much for our race during the last twenty-five years, therefore
>
> Resolved, that we invite the Free Mission Society of Boston, Mass., to fraternize with us, in our missionary work.

Duke William Anderson quickly persuaded the ABMC to modify the resolution by extending fraternal relations to the ABHMS in addition to the ABFMS.[53] This difference between the resolutions of the two black conventions does not imply that the members of the ABMC were less committed to the anticaste principles of the ABFMS. On the contrary, the ABMC passed several resolutions condemning racial bigotry and injustice.

> *Resolved,* that the spirit of caste and complexional hatred that has characterized this nation for the past fifty years, both in her political and ecclesiastical relations, is a paradox in the history of governments, which has been one of the chief causes of her punishments, and which, if continued, will destroy the institutions of the said government, and will represent us as a nation whose professions of liberty and equality are unmeaning.[54]

Numerous other resolutions on the "State-of-the-Country" and the establishment of exclusively black missionary associations in the South expressed similar sentiments.[55]

What was actually occurring at this meeting was the ascendancy of those who favored a union of the two black conventions without including the ABFMS, whose impediments from the black viewpoint included its anti-Masonic views. This fervent black commitment to freemasonry baffled the white leaders of the ABFMS. Their own disdain for secret societies precluded accepting black fraternal orders. They unfortunately did not un-

---

[52]Ibid.

[53]*American Baptist,* 19 September 1865; ABMC *Minutes,* 1865, 18, 20.

[54]ABMC *Minutes,* 1865, 16.

[55]Ibid., 11, 21.

derstand the social function of these organizations within the black community. In fact Prince Hall, a black Methodist preacher, led in the struggle to organize a black lodge in Boston as early as 1776. Clandestine black social networks such as the progeny of this Lodge often went unnoticed. But when there was any threat to their existence and viability, they found very creative ways of making their reality felt. These organizations provided mutual aid and group self-esteem. Many of the efforts toward black solidarity were often initiated and certainly supported by such groups.[56]

It can be said with reasonable certainty that most of those who spearheaded the drive for an all-black Baptist union were Masons or at least supportive of Masons. I find no evidence that any of them denounced either the Masons or any other fraternal order. They included Edmund Kelly, Duke William Anderson, Nelson G. Merry, and ABMC President Leonard Grimes. These veterans were supported by such rising younger ministers as William Thomas Dixon, Theodore Doughty Miller, and Rufus Lewis Perry. Perry drafted a ''Circular Letter,'' the public communiqué of the 1865 meeting, that emphasized the notion of black preeminence in the Southern mission field. They believed that the black Baptists were God's new reapers.

This Harvest Field is so marked off by geographical boundaries and local peculiarities that the labor of certain places devolves particularly upon certain laborers. Then, again, relative and denominational characteristics and interests enjoin the labors of certain fields or localities upon certain classes and denominations. This is emphatically true of the Southern field of labor to which we are to give special attention. All to whom we allude are of the same race, and perhaps, a great majority, professing Christianity, of the

---

[56]An interesting discussion of the role of black Masonic ties in black emigrationist activities can be found in *The Ancient Landmark* 3 (February 1854): 107. Although dated, William H. Upton, *Negro Masonry* (Cambridge MA: n.p., 1899) is still quite useful. For a fuller discussion of the social and existential uses of Masonic rites and camaraderie, see Abner Cohen, *The Politics of Elite Culture* (Berkeley: University of California Press, 1981). Despite the fact that his study focuses on Creoles in Sierra Leone, it is still applicable to the black American context. The best and most recent studies of black Freemasonry include Willian Allen Muraskin, *Middle-Class Blacks in a White Society: Prince Hall, Freemasonry and Middle-Class Realities* (Berkeley: University of California Press, 1975), and Loretta J. Williams, *Black Freemasonry and Middle-Class Realities* (Columbia: University of Missouri Press, 1980).

same denominational [Baptist] faith. Then, our duty as a denomination, and more especially as a Missionary convention, is plain. *We must occupy the field as effectually as possible.*[57]

Edmund Kelly, perhaps the convention's main proponent of an all-black merger, was selected fraternal delegate to the NwSBC's annual meeting, scheduled for June 1866.

The month after the ABMC solidified its desire for an all-black merger, the alternative movement for an interracial merger reached its high point, represented in a letter of William P. Newman to Nathan Brown, editor of *The American Baptist* and corresponding secretary of the ABFMS.

> We want a union of the bond and free, white and black, the finite and Infinite, that shall revolutionize the religious and political sentiments of this country. Upon us—upon our boards rests the responsibility of such a work. A concession of a part of our organized names will give us, I hope, a great equal-rights and gospel organization with the name of the *American Baptist Anti-Caste Missionary Convention*. We can rally one million of people to that sentiment and that number in harmony with God can convert the world, much more than a nation passing from barbarism to Christianity. The Lord aid us to effect such a work, that our children may die an hundred years old![58]

Sometime after writing that letter but before convening the NwSBC the following June, Newman retreated from this proposal, presumably because he heard of and supported the ABMC's all-black idea.

The following spring Edmund Kelly traveled more than a thousand miles from his home in New Bedford to represent the ABMC's position at the NwSBC. During the morning session of 4 June 1866, Newman gave notice that he would not "move the change of name of the Convention till next annual meeting.[59] A week later he wrote from Cincinnati that "in view of the anticipated union" of the two black conventions he "did not move an amendment to the 1st article of the convention according to previous notice."[60] In a time conflict described by the ABFMS as unavoidable, that

---

[57]ABMC *Minutes,* 1865, 26.

[58]*American Baptist,* 2 October 1865.

[59]NwSBC *Minutes,* 1866, 24-25.

[60]*American Baptist,* 19 June 1866.

society's board met in Chicago while the NwSBC was meeting in Nashville.[61] So Newman, who was supposed to represent the NwSBC to the ABFMS, was unable to attend. There is no indication that either body intended the conflict of dates, nor can we suppose that Newman's sentiments should have been changed by one more meeting with his Free Missionist friends, but it is certain that the occasion marked the passing of the best opportunity for an interracial Baptist missionary union.

Back in Nashville, Newman's "State of the Country" report to the NwSBC gives some clue to his weakening ties with his white comrades. In the poisonous climate of the Black Codes and the Ku Klux Klan, Newman had lost his trust in the Radical Republicans in Congress to right the wrongs of "a godless Executive and a syncophantic Cabinet," for the Executive Branch had "warped congress and encouraged the people in the rebellion." He bitterly denounced this renewed surge of the ideology and praxis of white supremacy.

> The caste class is dominant; the spirit of injustice rules; political corruption is the order of the day, and the professed friends of God and man, for the most part, are unwilling to accept the truth of human brotherhood, and the equality of men's rights. The doctrine that this is "the white man's government," is the doctrine of devils, and makes the people hypocrites, renders the government precarious, and if adhered to, will ultimately revolutionize the country.
>
> The Republican party never has done any more for *us* than it was compelled to do, to save its life. God emancipated us by the selfishness of *our oppressors,* and to him be the glory.[62]

As far as the Fourteenth Amendment was concerned, he believed that the Republican Congress "were as great usurpers as the Executive . . . because it handed us over, in our political rights, to *our* [Southern white] *peers and fellow citizens.*" Newman then appealed to the principles laid down in the Republican platform of 1866. The four principles of the Republican platform regarding black citizenship were actually the basis for the Fourteenth Amendment, passed by Congress on 13 June 1866 but not ratified by the states until 9 July 1868. The second article of this section of the plat-

---

[61]ABFMS *Minutes,* 1866, 14.

[62]NwSBC *Minutes,* 1866, 31.

form provided for "A representation in Congress, based on persons who are allowed by State to vote." This meant that the right to define who had the right to vote would be determined by state constitutions rather than the federal government. Newman foresaw what we now know to have been the beginning of a hundred years of the disenfranchisement of most Southern blacks. He concluded this report by calling for black solidarity. He declared that black people must "look out for our own interest in common with that of others, and stand by the people, who stand by God and the right."[63]

Newman put these words into action by appointing himself to serve on the NwSBC's Committee on the Union of Missionary Bodies, whose resolution was adopted by the NwSBC.

> That as principles are of no color, and the religion of Jesus does not respect the persons of men, we believe a union of all the Anticaste Regular Baptists of this country, North and South, is both expedient and necessary to a proper development of our resources as a denomination, and to make our influence felt in proportion to our numbers.
>
> We therefore recommend that three commissioners be appointed from this convention to meet with the American Baptist Missionary Convention at Richmond, Va., on Friday before the third Lord's Day in August, 1866, to consummate a union upon these principles.
>
> W. P. Newman
> Gustavus Brown
> J. F. Boulden
> R. DeBaptiste[64]

Newman and others were appointed as commissioners to the August meeting. Although the door remained open to a union with the ABFMS, relations remained cordial but circumspect until the ABFMS voted to disband in 1872.

Newman died of cholera on 3 August, before the union commissioners convened. Having lived to serve poor people, he died a pauper. Nevertheless his colleagues carried forward the plan he favored in his last days, the plan for a national union of black Baptists. Leadership of the commission-

---

[63]Ibid., 31-32.

[64]Ibid., 24-25, 30.

ers fell to Nelson G. Merry of Nashville. The others were Richard De-Baptiste, William Troy, Emanuel Cartwright, and Jesse Freeman Boulden. Merry was a good choice to head the delegation, because he had been active in both conventions almost from their inception. Of great usefulness also was DeBaptiste of Chicago's Olivet Church, who was more polished and articulate than Merry. Indeed, his friend William J. Simmons described him as "a man of Chesterfieldian manners and rare attainments in literary affairs."[65] It was his calm neutrality and intelligence that made him a successful mediator between Eastern and Western delegates, assuring a successful outcome—namely, the formation of the Consolidated American Baptist Missionary Convention (CABMC).

The Plan of Union committees of the two conventions met as scheduled in August in Richmond, Virginia. The brethren agreed that their problem consisted of "dissensions," "divisions," and "geography." Of the three, equal geographic distribution of finances and personnel was the issue most difficult to resolve. After much debate they agreed to "district the United States into four parts, of about nine states or more each." They devised a system of church government that was very presbyterial. They agreed "to have state conventions; in those conventions to have associations; with the design of having the churches report to the district conventions through associational letters, and through the district to the general convention."[66]

According to Edmund Kelly the delegates also agreed that "provision be made for a closer and more intimate relation between us and the three [home missionary] societies of whites at the North, viz., the American Baptist Free Mission Society, the American Baptist Home Mission Society, and the American Baptist Publication Society." Once they agreed to the principle that they "would endeavor to become one united body from Maine to the Gulf, not only in sentiment and practice, but as an organic body," and devised a palatable plan of union, they made provisions to challenge the right of the Northern missionary societies to collect money in the name of evangelizing black people without going through estab-

---

[65]William J. Simmons, ed., *Men of Mark: Eminent, Progressive, and Rising* (Cleveland: George M. Rewell, 1887; reprint, New York: Arno Press, 1968) 233.

[66]*National Baptist* (Philadelphia), 13 September; also quoted in Lewis G. Jordan, *Negro Baptist History, U.S.A., 1750-1930* (Nashville: Sunday School Publishing Board, National Baptist Convention, 1930[?]) 84-85.

lished black Baptist evangelistic agencies. They prepared to argue before both those societies and the public at large that monies for black evangelism would best be spent by aiding black missionaries who were under the direction of the Consolidated American Baptist Missionary Convention. Kelly told the white Baptists and the Northern white public that "our Society" is

> already in the field with colored laborers in the capacity of missionaries and Sabbath-school agents, who we believe, are better adapted to the wants of our people.[67]

With these sentiments in mind, the delegates also developed a missionary directory that was later adopted by the American Baptist Home Mission Society. They argued that the CABMC should be the only agency to appoint missionaries and Sabbath-school agents "for every state," and that they would only be "amenable to our board." The role of the white societies would be to give "their endorsal and support" to the CABMC's appointees. The delegates also agreed that all missionaries, Sunday school agents, and teachers "who are supported in part or altogether by these societies shall send to them duplicates of their quarterly reports" through the CABMC's corresponding secretary. The Union Committee felt "very hopeful of this plan" since the Northern societies had repeatedly made "generous proffers of aid in our [black] noble work of evangelizing the South and the world." They did not want to simply be a black home mission society, however. They planned to offer "a similar proposal to the American Baptist [foreign] Missionary Union in behalf of Africa." These proposals were later rebuffed by the ABHMS as well as the ABMU.[68]

In the meantime the CABMC held its first official meeting at Nelson G. Merry's First Colored Baptist Church of Nashville during the third week in August, 1867. The CABMC elected DeBaptiste as president, Merry as vice president, Rufus Lewis Perry of Brooklyn as corresponding secretary, and William P. Brooks of St. Louis as treasurer. It was agreed at this session that the corresponding secretary and a quorum of five members of the

---

[67]Ibid.

[68]Ibid.

Executive Board would be appointed from locations in and around New York City.[69]

There was considerable jubilation among black Baptists at the creation of their first united national body. There was some sorrow over the diminished hope of an interracial union, but not much. On the other hand, it is not surprising to learn that the new organization was beset with difficulties during the thirteen years of its existence. These problems were, however, largely the result of white denominational racism.

The denominational impact of Northern Baptist power, suggested in this chapter, becomes patently clear in the next. The ABHMS's Northern black colleagues were guilty in the society's eyes on three counts. Blacks were to be distrusted because "the black image in the white mind"[70] taught the ABHMS's white power brokers that blacks were incapable of self-government. Moreover, most Northern black Baptists were identified with those radical, nay anarchistic, Free Mission Baptist abolitionists, and therefore could not be trusted to share in the ABHMS's self-imposed burden of saving "North America for Christ." Third, blacks were part of that heathen element that was supposed to *be* saved and civilized; it was difficult for the Northern white missionary establishment to see how blacks could save themselves.

Lest these anticipations leave the impression that undue, reckless speculation now has center stage in this study, let us move to the next chapter where we can see how denominational racism raised its pernicious head.

---

[69]Jordan, *Negro Baptist History,* 85-87.

[70]For a superb discussion of this phenomenon, see George M. Frederickson, *The Black Image in the White Mind: The Debate on Afro-American Character and Destiny, 1817-1914* (New York: Harper and Row, 1971) 165-97.

4

Racial Conflict
and Racial Pride,
1866-1872

With the single exception of the integrated Free Mission Society, no organic ties existed between major black and white Baptist national organizations during Reconstruction or thereafter—until the predominantly white American Baptist Churches and the black Progressive National Baptist Convention became "associated organizations" in 1970, ninety-nine years after the failure of the merger between black and white abolitionist Baptists. As a result of the racial bitterness aggravated by Reconstruction politics, black Baptists could not even affirm church union with their most compatible protégés, the Free Missionists. By 1869 the die was cast. Richard DeBaptiste, president of the black Consolidated Convention, confessed that "in our organization we are separate, but we are one in the great principle of an anti-caste gospel for all the people on earth."[1] After examining the state of racial relations between the black CABMC and white Baptists we shall then be in a better position to understand the climate of separatist opinion that made this Christian merger untenable.

---

[1]ABFMS *Minutes,* 1869, 20. Two recent articles offer useful introductions to black Baptist ecumenism: Pearl L. McNeil, "Baptist Blackamericans and the Ecumenical Movement," *Journal of Ecumenical Studies* 17,2 (Spring 1980): 103-17; and J. Deotis Roberts, "Ecumenical Concerns Among National Baptists," *Journal of Ecumenical Studies* 17,2 (Spring 1980): 38-48.

Race consciousness was encouraged for different reasons by both black and white Baptists between 1866 and 1872. The development of this prevailing attitude among white Southern Baptists is well known,[2] and the literature suggests a similar situation in white Northern Baptist Reconstruction activities. Racial attitudes among black Baptists have, however, received little attention. In this chapter I consider why and how racial and religious separatism received theological and ideological justification among black Baptists who belonged to the new Consolidated Convention.

The merger of the two black conventions was justified by the participants on three grounds. First, the former abolitionist white Baptists in the Home Mission Society and the Southern Baptist Convention had given little past evidence that they were able to accept the idea of the "social equality" of fellow Christians who were black. Second, Southern black Baptists could more easily and "naturally" accept indigenous rather than white leadership. Finally, Northern black Baptists felt a natural right and inclination to have primary responsibility for the evangelization and perhaps also the education of black Southerners. They believed that they had this right because (along with the white members of the American Baptist Free Mission Society) they were former abolitionists, because many of them were former slaves, and because they were all of African descent. This overall separationist posture of the leadership of the CABMC was revealed in the struggle against what they called "proscription" (1) within the power structure of the ABHMS, (2) in the development of Baptist educational institutions for former slaves, and (3) in the financial policies of the ABHMS.

The Issue of Black Membership
on the Home Mission Society's Board

As with other denominational agencies devoted to the same work, the ABHMS from time to time appointed black members to its executive board. The Reverend William T. Dixon of Brooklyn was the first black minister to be designated a board member. The ABHMS was founded in 1832 and

---

[2]See John Lee Eighmy, *Churches in Cultural Captivity: A History of the Social Attitudes of Southern Baptists* (Knoxville: University of Tennessee Press, 1972); H. Shelton Smith, *In His Image, But . . .: Racism in Southern Religion: 1780-1910* (Durham NC: Duke University Press, 1972) 264-66, 273-74, 281-82. The significant monograph dealing with Southern Baptist racial attitudes during the period under discussion is Rufus B. Spain, *At Ease in Zion: Social History of Southern Baptists, 1865-1900* (Nashville: Vanderbilt University Press, 1967).

Dixon was elected in May 1867. This election received much publicity in denominational newspapers and reopened the old charge of "proscription" against the ABHMS; its paper, *The Examiner and Chronicle,* aware of this charge, defended the motivation of the Board's Nominating Committee in phrases consistent with the prevailing racialism of those times.

> Mr. Dixon is one of the "rising race," but was not on the board for that reason, but because he is a representative man of his complexion, and because the expeditious and effective way for the Home Mission Society to reach the perishing of that complexion is to put their harness on this man. So as to Mr. Hazehuhn—he was not chosen because he is a German, but because his appointment is the nearest path to the German element. The nominating committee very properly regarded the Home Mission Society, as a fisher of men, and therefore made these selections in the way of bait. Good.[3]

From the black viewpoint the problem was that black leaders were not consulted in the nominating process. Their preferred candidate was probably Rufus Lewis Perry, the most radical black Baptist of this period, who held the most important office in the CABMC, that of Corresponding Secretary.[4] The election of the more moderate and less prominent Dixon was an obvious insult both to Perry and to the CABMC. Dixon also felt somewhat slighted by the Examiner's explanation of the Nominating Committee's choice of himself. He told the *Christian Times and Illinois Baptist* that

> he did not believe that he had been elected as a tool because he was a black man and color at a premium. He would say that while [he] was [a member of] a convention [of black Baptists from every] state of the United States, yet they [the Consolidated Convention] had failed to do what they wished to do in educating the freedmen. His convention was not composed of rich men.[5]

---

[3]*American Baptist* (New York), 4 June 1867.

[4]Biographical sketches of both Dixon and Perry can be found in William J. Simmons, ed. *Men of Mark: Eminent, Progressive, and Rising* (Cleveland: George M. Rewell, 1887; reprint, New York: Arno Press, 1968) 495-99, 425-29. Another sketch of Perry appears in Albert W. Pegues, *Our Baptist Ministers and Schools* (1892; reprint ed., New York: Johnson Reprint, 1970) 375-80.

[5]Quoted in *American Baptist,* 4 June 1867.

This issue simmered among black Baptists without much public comment until the 1869 meeting of the ABFMS. When the Free Mission Society's Committee on Home Missions presented its report, Charles Satchell of Louisiana, its black chairman, attacked the ABHMS's practice of tokenism. The ABHMS as well as the SBC had delegates present. As usual, Satchell identified strongly with the anticaste principles of the ABFMS, and reported that

> the Free Society had more [of] the confidence of the freedmen in Louisiana than any other association. It was true that the Home Mission Society had men there—they had colored men on their board—but they were a cypher, and the people had no confidence in the board. The Home Mission was not in the position to effect for them the same amount of good as [the ABFMS].[6]

Satchell also used this occasion to remind the two white denominational officers that he himself had not been treated by white ministers as an equal, but that he had always invited white ministers to preach in his pulpit. In thirty years of ministry, "he had not yet received the first invitation to preach in one of their pulpits, either at the north or at the south." Furthermore, he declared, he would rather associate with the ABFMS because "they are working for *church equality,* not social equality; that will follow by-and-bye." In error, he denounced the ABHMS because it "had not, to his knowledge, a single missionary in Louisiana."[7]

James B. Simmons immediately came to the defense of the ABHMS, of which he was an officer and fraternal delegate.

> Rev. Messrs. Dixon [elected in 1867] and [Leonard A.] Grimes [elected in 1869], the colored members of the board of the Home Mission society, are not mere cyphers. They are on committees to which is entrusted work of vital interest to their race, and they are perfectly familiar with the workings of the society.[8]

---

[6]*American Baptist,* 1 June 1869.

[7]Ibid. J. W. Horton, the ABHMS's first missionary in Louisiana, had labored there in 1865. Jeremiah Chaplin and Mark Bryant served the Society between 1866 and 1868. Although Charles Bradley served for a short time in 1867, Jeremiah Chaplin's classes in theology became important mainstays for black ministers who were wrestling with Scripture. See the ABHMS *Reports* for 1865 through 1869, especially ABHMS *Reports,* 1868, 12.

[8]*American Baptist,* 1 June 1869.

The Free Mission Society was quick to use this occasion as a way of celebrating the long, congenial affiliation it had had with the black Baptists in contrast to the ABHMS's discriminatory indifference. Corresponding Secretary Nathan Brown wrote in his annual report that

> among the names of the founders and early supporters of the society we find many honored colored ministers, whose efforts for the redemption of their race have been in unison with ours ever since they joined us in organizing this channel of missionary operations.[9]

Brown reminded his readers that Charles Satchell and Wallace Shelton, who were black ministers, "were members of the board twenty-five years ago and are members now." Other black ministers who had more than twenty years of service on the ABFMS's board included Jeremiah Asher (who died in 1865), William P. Newman (who died in 1866), Duke William Anderson, William Troy, Sampson White, William Spellman, Henry L. Simpson, and Samuel H. Davis. These ministers had not only served on the board before the Civil War, but they had also served as ABFMS missionaries from time to time.[10]

The Controversy Over the National Theological Institute

Black leaders also thought they saw ecclesiastical "manifest destiny" at work in the ABHMS's unsuccessful effort to take over the National Theological Institute.[11]

The National Theological Institute was organized and located in Washington, D.C., as an independent educational society in December 1864, for the purpose of educating freedmen for the Baptist ministry. This society began operation early in January 1865, but was not chartered by the United States Congress until 10 May 1866. This charter was amended on 2 March 1867 in order to expand its operations to include the function of

---

[9]ABFMS *Minutes*, 1869, 9.

[10]Ibid.; also see *American Baptist*, 16 June 1870.

[11]The story about the development of this organization cannot be found in the major histories of North American Baptists.

a college. Its name was then changed to The National Theological Institute and University.[12]

Once this institution was started by the Reverend Edward Turney, D.D., Baptist ministers—largely from Boston—began to seek control both of Turney's school and of the NTIU itself. Several of these leaders supported the Northern Baptist Education Society, which "was organized in 1829 to replace the Massachusetts Baptist Education Society and to widen its usefulness by having branches in all the New England states."[13] Justin D. Fulton, pastor of the Tremont Baptist Church of Boston, was one of the major supporters of the Baptist Education Society and became one of the first presidents of the University. Other Boston area ministers also became officers of the Institute.[14] Fifteen of the thirty-five members of the Board of Managers and eleven of the fourteen members of the Executive Committee lived in Massachusetts. Moreover, Massachusetts Baptists usually gave more than any other single state to this cause. In the 1867-1868 fiscal year, for instance, donations from Massachusetts amounted to $5,730.43, more than fifty percent of the total contributions received from seventeen states.[15]

By contrast, the Corporate Board, the legal trustees of the University, had a majority of its twenty-one members residing in the District of Columbia. There were only two black members of the corporation, Leonard A. Grimes and Duke William Anderson, who also served on the executive committee. There was one black vice-president, Rufus Lewis Perry, and two black members on the Board of Managers, Theodore Doughty Miller, and William Thomas Dixon. Only five black ministers held official positions in an organization that was founded to educate black ministers.[16]

The racial profile of the University might have been excused by black Baptists and white abolitionist Baptists if the powerful Boston faction of

------

[12]Charles H. Corey, *A History of the Richmond Theological Institute with Reminiscences of Thirty Years' Work among the Colored People of the South* (Richmond: J. W. Randolph, 1895) 53-54.

[13]Robert G. Torbet, *A History of the Baptists,* 3rd ed. (Valley Forge PA: Judson Press, 1963) 317.

[14]NTIU *Proceedings,* 1868, 3, 4, 8.

[15]Ibid., 3-4, 45-53.

[16]Ibid., 3-4, 53.

the Board of Managers, especially its executive committee under the leadership of Justin D. Fulton (hence "Fultonites") had not tried to take legal possession of the Institute. Their motives for trying to take over the Institute, although complex, largely centered around the Institute's controversial superintendent, the Reverend Edward Turney, who had formerly taught theology at Madison University in Hamilton, New York. Their actions also flowed partly from their desire to subsume the work of the Institute under the ABHMS.

Many of the Massachusetts ministers who were officers and members of the Board of Managers, as supporters and graduates of professional schools such as Newton Theological School, Madison University, and Rochester Theological Seminary, were deeply committed to a learned ministry. Turney, even though he had taught at Madison, and the District of Columbia faction within the Institute's leadership, who sided with Turney (hence "Turneyites"), did not have such a heavy investment in forcing classical theological and undergraduate curricula on the freedmen ministers, who were at a distinct disadvantage in mastering such material.

After the Institute was chartered as a national university in 1867, the tensions between the Fultonites and Turneyites increased. In a move to gain financial independence from the Fultonites, Turney encouraged the Corporate Board to request Congress to amend the Society's charter so that it could sponsor a university and be eligible to receive funds from the Freedmen's Bureau. According to the *American Baptist,* members of the Boston faction subsequently began to oppose Turney openly. They tried in 1867 to seize legal control of the Institute at Washington by moving its corporate headquarters to Boston because "they opposed and condemned the chartering of a university, and set themselves against the carrying out of the provisions of the congressional act."[17] Turney had already solicited $9,000 from General Howard of the Freedmen's Bureau to be used solely for the Washington school. This money was seized by Zalmon Richards, the National Institute's treasurer, in behalf of the Boston executive committee. This move, as well as the attempt to seize corporate control, was illegal since the Fultonites did not have "the sanction of the trustees, who were incorporated as a board in Washington." According to Turney, "the orig-

---

[17]*American Freeman,* 3 March 1870. (This newspaper merged with the ABHMS's *American Baptist* in 1870, and took charge of the "secular department" of the *American Baptist.*)

inal bill seeking an act of incorporation, was drawn by myself. It provided that the corporation should be under the jurisdiction of 'the laws of the United States in force in the District of Columbia.' ''[18]

Turney lamented the fact that ''on the 1st of May 1867, a company of men, about twenty in all, and most of them residents of Boston and vicinity, convened in that city'' in order to transfer ''the seat of operations'' to Boston. These Fultonites then issued a direct challenge to the legal authority of the Corporate Board. But they underestimated the influence that Turney and Edgar Harkness Gray, pastor of Washington's North Baptist Church and chaplain of the United States Senate, had on the Corporate Board. The corporation's executive committee met on 6 May and ''utterly repudiated the proceedings of the Boston meeting.''[19] These trustees also successfully sued the Fultonites in an effort to have the restricted funds that were granted to the National Theological Institute and University by the Freedmen's Bureau returned to Washington. This dispute lingered for almost three years until the case was settled in favor of the Turneyites. The Fultonites did not try another direct assault until 1870.

The Boston leaders, who were all prominent members of the ABHMS, persuaded the ABHMS in its May 1870 meeting to ask Congress ''to annul and declare void the Charter of the National Theological Institute and University'' by arguing that it needlessly duplicated the work that the newly established Wayland Theological Seminary (Richmond, Virginia) performed in behalf of the ABHMS, and ''the Baptist denomination.''[20] The ABHMS had recently established a department of education in its executive board, which was placed under the direction of Corresponding Secretary James B. Simmons since he was already in charge of the ABHMS's operations in the South.[21]

Once the ABHMS committed itself reluctantly, but fully, to developing and controlling the denomination's educational work among the freedmen, Fulton secured the permission of his faction within the Institute to merge with the ABHMS, having already arranged that the Board of Man-

---

[18]*American Baptist,* 17 March 1870.

[19]Ibid.

[20]ABHMS *Report,* 1870, 7.

[21]ABHMS *Report,* 1869, 22-23.

agers would meet in Boston on 20 May, the day after the ABHMS met in the same city. However, Congress did not revoke the original charter of the Corporate Board, whose recording secretary happened to be Edward Turney, and whose most prominent member was Edgar H. Gray, the influential chaplain of the United States Senate.

The legal squabbles that ensued between 1867 and 1870 obscured the fact that the work of the Institute had been divided, de facto, among two parties. Turney and the majority of the Corporate Board retained legal and local control of the Washington school and the contributions of the Freedmen's Bureau to that enterprise. Justin Fulton and the Board of Managers cooperated with the ABHMS in establishing Wayland Theological Seminary under the Reverend Silas B. Gregory in an attempt to compete with Turney's school. They also succeeded in controlling the work of the Institute outside Washington.

The Institute, as a national education society, maintained schools in Richmond, Virginia, St. Helena, South Carolina, and Augusta, Georgia, as well as in Washington. Schools were established at these "important points, so that the more influential pastors of churches might be helped without removing them from their work and from their pastoral charges." [22] The Institute also established "Ministers' Institutes," which conducted intensive, short-term courses in theological studies. Such institutes were first used successfully before the war by the ABHMS in its work in the West, especially the work developed by the famous John Mason Peck. The Fultonites strained to make sure that the curricula of these institutes focused on classical theological studies.

But Turney was not willing to concur with this truncated view of theological studies, especially when aspiring black ministers often did not know how to read and write. Besides trying to become eligible to receive funds from the Freedmen's Bureau, Turney also sought to amend the National Institute's charter in 1867 to allow it to offer basic normal and undergraduate courses. The Fultonites, however, had different plans in mind that became fully visible after the May 1867 meeting. They sought to restrict Turney's activities "to the theological department; and, next, to secure the services of a competent teacher for the academic." [23] They contended that

---

[22]Corey, *A History of Richmond Theological Institute*, 54.

[23]NTIU *Proceedings*, 1868, 19.

Turney accepted this arrangement whereby he would head the theological department and the Reverend William T. Johnson of Washington would head the academic department. Johnson also happened to be a member of the Corporation. In a meeting of the Executive Committee in Washington on 12 September, the Committee claimed in its 1868 report that it took this action

> when . . . a publication appeared, in September [1867], in one or more of our denominational newspapers, and in a printed document, widely circulated, wherein Dr. Turney claimed to have under his care, and depending on him *alone* for support, twenty-six schools and 1,700 scholars, for whom, virtually, he then solicited pecuniary aid, the Committee could regard such procedure only as a departure from the terms on which he had received his appointment.[24]

When the Executive Committee discharged Turney for his recalcitrance, the leaders of the ABFMS and the CABMC quickly responded, because both had delegated their educational work to what was known as "Turney's Association,"[25] since Turney was the actual founder of the University. Both groups participated in the work of the Institute through their support of the small theological school that was conducted by the Reverend Duke William Anderson, pastor of the First Colored Baptist Church of Washington, one of the major leaders in both the ABFMS and the CABMC and the first black trustee of Howard University.

Both the CABMC and the ABFMS harbored the dream that a national black Baptist seminary and university could be established in the District of Columbia. Then the Fultonites successfully aborted this plan by dismissing Turney. The ABFMS's executive board lamented the university executive committee's dismissal of Turney as a repudiation of a sounder pedagogy, and as a frustration of the larger plans to build a black university.

Dr. Turney, appreciating the importance of giving to our brethren of the

---

[24]Ibid.

[25]As early as 1866, Turney pleaded with the Home Mission Society to support his Association. "The Object of the Association was to give such men a proper general instruction in Christian doctrines, preaching, and the general management of churches. At the time the Association began to work, no similar organization existed, and no arrangement for the establishment of schools had been made." See ABHMS *Report*, 32.

south the highest advantages of education, had devoted himself for two or three years to the establishment of such a school as would fully meet their wants, and had obtained from congress the necessary charter for a university. Unfortunately, the board with which he is connected seem to have repudiated his enlarged plans, and manifest no disposition to carry out the provisions of the charter. Under these circumstances it becomes more important than ever that our society should sustain Bro. [Duke W.] Anderson in carrying on the Free Mission school already established.[26]

But they did not believe that such a move would frustrate the desire of the black leaders to establish a national Baptist university for black Baptists.

It is probable that the consolidated convention of colored Baptists, if disappointed in their expectations of a university under the instruction of Dr. Turney, will in the course of a few years establish one of their own; and until such time it seems the absolute duty of this society to lend its aid to Bro. Anderson, and perhaps to others who may be engaged in the like work of instruction further south.[27]

Black Baptist leaders were deeply disappointed about the action of the National Institute's board of managers. As early as 1865, the black American Baptist Missionary Convention had "voted to cooperate with"[28] Turney in his pioneering effort in Washington. When Turney was dismissed, Duke Anderson, reflecting the sentiments of his fellow black Baptists, condemned the Boston committee, and accused its members of collusion with the ABHMS to frustrate the black desire for a national university. According to Anderson,

The Boston Board have turned Dr. Turney away, but it will do him or our work no harm. Their scheme appears to be to blend the rebel element [white Southern Baptists] with their instructors, and thereby teach the colored men in such a way as will prevent them from becoming competent and capable. This is the great object of the South, and we want the *American Baptist* to speak out clear and bold.[29]

---

[26]ABFMS *Minutes*, 1867, 8-9.

[27]Ibid., 9.

[28] ABMC *Minutes*, 1865, 24; ABHMS *Report*, 1866, 33-34.

[29]*American Baptist* (New York), 15 October 1867.

Anderson was not speaking just for himself.

In response to the proscriptive implications of this latter controversy, the CABMC in 1869 organized the Consolidated American Educational Association under the direction of Rufus Lewis Perry and William Thomas Dixon. This association contributed to the support of schools, mostly elementary and secondary schools, in the former slave states, a project constantly plagued by shortage of funds.[30] Despite the proscriptive activities of the ABHMS and the Fultonites within the NTIU, the CABMC was determined at least to influence—since it was prohibited from directing—the shaping of denominational educational policies. To this end in 1871 Corresponding Secretary Rufus Lewis Perry founded and edited the *National Monitor* as a denominational newspaper and the *Sunbeam,* which was one of the first efforts of black Christians to create their own religious education literature.

The Consolidated Convention's major ally in its fight against the ABHMS and the Fultonites was, as usual, the ABFMS. In accord with Duke Anderson's challenge, *The American Baptist* did "speak out clear and bold" throughout the three-year duration of the NTIU controversy. It carried editorials and articles that severely chastised the cultural and denominational imperialism of the ABHMS and especially of the Fultonite forces within the Society. In response to a rather tinctured story (which contended that "Dr. T. got a bill through the senate, vesting the whole property and control in himself and associates")[31] in the Freewill Baptist paper, the *Morning Star,* the *American Baptist* raised a significant question.

> Has it come to be an established rule that philanthropic workers among the Baptists are not to be tolerated, and spoken of only with a sneer, unless they have placed themselves under the protection of some aristocratic organization, or at least under the patronage of Boston ministers? . . . We should be very sorry to see such a despotism established over Baptists, that congress could not incorporate a university among them without first asking leave of some "ministerial conference," acting as a sort of episcopal bench for the denomination.[32]

---

[30]CABMC *Report,* 1872, 26.

[31]*American Freeman* (New York), 3 March 1870.

[32]Ibid.

The Free Missionists deeply resented the presbyterial impulse within the ABHMS, and after 1846 never seriously considered the possibility of reuniting with it. In 1872, just before its demise, the ABFMS did, however, merge all of its foreign mission work, except its African missions, with the American Baptist Missionary Union, closely tied to the ABHMS. Turney died the same year that the ABFMS ceased its work and his school apparently died with him. But in 1872 the wealthy ABHMS had lent a strong hand to those leaders within its ranks who later organized the National Baptist Educational Convention.[33]

The Controversy
over the Home Mission Society's Financial Policies

Nothing gave greater impetus to the separatist tendency among the black leaders of the CABMC than their belief that they had the right and responsibility to share in the administration of all Baptist funds collected in the name of aiding the freedmen. This conviction ran counter to the nationalistic aspirations of the ABHMS. The CABMC leaders, while condemning tokenism and cultural imperialism within the ABHMS, also repeatedly challenged its right to administer the funds given to it for Southern education and evangelization without being accountable to black Baptist leaders. Between 1867 and 1869 the leaders concluded that the white leadership of the ABHMS would not share the control of the Society's Freedmen's Fund with any other agency, even if that agency were headed by several educated black leaders who were former slaves.

The controversy over the allocation of the Freedmen's Fund began in the 1867 autumn meeting of the CABMC in Nashville, Tennessee. The Reverend R. R. Whittier, a white minister, reported in the ABFMS's *American Baptist* that the CABMC leaders were disappointed because they "expected more assistance directly from the Home Mission Society than they realized during the past year. It appears they understood Dr. Backus last year at the Richmond convention to promise large assistance, hence their indebtedness."[34] The controversy surrounding the allocation of these funds centered on what Jay S. Backus, one of the two corresponding sec-

---

[33]This Convention eventually led to the formation of the American Baptist Education Society in 1888. See Albert Henry Newman, *A History of the Baptist Churches*, 476-77.

[34]*American Baptist*, 3 September 1867.

retaries of the ABHMS, actually promised the black Baptists at the 1866 meeting when the two black conventions merged to form the CABMC.

The 1867 minutes of the CABMC have not been found, so the wording of Backus's offer is unavailable. Documentation of this controversy begins with the September 1868 issue of *The American Baptist,* in which coeditors Rufus Perry and Nathan Brown published the full minutes of the CABMC's meeting of the previous month. Included in the record was a request by Perry, written in May as corresponding secretary of the CABMC, to his two counterparts in the ABHMS. The reply of Jay Backus is also included, as are other items revealing the CABMC's reaction to Backus and the Society.[35]

Perry asked the ABHMS for $1,700 to clear a large debt and proceed with the Southern work. Perry contended that his convention had indebted itself for $1,300 because it moved on the basis of assurances from Theodore Doughty Miller, who supposedly had information from Backus that the ABHMS would extend that much aid. According to Perry, "This request is made the more hopefully in view of the fact that through a misapprehension of the full force of a supposed promise of funds on the part of Dr. Backus, by T. D. Miller," the CABMC still believed that the Society would come to its aid. In making the request, Perry anticipated that the most serious objection would not be to the gift of money itself but to the fact that a competing national black organization was making the request. Accordingly he gave considerable attention to the stature of the CABMC.

> The Consolidated American Baptist Missionary Convention, of which I have the honor to be corresponding secretary, has a constituency of about 100,000, among whom there are two hundred ministers of the gospel of our Lord and Savior Jesus Christ. Though numerically strong, with a corresponding influence among the millions of our recently free brethren— brethren according to flesh as well as the spirit—we are pecuniarily feeble and comparatively helpless in all instances wherein money is absolutely needed to accomplish the end of our missions. Were it not for this one hindrance our accessions to the church in our several fields of labor in the south, would amount this year to ten thousand (10,000) hopeful converts with

---

[35]Between August 1868 and Perry's founding of the *National Monitor* in 1867, the *American Baptist* was the official newspaper of both the Consolidated American Baptist Missionary Convention and the American Baptist Free Mission Society.

convenants made with God and sealed by Christ with his atoning blood, by themselves with scriptural baptism, and walking in newness of life. This, therefore, is to ask an appropriation as liberal as your more able treasury will admit, to aid us. We verily believe that what you may commit to our trust will yield four hundred per centum more than it would if expended by your board among us in the ordinary way.[36]

The "ordinary way" apparently refers to the ABHMS's support of its own appointees in the field. Perry hastened to say that he was not suggesting that the Society withdraw those missionaries. But he did believe that the CABMC was the ideal agency to pursue Baptist missions among black Southerners.

But we labor under fewer disadvantages than you, as a society, and so far as the availability and efficiency of laborers, fields, and material to work upon are concerned, we pray you to recognize our being, to let us be, help us to be.

Perry gently reminded the Society's secretaries that the black Baptist organization was necessary because of racial prejudice and then reasserted the special qualifications of the leaders of his own group.

We have many good managers among us capable of shaping and pushing forward a successful missionary work. These, from facts already stated regarding social antagonism, are far better fitted to manage than to be managed in their internal affairs by those who are so far removed from them socially.

The CABMC, then, was asking for a lump sum grant to be controlled completely by the black convention, with the provision of full reports to the white Society.

In his June reply Backus outlined the terms of his promise and denied that either he or the ABHMS's executive board could be bound by his word when the CABMC did not meet the stipulations of the offer.

So far from admitting that we are under the slightest obligation from anything that I proposed or promised in Richmond, I have always felt. and do now, that what I asked for was all refused, and that after I left, others were allowed to represent me and my brethren of their Baptist indepen-

---

[36]*American Baptist,* 29 September 1868.

dence; and so I was cast out and my request with me. I do not blame the
brethren of the convention, they were misled and I hope they will see it
and accept the proposition now or hereafter, that we may work together in
the Lord.[37]

The terms of the original proposition can only be imagined, but it is certainly not inconceivable that Backus proposed that black Baptists should
not form a national organization but rather should merge with the ABHMS.
In any case Backus reported on his board's action on Perry's request.

> Every man in the board seemed disposed to do all that would be proper
> or true to his office, or trust, but finally agreed that, unpleasant as it was
> to decline they could not see it wise to grant the request, as it would be
> without constitutional authority, without *precedent*, and what was worse,
> would be to establish a precedent.

The ABHMS feared it would be inundated with requests from the "five or
eight" black state conventions or associations that had been founded in the
former slave states since 1866. It also, according to Backus, feared that it
would be plagued by other "missionary societies north and south, and by
the German conventions, and the Swedes and French, and all others."

Backus then admitted that this issue was only secondary; the main issue was that his board would not have the last word as to how such monies
would be disbursed. They preferred to pay the CABMC's missionaries directly, not through the medium of the Convention itself. Backus reminded
Perry that "as I suggested to you, could the matter have been put in shape
to pay on receipt of reports of service as we helped before, it would have
relieved the thing."[38] The ABHMS wished to keep control of the Baptist
Freedmen's Fund, which the CABMC believed belonged to the entire denomination. Furthermore Backus and his colleagues would have preferred
that the CABMC had not come into being and consequently had little interest in its success or solvency.

About Backus's letter, Perry commented that "while the spirit and tone
of this reply may be regarded as commendable, it does not take up and reason away as illegitimate or unjustifiable, the grounds on which our application was based. It is seemingly evasive, but your secretary's acquaintance

---

[37]Ibid.

[38]Ibid.

with the writer rather forbids the charge of an intentional evasion." Perry then praised the ABFMS for its unconditional grant of one hundred dollars. Perry emphasized that his board had not asked for this assistance from the ABFMS, but that it acted after hearing from Perry that his board needed money. Perry commended the ABFMS for its Christian charity. "This body of brethren, though their gift be small, gave what they had," he wrote, "and allowed no constitutional technicality to hinder them from practical sympathy and from affording some relief in our pecuniary embarrassment." Perry urged his brethren to accept aid from white Baptists only if they "feel it is a privilege to aid us directly."

Perry then reported that the Board had recommended that all pastors and missionaries of the Convention pledge to take up "Quarterly collections." Both he and the Board felt that this method would be "the first and most successful step towards the necessary, desirable and praiseworthy end of self-reliance." Perry argued that this approach would be necessary because most of the white brethren were not interested in encouraging real black Baptist independence, and in effect practiced "taxation without representation."

> The fact that we must become more self-reliant is too plain, and the neglect of it is too threatening for us to stand idle or passive. Our white brethren, with the exceptions already mentioned, are bound together as such for the defence and perpetuity of their own distinctive interests. They are true to themselves. They not only retain all they have, but draw more from us than they appropriate directly to us.[39]

Richard DeBaptiste referred the Executive Board's report to a committee, which dealt at length with the matter of the ABHMS's refusal to aid the CABMC. The committee maintained that the ABHMS had tacitly agreed to cooperate with both of the former black conventions, but had withdrawn support when the two were merged. In order to counteract and condemn the ABHMS's proscriptive behavior, the committee recommended to the Convention that

> the board be instructed to send out an appeal, first, to the societies that ask and receive funds for us, founding the appeal on the terms of cooperation which, in substance, were passed or adopted two years ago; excepting the

---

[39]Ibid.

American Baptist Home Mission Society, whose executive board has, according to the report of the executive board, already refused to aid us in those terms.

The committee passed a resolution that in effect provided for special appointments of black missionaries who would be supported by the monies collected from either white sister societies or the general public. This same resolution threatened to embarrass any white sister society that refused to support the CABMC.

> In case these societies refuse to aid us, the Board then appeal directly to the persons contributing to the societies for our benefit as a people, making known such refusal; and also publish the appeal in every Baptist paper in the United States, and request every other desirous of seeing us maintain ourselves, to copy it.[40]

As it turned out, this threat came too late. The ABHMS had already suffered a substantial decrease in contributions to its Freedmen's Fund partly because of the postwar financial slump and partly because of increased competition from other Baptist societies, especially from the CABMC itself, which reported in 1869 that it had received $21,213.51 in comparison to $4,786.98 that the ABHMS received during the same 1868-1869 fiscal year.[41]

The existence of the CABMC obviously posed a threat to the ABHMS's monopolistic aspirations. In order to counteract this threat, the Reverend James B. Simmons, Backus's cosecretary in charge of the Society's Southern work, made several attempts to discredit the CABMC leadership by subtly characterizing it as dishonest, divisive, and even un-Christian since it advocated black tribal consciousness. He began his counterattack in April 1868, around the time that Perry initially requested funds from the ABHMS.

Simmons published a copy of his letter to the Reverend Warren Randolph of Philadelphia, his classmate at Brown University. Answering Randolph's question about Simmons's changed opinion regarding strategy for the Southern mission, Simmons stated,

---

[40]Ibid.

[41]CABMC *Report* 1869, 17; ABHMS *Report*, 1869, 53. Also see chap. 3, footnote 9.

I always felt that any individual Baptist or any company of Baptists, had a primary right to educate all the freedmen they could. I had not at that time, perhaps, properly considered the disadvantages which would attend two *national* organizations engaged in doing the same work.[42]

Simmons then wrote that he felt obliged to yield to the ABHMS's decision in its Boston meeting of 1866 "that the denomination approved of but one national organization." Since he had become one of the Society's secretaries he had learned some facts that convinced him that the Society had made the right decision. Simmons did not elaborate, but he left the impression that either the black Baptists, the Turneyites in the NTIU, or the Free Mission Baptists were not quite as solvent or honest as the ABHMS establishment. In later portions of the letter, arguing against the creation of black-managed schools for ex-slaves, it became clear that Simmons regarded the leaders of the CABMC as weak if not unscrupulous managers.[43]

In 1869 Simmons was forced to address the entire issue of the ABHMS's proscriptions against the CABMC when he came before the 1869 annual meeting of the American Baptist Free Mission Society. Charles Satchell, acting as chairman of the Committee on Home Missions, submitted a report to the ABFMS that condemned the imperialistic aspirations of the ABHMS on the grounds that it offended the principles of local autonomy. Because, Satchell's report argued,

the colored people themselves fully comprehend their own wants, and the means and measures but calculated to make the gospel a practical benefit, which can be effected through local organizations already in operation; and believing, as they do, that the time has come, when they must assume the responsibility, and, as agents in their elevation, work out, under God, their own destiny.[44]

Black Baptists therefore believed that the ABFMS and the CABMC were the only "effectual door" for "the elevation and Christianizing of this class of people." Satchell even insisted that it was impossible for Northern societies to gain a foothold among potential black converts unless they operated on the anticaste principles of the ABFMS. Satchell's report was

---

[42]*Macedonian and Record* (New York), July 1868.

[43]Ibid.

[44]ABFMS *Minutes,* 1869, 14.

adopted during the morning session of 17 May, with, however, both John Lansing Burrows and Simmons opposing its adoption.

During the afternoon session Simmons and Burrows were confronted with a resolution by the Reverend R. Cheney, a veteran white Free Missionist, condemning caste in the American churches and declaring "that God demands immediate repentance of this as of all other sins." Burrows attacked the resolution, which Cheney then defended.[45] Burrows characterized Cheney's speech as "one of the most dangerous and heterodox" speeches he had ever heard, but black leaders of the ABFMS and the CABMC spoke in support of the resolution. Rufus Perry was the most direct and lucid. Perry condemned the ABHMS's refusal to share the responsibility of disbursing the monies it collected, in the name of helping black people, with the black CABMC.

> The Consolidated Convention was organized for specific purposes. There are a number of antagonistic societies in the field for the avowed object of helping the colored people, but their actions have been such as to produce discord amongst them. At the close of the war, societies sprung up all over the country for the help of the freedmen; and hundreds of thousands of dollars were subscribed, *but the freedmen never got it.* What has become of it? Where did it all go to? Our convention has sent out a number of colored men as preachers, and they have done a good and great work. Ten thousand souls were brought into the church, and only $2,000 of money raised. The Home Mission's expenditures in this field were about 50,000, and they only received one-tenth as many as we did. We not only get the work for this money, but the funds are left in the hands of poor colored men, who are thereby enabled to support their families.[46]

In reply Simmons stated, correctly, that the ABHMS had both black and white missionaries in the field. But this was hardly a response to Perry's undisguised anger about the ABHMS's attempt to sabotage the work of the CABMC.

Apparently Simmons did not recall at the time exactly how many of the Society's Southern missionaries were black. In an ostensible attempt to rectify this oversight, he cosigned a letter to the members of the CABMC

---

[45]Ibid., 15-16. Burrows was a Southern Baptist leader and editor of the *Religious Herald* (Richmond).

[46]*American Baptist,* 1 June 1869.

with Jay Backus on 8 September 1869. The actual purpose of the letter was evidently to defend the Society's practice of hiring missionaries on the basis of "qualification" rather than color.

> We believe in the text: "If ye have respect to persons, ye commit sin." We suppose it right, however, to have to respect *qualifications* in selecting and supporting laborers. Our records . . . show that, of twenty-three men appointed at one Board meeting, seventeen were to labor among the freedmen, and eleven of the seventeen were good and able colored men. Two of the members of our Board are also colored men.[47]

Simmons and Backus neglected to indicate, however, what criteria were employed to determine "qualification" for missionary labor. In reply President Richard DeBaptiste reasserted the charge of Perry and others that the society was sabotaging the Consolidated Convention.

> NOTE—If this communication is an open, unreserved expression of the Board of the Am. Bap. Home Mission Society, as we have been informed it is, then we have only to thank God for the existence of a spirit and liberality on the part of the Society which we feared did not exist. But we shall look to the future course of the A.B.H. Society for a practical expression or a faithful carrying out of what is expressed as the views and policy of the Board. Hitherto they have not in any respect aided us in our work, but their course has been seriously detrimental to our position and influence as a missionary body having the first claims to help in our work among ourselves. The principle of helping us to help ourselves, regarded by the intelligent of every denomination as the best, has hitherto been totally ignored. But now that we are authorized to hope that hereafter we will be seen and encouraged and aided in going forward in the development of self-reliance, we have only to say, looking up and hoping, Thank God![48]

There the matter stood, so far as the record shows.

These documents demonstrate both the frustration of the black leadership and the patronizing behavior of the ABHMS's officers. As we study all three issues described in this chapter—black members on the Society's board, ministerial education of former slaves, and management of the Southern mission—we can understand the dismay of the black leaders as

---

[47]CABMC *Minutes,* 1869, 16.

[48]Ibid.

they tried to accomplish the work to which they believed God had called them. Imagine their perception of huge numbers of freed blacks awaiting either conversion or the regularizing of their religious lives. Many black Baptists believed that the CABMC could judge better than the ABHMS how to evangelize the Southern brothers and sisters and how to raise up a ministry among them. Even if we allow full measure of institutional pride, there is still every reason to think, in view of the previous history of race relations, that the black leaders were correct.

The CABMC's condemnation of denominational proscriptions between 1867 and 1872 was more than a reactionary movement. These issues provided occasion for expression of the theological belief that the ABHMS's behavior was an affront to Christian charity and therefore sinful. Rufus Perry, perhaps the major theologian of the black Baptists, saw the issue as nothing less than true faith versus idolatry.

> The [Southern Mission] field must be occupied [by black missionaries], for God has declared it by his providences; and unless we occupy it, strangers will come in and introduce strange gods. This was the case with the children of Israel whenever they ceased to worship, or turned their backs to the God of their fathers.[49]

Perry based his argument not only on Scripture but also on the experience of God's people, as he took up the issue of the worth of black Baptist ministers as religious and social leaders.

> Experience, also, admonishes us not to put our trust in those who proscribe us, and commit to them the leadership of our missionary work, or make them the architects of the social and religious fabric in which we are to dwell as a race.[50]

The black Baptist abolitionists of the antebellum period had become the black religious separatists of the Reconstruction era.

---

[49]*American Baptist,* 22 September 1868. Leonard I. Sweet (*Black Images of America, 1784-1870* [New York: W. W. Norton, 1976] 69-147) makes a good effort to understand the integrationist strand of black religious thought, but he fails to comprehend the roots and the depths of black separatism. The roots lay in a pronounced, often biblicistic, identification with the schemes of providence in both the Old and New Testaments.

[50]*American Baptist,* 22 September 1868.

The struggle for autonomy, however, did not always result in racial unity. Once the separatist disposition gained institutional expression in the form of a national black Baptist denomination, it assumed other, uncontrollable forms that caused the dissolution of the CABMC itself in 1879. But this separatism harbored little resentment against white people for the wrongs they had inflicted on blacks. The leaders of the Consolidated Convention understood that they had to wage an vigorous ideological campaign for both ecclesiastical and secular rights, for the very people who controlled white denominational monies and political influence also had a direct influence on the moral and political tone of American public opinion. The interplay between the separatist spirit and the prophetic politics of the Consolidated Convention will be examined in the next chapter.

5

The Reconstruction Ideology of Black Baptists, 1869-1879

It would be a mistake to think that all of the problems of the Consolidated Convention were caused by antagonists outside its fellowship. Severe internal controversies during the 1870s led to the CABMC's demise in 1879. There were four main areas of disagreement: sectional attitudes, national politics, financial support, and internal governance. These controversies masked the continuation of the intense ideological struggle over the expenditure of the moral capital blacks earned during slavery. Several questions confronted Black Christendom, and Black Baptists in particular: Should the rituals and folkways of slave culture be abandoned? Would the former slaves receive reparations? Could the majority people envision a day when the exalted doctrine of human equality of both the revolutionary era and abolitionism would become a daily praxis rather than a tragic and vacuous shibboleth, a remnant of a dead Romanticism?

Black Baptists discovered that chattel slavery, with its odious advocacy of America as a white *Herrenvolk* democracy, had spread into nearly every crevice of the body politic. Oddly enough, however, the most painful fissure they endured was among themselves. Learning from the supposed success of the Abolitionist movement, Northern black Baptists, like blacks in other denominations, tried to forge their own version of Romantic social reform. They, too, dreamed of creating a "Christian America."[1] But their Christian America would most definitely be a multiracial society. They were not trying to create an integrated society that would eliminate color differentiations. They wanted the nation to respect and accept them as African-Americans. Some black Baptists concluded, however, that the nation would not accept them because most black people simply did not project a white middle-class image that Victorian America required. Those who espoused these views were those who simultaneously had acquired white organizational and cultural skills in the crucible of the antislavery struggle in antebellum America. Those who had found somewhat different skills under the slave regime had a significantly different outlook. An examination of this ideological struggle as it took place within the black Baptist Consolidated Convention will provide a profile of the religious angle of the larger historic struggle for dignity.

Sectional Tensions and Rivalries

Of the four areas of dispute that led to the dissolution of the CABMC, none ran deeper or lingered so long as the peculiar problem of sectionalism. More than any other factor, sectional loyalty defined friend and foe in a power struggle between black Baptists schooled in the radical politics of Northern abolitionism and those who had survived the rule of the Southern slave regime by accommodating to it. The sectional bitterness that crept into most CABMC activities is somewhat surprising since many "Northern" black leaders had fled or migrated from the South. Despite this fact, however, there was a pattern of unabashed Northern black elitism, which undoubtedly contributed to the heat of debate. The impact of this class consciousness was telling, and continues to linger today. Some observers may argue that it has now lost much of its importance within the Afro-American Baptist community, but that it has caused serious divisions in this community is not debatable. Class consciousness played such a large role in the collapse of the CABMC that we must describe its nature in order to understand how apparently trivial matters sometimes became important.

---

[1]Robert T. Handy, *A Christian America: Protestant Hopes and Historical Realities* (New York: Oxford University Press, 1971) and Leonard I. Sweet, *Black Images of America, 1784-1870* (New York: W. W. Norton, 1976).

The problem began when Emancipation brought freed slaves and Northern blacks together. The informal gatherings of the "invisible institution" often became visible Baptist churches, usually without any direct supervision by Northern missionaries. But when slave congregations did not exist, the black missionaries sponsored by the CABMC—among them Edmund Kelly, Sampson White, Charles Satchell, Jesse Freeman Boulden, Arnold B. Williams, and Israel Campbell—were particularly adept at forming freedmen into Baptist churches. These missionaries, former fugitives who tended to look on slave culture as defective, challenged the "old ways" of slave religion. In the process they came into conflict with popular but uneducated ex-slave preachers, some of whom had developed considerable local and regional power and (at least nominally) became affiliated with the CABMC.

Despite the personal acrimony and institutional risk, the missionaries were unsparing in expressing their aversion to the excesses, especially the unrestrained ecstasy, of slave religion. It is difficult to discern who among this representative group had the least or the most intense repugnance toward the old way. Let Charles Satchell speak for all of them. His own referent was blacks in New Orleans. His report, as interpreted by Rufus Perry, appeared in *The American Baptist* in June 1868.

> In addition to the vices and irregularities inseparably attendant upon the state of slavery, there have been the "church mothers," "gospel mothers," and "old sheppards," officials [of the congregations] quite outside of the New Testament arrangement, but who nevertheless claim to be under the special influence of the Spirit, and exercise an authority, greater, in many cases, than that of ministers. If a member can keep on the right side of these gospel mothers, he need *not* have *no* fear of church displeasure; but woe to that disciple who is so unfortunate as to be out of their favor. Then, again, there are bad men under the garb of preachers, who go around imposing on the ignorance of the people, baptizing them for a fee of five dollars, or performing some other spiritual service by which they can rob them.[2]

Accordingly the members of Satchell's small association had pledged themselves to root out every religious practice that could not be found in Scripture. Perry urged other likeminded ministers to form associations to

---

[2]*American Baptist,* 26 June 1868.

reform the ignorant and superstitious ways of erstwhile slave congregations.

> Old habit and customs will doubtless linger long in some places, but scrip-
> tural education and an enlightened ministry, with the blessing of God, will
> in time overcome all these evils, and raise the people above the power of
> superstitions or designing men.[3]

Another instance of sectional tension occurred when William Troy,
general agent of the CABMC, visited Savannah, Georgia, and received the
"cold shoulder" from most of the local ministers, especially from William J. Campbell, the influential (and old school) pastor of the famous First
African Baptist Church.[4] N. D. Sweet, the Episcopal layman with whom
Troy was staying, told his guest that he was being snubbed because he was
a "Yankee nigger." Troy's lengthy response to this particular action re-
veals the major elements in dispute.

> I know there is such a feeling amongst some of my people. The Lord have
> mercy upon them. What of it, if I am a Yankee [in sentiment rather by
> birth]? What has the Yankee done to the negro, north or south? This ques-
> tion is to be decided, and I propose to fight out along this line. I am dis-
> posed to think the light that enemies have held up "the Yankees" in, has
> caused some of our watery-brained black men to become frightened, and
> try to turn up their noses also at the Yankees. Well, if we are to have men
> of our own kith and kin to fight, we shall grant no quarter for them. We
> shall put the same old anti-slavery truth to them, and seek the young of the
> race and set them to think on God and man, caring not where a man is born;
> whether in Yankeedom or Lapland, thro'out the whole of God's domain,
> he is a man and a brother. Sectional controversy is what the Christian can
> take no pride in. The doctrines of the Bible are clear and positive. "God

---

[3]Ibid.

[4]According to Emanuel King Love, later pastor of this church, Campbell had 4,000
members, and "controlled the surrounding country. He controlled from Savannah to Dar-
ien, Brunswick, and all the country adjacent to Savannah. His praise was on the tongues
of everybody, and especially the saints. His people would do just what he told them to do.
When he spoke it was law. If he said a thing was wrong, all the world could not make his
people believe otherwise. It would have been an insult to have attempted it." Campbell
suffered a stroke shortly before the great controversy in First African, which occurred in
1877. See *History of the First African Baptist Church from Its Organization, January 20th,
1788, to July 1st, 1888* (Savannah: The Morning News Print, 1888) 58-59.

hath made of one blood all nations of men,'' black and white. I have much more to say on this subject, for I see plainly that we shall be called upon to war against the spirit of caste I have alluded to. I am a citizen of the world, God's free man.[5]

The following month Charles Satchell voiced his approval from Louisiana and added his own observations. Satchell argued that the Free Missionists were having ''great trouble'' penetrating the South because of an ''imperfect'' Southern ministry. ''From this source,'' he added,

> we shall have trouble for some time to come; men wedded to the old customs of the country, ignorant, selfish and domineering, and who can only live by keeping the people in a state of ignorance to uphold their pretensions. They ignore everything like system, have no respect for moral obligations, and poison the minds of the people against every thing of northern origin, as Yankee measures to cheat slaves out of their money.[6]

A lesser-known black pastor was more candid about why he differed from the old preachers and deacons who had had no other religious training except what was ''taught'' to them by law-abiding Southern white deacons and pastors. ''Whatever qualifications I had for the pastorate, and my ideas of church polity,'' Peter Randolph wrote, ''had all been received in the North and not from the South.'' Randolph singled out the problem of unconsecrated slave marriages and the powerlessness of female members as two of the most vexing problems that greeted him when he left Boston to become the carpetbag pastor of the Ebenezer Baptist Church of Richmond. He settled the first problem by assisting freedmen to get married ''properly.'' He immediately moved against the second problem by insisting that men and women, and families, should sit together during worship. This was a direct challenge to an old Southern tradition. He later made sure that women were allowed to vote and speak in church meetings. According to him, his innovations were ''a new state of things, and soon my church was named the 'aristocratic church.' ''[7] Many of these Baptist churches pastored by black carpetbaggers earned the reputation for having Northern

---

[5]*American Baptist*, 23 February 1869.

[6]*American Baptist*, 23 March 1869.

[7]Peter Randolph, *From Slave Cabin to the Pulpit: The Autobiography of Rev. Peter Randolph* (Boston: James H. Earle, Publisher, 1893) 88.

sentiments that smacked of what we might now call ''cultural paternalism.''[8]

On the national level, black leaders of the Consolidated Convention were not embarrassed to mention the differences between themselves and recently freed Southern brethren. The contrast was usually cloaked in a call for the support of an enlightened black national denomination that had the patience to deal with the ignorant Southern brethren. While visiting the state of Mississippi in July 1870, Rufus Lewis Perry sent a personal note to Nathan Brown, white corresponding secretary of the ABFMS.

> We must try to sustain a general missionary in this state, one that has the cause of Christ at heart. Our people are not rational enough here to act from principle; they are impulsive, and go as their feelings, not their reason moves them, and their feelings are often at the mercy of the designing.[9]

Despite these lamentations of Yankee-minded national leaders, the Southern brethren obviously had some ground for suspecting the Northern CABMC brethren. The Northerners were, after all, trying to change religious practices hallowed by generations of black Southern tradition. Moreover, the CABMC's constant requests for money were not matched by a comparable and visible harvest that had any immediate effect upon black Baptist life in the South. The changes that did come, such as the formation of associations and state conventions, were largely carried out by local preachers. Although the CABMC did support some of these preachers, it tended to support only those preachers that its leaders had known before the war. That excluded most of the Southern brethren. This cleavage between North and South exacerbated other areas of dispute, such as differences over national politics, and contributed largely to the disappearance of the CABMC.

Religion and Politics

In the final days of 1868 the leaders of black America were beginning to notice that many of their old abolitionist friends were falling away from the frontline of social justice because of death, old age, or weariness. They were then faced with a question whose answer would determine much of

---

[8]Ibid., 89.

[9]*American Baptist,* 28 July 1870.

the course of Afro-American history for the next one hundred years. Where were black plebeians to turn for moral and economic support in a country so steeped in laissez-faire economic and social views that it acted either too slowly, or not at all, against the lawlessness of Southern white secret societies, government officials, and private citizens who were depriving many blacks of basic human rights?

Regardless of social status, political views, or religious beliefs, blacks—North and South—were faced at the end of 1868 with abundant evidence that emancipation was more a military enactment than a political reality. As one black Baptist leader put it, one month after the election of General Ulysees S. Grant as president of the United States, the nation still held "its colored citizens in political slavery." But the Reconstruction policies of the almost-impeached President Andrew Johnson had convinced black leaders that even former white Southern Union sympathizers were to be distrusted once they acquired political power. Although blacks participated rather vigorously in the Presidential campaign of 1868, some black leaders argued that the greatest victory of all lay ahead: Would the new Congress reconsider the 1866 Congressional decision to phase out the Freedmen's Bureau by 1869? Would the Congress pass a proposal for an amendment to the Constitution that would grant blacks the right to vote in all the states of the Union? Would the states then ratify it? More broadly, would white America—North and South—accord Afro-Americans civil and political equality? In a spirit either of deep political cynicism or of unrequited optimism, some black religious leaders disclaimed interest in *social equality*. They trusted in the religious promise of a brighter day either on earth or in heaven. Whether they were premillennialists or postmillennialists, few Baptist leaders foresaw any prospect for positive answers to these ominous questions in the 1870s.

As theological timekeepers predicted both weal and woe, the political evangelists of the Consolidated Convention began to provide both ecclesiastical and social leadership for the former chattel slaves. Indeed, by 1876 all of the Southern states, with the exception of Florida, had a black Baptist state missionary convention. Kentucky led the way in 1865, North Carolina organized in 1866, and was followed by Virginia and Arkansas in 1867, Alabama in 1868, Mississippi in 1869, Georgia in 1870, Tennessee and Louisiana in 1872, Texas in 1875, and South Carolina in 1876. Florida did not organize until 1883. Except for Florida, Southern black

Baptists followed the pattern of establishing state conventions shortly after the federal government readmitted their states into the Union.[10]

The black preachers who organized these state conventions responded positively to a black demand that they address the people's material as well as spiritual needs. Their evangelical theology, however, constantly provided a sledge hammer to drive a wedge between those who saw no distinction between religion and politics and those who did. The Reverend James T. White, born and reared in New Providence, Indiana, is a case in point. He was a black carpetbagger who competed initially with the Reverend George Robinson, perhaps the most popular antebellum black preacher in Arkansas. White was a very literate person. Robinson, on the other hand, had very little, if any education.[11]

The primary issue between Robinson and White seemed to involve conflicts over clerical style and evangelistic territory rather than any ostensible political differences. But ideological differences actually exacerbated the split within the Arkansas state convention once it was organized in 1867. It was a fundamental split between the old guard and the slightly "uppity" black Northern missionary in the postwar South. White became the pastor of the First Colored Baptist Church of Helena, and won a seat in the Arkansas State Senate in 1868. During that year, the political struggle in Arkansas was so intense between Democrats and Republicans that several local associations were unable to hold their meetings. Radical black Republicans were especially susceptible to the harassment of popular local white Democrats. Wilson Brown, pastor of the First Colored Baptist Church of Little Rock "before the slaves were freed,"[12] refused to permit the black Arkansas River Union Baptist Association to meet in his edifice as previously agreed. Brown refused because "there was so much political excitement that he thought it unsafe for us to meet there then—especially as some of our ministers were taking active part in politics."[13] It is unclear

[10]I compiled these data from published minutes and state histories of these organizations that are too numerous to mention. The most complete collection of these minutes is in the Library of the American Baptist Historical Society in Rochester, New York.

[11]John Franklin Clark, *A Brief History of Negro Baptists in Arkansas: A Story of Their Progress and Development, 1867-1939* (Pine Bluff AR: n.p., 1938[?]) 7-13.

[12]Ibid., 7.

[13]Arkansas River Union Baptist Association, *Minutes,* 6.

whether or not Brown was for or against political evangelism. But this state convention was clearly divided about what strategy should be pursued.

From antebellum times through Reconstruction and into the Gilded Age there were strong disagreements among black Baptists on political questions. At one level the dispute raged over whether ministers should engage in political action and disseminate political opinion. At certain times the dispute dealt with particular positions on certain issues. In both cases the potential for ecclesiastical disruption was enormous.

The Northern-oriented leaders of the CABMC, most of them schooled in abolitionist politics, placed great value on the franchise and attendant political activity. One of the most vigorous proponents of black Christian politics was Rufus Lewis Perry. Born a Tennessee slave in 1834, Perry secretly educated himself, fled to Canada, and became a school master. Ordained in 1861 after theological training in Kalamazoo, Michigan, he was during the 1870s the CABMC's spokesman and most influential leader.[14] At one point he was editor or coeditor of four publications while simultaneously serving as corresponding secretary of the CABMC. From his Brooklyn base he reigned like a bishop, using his pen in lieu of other symbols of office.

Perry wrote most of his political opinion during the rapidly shifting events of Reconstruction. He was very sensitive to what was later called "the betrayal of the Negro."[15]

> [The nation's] undisputed claims to civilization, honesty and Christianity as a nation will ever be dated by future generations from the time when congress shall by appropriate legislation secure to all citizens of the United

---

[14]Elias Camp Morris, the first president of the National Baptist Convention (1895), testifed that the secretary of Baptist gatherings was usually the most important figure. He said, speaking of an earlier period, "Back in those days there were only a few competent men to fill the position of Secretary, hence that office was considered of more importance than the presidency, and even until now [1901], with many of our people the art of good penmanship is termed education." See his *Sermons, Addresses, Reminiscences, and Important Correspondence, with a Picture Gallery of Eminent Ministers and Scholars* (Nashville: National Baptist Publishing Board, 1901) 144.

[15]See Rayford W. Logan, *The Betrayal of the Negro: From Rutherford B. Hayes to Woodrow Wilson*, enl. rev. ed. (London: Collier-Macmillan, 1965).

States, irrespective of race, color or previous condition, such equal rights
and privileges as are peculiar to a republican form of government.[16]

Perry believed, as a devotee of ecclesiastical and political republicanism,
that quietism was not only the quickest way to lose one's natural rights,
but amounted to sinfulness and cowardice of the worst sort. He called attention to the upcoming meeting of the National Convention of Colored
Citizens that was scheduled to meet on 13 January 1869 in Washington,
D.C., urging "firm, clear-headed, sagacious" black leaders to attend.
Nevertheless, he argued, whatever the results of that meeting,

> the colored men of this nation owe it as a duty to themselves and their
> households, to keep before the national congress, their manly and strong-
> est protests against the political outrages to which they are subject.

Perry told his readers that if they protested against political oppression, "the
God of justice will lead them to victory."[17] He saw voting as a sacred duty
that black Baptist leaders must teach their people to secure by becoming
more educated and more religious. Being religious was synonymous with
being moral. "We learned from observation," Perry wrote,

> that the only way to make the ballot a blessing is to educate and Chris-
> tianize the voter. Education and piety are the only influences to which the
> ballots of the masses will yield and be governed for the general good of
> the people, the strength of government and the development of national
> resources.[18]

Perry believed that it was the will of God that black citizens would become
the leaven that would raise the nation from its depraved condition. He had
already replied in his 1868 Annual Report to all those, including some of
his black brethren, who either had no faith in black self-government or were
impatient with it.

> To know that God is working for any good object, is to regard it as accom-
> plished and rejoice over the result. Although the work of our hands be slow

---

[16]*American Baptist,* 29 December 1868.

[17]Ibid.

[18]*American Baptist,* 26 May 1870.

and doubtful, yet there is a power behind the throne whose will cannot be resisted.[19]

Not all Baptists were as sure as Perry that piety and politics could or should be married. Southern white Baptists were interpreting ''spiritual'' to mean ''nonpolitical.'' They often charged their Northern coreligionists with an unholy mixing of religion and politics.[20] Among black Baptists this issue surfaced in the spring of 1871 when Rufus Perry locked horns with George Washington Dupee, one of the strongest black preachers in the nation and pastor of the Washington Street Church in Paducah, Kentucky. Dupee was an ex-slave preacher who seldom ventured into the North. He was also a conservative political activist who preferred to work behind the scenes rather than to risk raising the ire of his white Southern neighbors.[21] The controversy began when Dupee wrote an open letter to Perry, who printed it in his newly created biweekly denominational newspaper, *The National Monitor*.[22] The issue containing Dupee's letter and Perry's answer is not extant, but we do have two issues containing some responses to the original exchange. Unfortunately there is no extant correspondence supporting Dupee, who apparently criticized Perry for encouraging ministers to take public positions on political issues.

The strongest printed criticism of Dupee's position came from William H. Banks, a black carpetbagger and pastor of the Ebenezer Baptist Church of Wilmington, North Carolina. Banks was a young man who had gained so much prominence in the CABMC that he was its host in 1870. Banks dismissed Dupee's conservative ideology.

---

[19]CABMC *Report*, 1869, 7.

[20]*Watchman and Reflector* (Boston), 9 June 1870.

[21]William J. Simmons, ed., *Men of Mark: Eminent, Progressive, and Rising* (Cleveland: George M. Rewell, 1887; reprint, New York: Arno Press, 1968) 599-607. Victor B. Howard (*Black Kentucky: Emancipation and Freedom, 1862-1884* [Lexington: University Press of Kentucky, 1983] 155-56) places Dupee in a distinct minority among black leaders. Dupee believed that blacks needed to make a distinction between holding political office themselves and achieving ''simple justice.'' It is important to note that other black leaders tolerated Dupee's position; they simply disagreed with his strategy. See Elijah P. Marrs, *The Life and History of the Reverend Elijah P. Marrs* (Louisville: Bradley and Gilbert, 1885) for an illustration of a black Baptist preacher who believed that religion and politics are inseparable.

[22]*National Monitor*, 21 May 1870.

> I feel proud, Brother Perry, of your reply to Rev. G. W. Dupee; for I really
> think as you do: that a minister has to preach politics—not party, but *per-
> sonal* politics; for, if he did not, one part of the people would be found
> living on the other part. Every minister should preach [as much] politics
> as are necessary for good government.

Banks believed that the pulpit is a watchtower from which the pastor sounds
the alarm when evil is about to threaten the well-being of his flock. "Suppose," he asked, "a minister sees a national trouble approaching, such as
would depress him, as well as all others—would it not be in his line of pulpit duties to give the alarm?" He then turned to the reason why he felt some
people attacked black ministers for using the pulpit as a watchtower to alert
the people.

> As soon as the good minister sees things going wrong, his heart at once
> begins to feel, and then he begins to preach, and then the evil ones begin
> to try to kill his influence and usefulness as a minister of the Gospel, by
> charging him with preaching politi[c]s in the pulpit.[23]

Banks felt it was imperative for "preachers, newspapers, and every other
[political] machine to do as much as possible to repair wrongs when they
see them." He thought it absurd to believe that any influential person could
avoid commenting on politics as the Reverend Mr. Dupee believed.

Beyond the general question of "mixing" religion and politics, black
ministers expressed themselves on particular issues. For instance, they took
sides in 1872 against the Liberal Republican ticket, a conservative slate
endorsed by most Democrats. The Liberal Republicans opposed corrup-
tion in the Grant administration as well as "Negro rule" in the South. They
favored rapid restoration of the white franchise. They nominated Horace
Greeley, while the regular Republicans (radicals and moderates) renomi-
nated Grant.

Black leaders of the CABMC were not silent on this issue. Although
they repeatedly voiced their objections to supporting blind party loyalty,
they still placed their trust in the Radical Republicans who had already delivered on many of their promises to the black electorate. The Convention
expressed its sentiments in a lengthy resolution passed during its 19 Oc-

---

[23]Ibid.

tober session in St. Louis, seventeen days before the Presidential election on 5 November.

> And *Whereas,* Next November is the time when every man, black as well as white, shall say by the ballot who shall rule these United States; and
> *Whereas,* the colored part of the inhabitants, during all the years of the past history of this country, shall, for the first time by their suffrage, consent as to who shall govern them. Therefore, be it
> *Resolved,* That we will honor God, show our appreciation of the rights and privileges given to us, and to show our utter detestation of all the new departures of the so-called Liberal Republicans—believing, as we do, that every step out of the Radical Republican party is a fast retreating step back again to the land of whips for our own backs, to labor unrequited, to all the laws forbidding the peaceful enjoyment of our rights as American citizens—by urging our colored fellow-citizens to cast their ballots for President U. S. Grant and for Hon. Henry Wilson, for the Vice-Presidency of these United States.[24]

The Convention also expressed itself on another matter of pressing importance—a civil rights bill. Although Jim Crow legislation did not reach its zenith until the 1890s, blacks experienced various sorts of pernicious discrimination. The Convention called on Congress to do something about this.

> We pray that all the privileges accorded to other citizens, such as steamboat, hotel and railway accommodations, may be secured to us by the speedy passage, when Congress shall have assembled, of the supplementary civil rights bill.[25]

Before defecting to the Liberal Republicans, Radical Republican Charles Sumner of Massachusetts had introduced a bill in 1870 that sought to protect blacks from discrimination in housing, jobs, hotels, restaurants, places of amusement, public conveyances, juries, and incorporated church or cemetery associations. This bill drew the CABMC's endorsement in 1872. After being bottled up in the Senate Judiciary Committee, the bill was moved out when Grant offered half-hearted support in 1873. Mem-

---

[24]CABMC *Report,* 1872, 17-18.

[25]Ibid., 18.

bers of the Consolidated Convention lost little time in lobbying for the new bill.

Among the most vocal supporters was William E. Walker, a pastor from Trenton, New Jersey, and sometime missionary and agent of the Convention. Walker frequently sent editorial letters to his close associate, Lewis H. Douglass, brother of Frederick Douglass and copublisher (with his brother) of the *New National Era and Citizen*. In one such letter Walker raised the question, "What Do the Colored People Want?" For him the answer was quite simple: Equality of Rights.

> Equality of rights in a Republican form of government, is the life blood of human existence; it is the apex of man's ambition to attain—without it life is but a myth at best. Man is not free after leaving the land of Egypt until he reaches Canaan. Now, to secure the fruit of this land, which is equality, we want—first, purity of purpose; second, concentrated action; third, combined consolidated, determined perseverance.[26]

Walker cautioned black voters not simply to be satisfied that white friends would do right by them. He declared, "Rights can never be secured or obtained by passiveness, inactivity, or indifference."

Shortly after he wrote this letter, Walker penned an "Address," at the request of black New Jersey leaders, asking their Congressional representatives to support the pending Civil Rights Bill. He asserted that blacks looked to the Republicans for "redress,"[27] and that the Republicans, in turn, looked to blacks for support. They received two public replies in the *National Era* from Radical Republicans. Senator F. T. Frelinghuysen wrote that he had voted for the civil rights bill during the last session of Congress

---

[26]*New National Era and Citizen* (District of Columbia), 23 October 1873. In antebellum days, Walker, a native of Fredericksburg, Virginia, traveled back and forth across the Mason-Dixon Line continuously. He attended Oberlin College. His name appears in the ABMC *Minutes* for the first time in 1859. He was an abolitionist. His reputation as a scholar preceded him. He was asked to write the 1860 Circular Letter. His essay on "The History of the Church in Africa" was published in *The Anglo-African Magazine*, 2,2 (February 1860): 68-73. It manifested a sound introductory knowledge of church history as it was known then. See ABMC *Report*, 1860, 25-27. Walker, like Perry and most of the former abolitionist members of the the CABMC leadership, was an avowed black cultural nationalist. He expressed definite romantic views of black racial equality, if not moral superiority, in both the Circular Letter and the historical essay.

[27]*New National Era and Citizen,* 11 December 1873.

and attached amendments of his own to it. He cautioned the black New Jerseyans that the Bill had to undergo "a full and thorough investigation before the Judiciary Committee, so as to prevent its being set aside by the Supreme Court."[28] Representative Walter W. Phelps concurred with the Senator's judgment.

The Senate passed the bill in May 1874, but it ran into greater difficulty in the House of Representatives, which adjourned before taking action. In the interim, supporters tried to convince House opponents that the bill's clause advocating nondiscrimination would not amount to voting for social equality. Yet other supporters of the bill, blacks as well as whites, felt this clause should be deleted in order to ease passage of the bill. Washington Dupee became one of the boldest black Baptist exponents of this view. He met with fierce opposition not only from other ministers but also within his own congregation in Paducah, Kentucky. We have a report of this opposition from William Walker, who was in Paducah attending the Colored Baptist Kentucky State Convention of which Dupee was then president.

According to Walker, Dupee published an editorial in his own paper, *The Baptist Herald,* "in which he opposed the Civil Rights Bill, especially the school feature of that bill." This unusual position "brought down upon him the indignation of a vast number of his parishoners [*sic*], who threatened to punish him for his opinions as expressed, but recourse was taken to law." The authorities imprisoned Dupee, who was denied bail, in order "to keep the peace." Thereafter Dupee's "premises and person [were] guarded at night for several days."[29]

This incident deepened the cleavage that had already developed between the black Radical Republicans of the CABMC and local conservative Southern schismatics who followed the leadership of Dupee and Elder Nelson G. Merry of Nashville, Tennessee. The bill itself was signed into

---

[28]Ibid.

[29]*New National Era and Citizen,* 15 October 1874. According to E. Merton Coulter, "the Democrats could always depend on a few negro [*sic*] supporters." See his *The Civil War and Readjustment in Kentucky* (Chapel Hill: University of North Carolina Press, 1926) 438. Coulter quotes an Owen County Negro as having said, "'I'se a Democrat, dyed in de wool, I'se an honest nigger, and votes wid my friends. I has plenty while dese Radical niggers, half of 'em hab no meat at home.'"

law in 1875, only to be declared unconstitutional by the United States Supreme Court in 1883.

Financial Problems

In presenting to the CABMC the 1872 annual report of its executive board, Rufus Perry also lost no time in delineating the primary problem that confronted the Convention. Perry complained that the members had failed to support the Convention with their money.

> In every instance where you have given cheerfully and liberally, there has been a corresponding result of blessed fruits. On the other hand, wherever you have left the board without means to work with, there, at that point, is a barren field—a blank in our missionary history. This could not be otherwise. It is the legitimate result of cause and effect.[30]

According to Perry the annual report for 1871 was not printed until the middle of September 1872, almost a year after the meeting. The CABMC had to stop printing the *National Monitor* and the *Sunbeam* because its members had failed to give the money they pledged at the 1871 meeting in Brooklyn. Perry did not cite the cause of this lack of support, but stated that the Executive Board

> began to perceive a threatening indifference on the part of many of our ministers, and to apprehend the approach of the death of the Convention, which must inevitably follow, when contributions from our churches and other supporters of the Convention are, by any means, cut off.

Perry told the Convention that had it not been for the "efficiency of the Board" and the support of congregations such as the Olivet Baptist Church of Chicago, whose pastor was Richard DeBaptiste, the Convention's president, the mission rooms of the CABMC might have had to be closed. Perry reminded the Convention that Olivet had suffered greatly from the ravages of the Great Chicago Fire of October 1871. Nevertheless, in the light of its financial crisis, the board sent out an unsuccessful circular asking the churches to live up to their pledges. Charles Graham, the vice president of the Convention, even lent the CABMC $200. "Your secretary employed his own private means as far as he could do so," Perry added.

---

[30]CABMC *Report,* 1872, 8.

As far as the disbursement of funds was concerned, the board directed the treasurer to pay local bills and incidental expenses from the funds of its affiliate, the American Educational Association, "whose department was less embarrassed." The board also had to cancel all missionary commissions that legally bound it to pay the salary of those commissioned. As if to save face and grasp for hope, Perry offered a pious exclamation.

> But after all, we have reason to thank God for what he has done for us, and enabled us to do for ourselves and for his glory. Through his kind providence, he has broken the shackles that bound us and our brethren in a degraded slavery for two hundred and fifty years, and lifted us to the elevation of full citizenship with all its civil and political rights and privileges, and placed us in a position to prove ourselves worthy of our high calling, and labor with success for the spread of the kingdom.[31]

One more grasp for hope and for a sense of accomplishment was apparent in Perry's summary and recitation of the accomplishments of the CABMC since its formation in 1866. Based on his review of the records between 1866 and 1872, Perry claimed that the CABMC had hired 209 missionaries who had worked in twenty-four states. They had traveled 102,489 miles, preached 15,000 sermons, baptized 12,012 converts, formed ninety-five new congregations, and forty-six new schools. The CABMC had also given employment to seventeen "colored persons" in its Brooklyn office. It had also collected $94,000 which had either been paid directly or through its various missionaries.[32]

Later on in his report Perry gave the financial picture for 1872. Gross receipts for the year ending on 30 September 1872 amounted to $4,039.03. Donors designated $2,633.60 of this total for educational purposes; and $130.21 for the printing department. That left $1,265.22 for general purposes, including the hiring of missionaries, which was usually the largest item in the CABMC's budget. In the midst of reporting these figures Perry said that "all the money received at the mission-rooms, but $153.52, was collected or given by friends in the North. The money sent in by churches in the South was only $53.52."[33] This latter amount came from Virginia,

---

[31]Ibid.

[32]Ibid., 9.

[33]Ibid., 10-11.

North Carolina, and South Carolina. As if to list the Convention's antagonists, Perry cited the states of Alabama, Tennessee, Kentucky, and Missouri as having given nothing during the previous fiscal year. He failed to mention the states of West Virginia, Florida, Mississippi, Louisiana, Arkansas and Texas. Perry never mentioned the political differences between himself and George Washington Dupee nor did he state that the Southern brethren primarily represented themselves through their local associations. At any rate the CABMC responded to this situation by once again commencing a pledge campaign which resulted in a list of pledges amounting to $575 from eight-nine persons. But only six persons who pledged actually paid during the meeting of the Convention, and that amounted to only twenty-one dollars.[34]

The Nagging Problem of Governance

In view of the CABMC's grim financial situation, its leaders attempted to form a closer relation with the Southern black brothers and sisters. They went about this in the wrong way, however. They thought that a restructuring of their operation would solve this problem. They failed to recognize that the Southern leaders, who were often victimized by white associations, were suspicious of any body larger than themselves that sought to manage their affairs. Nevertheless, the CABMC appointed a Committee on Fields and Missions to divide it into districts. This was an admission that the state convention and associational system agreed to in 1866 had failed. The pressure to abandon the old system was not only economic in origin. It came largely from the Executive Board. Originally the Executive Board's report suggested that the CABMC simply divide the South into four districts. But the Committee on Fields and Missions, chaired by Simon P. Anderson of Missouri, rejected this suggestion. The Committee believed that the need for home missions was a national problem, not just a Southern problem. So it added two huge districts to cover the rest of the country.

Each of these six districts were to have district and local executive boards. The boards were to be located in Richmond, Savannah, St. Louis, Louisville, Chicago, and Philadelphia. The Committee left the power of appointing district secretaries up to the Executive Board rather than the lo-

---

[34]Ibid., 25.

cal executive boards. But it insisted that the salaries of these district secretaries were to be raised by the local boards. The district secretaries in
turn were "to proceed to organize their respective boards, from the best
working material at command." The missionaries were to be under the direction of the district secretary and his board. The district secretaries were
directed, however, to "immediately duplicate" the reports of the missionaries and send them to the Executive Board. In short the power of the Executive Committee, based primarily in the Northeast, was to remain intact
even at the peril of offending many of the local leaders. The presbyterial
structure of this arrangement also made the Committee's proposal subject
to attack. It is unclear from the 1872 minutes whether or not there was much
controversy regarding this proposal. In any case, it was adopted. Perhaps
the most serious strategic error made by the Committee was to suggest
names to fill the positions of general state missionaries without having them
confirmed by state conventions.[35] Practically all of these appointees were
former antebellum associates of the members of the Executive Board.

Reaction to this presbyterial restructuring was swift and decisive,
spelling the doom of the CABMC. The Western brethren were the first to
respond. Led by William H. Howard of Lexington, Missouri, they formed
the Baptist General Association of Western States and Territories in a
meeting at Mexico, Missouri on 15 January 1873.

But the more ominous schism came from the South. A new organization was formed at the third annual meeting of the Sunday School Convention of Tennessee. The new body was called the Missionary Baptist
State Convention of Tennessee, North Alabama, North Mississippi, East
Arkansas, and Kentucky. It is not coincidental that this group met at the
First Colored Baptist Church in Nashville, where Nelson G. Merry served
as pastor. Merry and Dupee were leaders of this faction, but endeavored
to remain behind the scenes until they knew they had enough troops to
launch a new enterprise. The official call for a new Southern organization
came from the First Missionary Baptist Association and Convention of
Kentucky. Dupee was the moderator of this body but sent Elder J. F.
Thomas to be its representative at the 9-13 October 1873 meeting of the
Tennessee Sunday School Convention.

---

[35]Ibid., 29.

During the course of the meeting, Thomas was asked to speak. He delivered "his message in a few pointed remarks." After he spoke the Committee on Resolutions passed four different resolutions concerning Thomas's visit. The assembled brethren resolved to thank Thomas for coming, concurred that they would work with the Kentucky Convention "in matters of important for the true advancement of the Gospel" throughout their common territory, and endorsed Dupee's newspaper, the *Baptist Herald.* Later in the meeting the brethren also voted adopt Thomas's call for the reorganization of the Northwestern and Southern Baptist Convention. Thomas's resolution pointed to the failure of the CABMC to establish and mount an effective missionary organization as the primary reason why blacks west of the Appalachian Mountains should form a Baptist convention. The resolution read,

> *To the Baptists of the Northwestern and Southern States:*
> *Whereas,* The vast field of missionary labor embraced in the above-named territory, has been shamefully neglected since the organization of the American Baptist Missionary Convention, which has failed to carry out the object for which it was formed; Therefore,
> 1. *Be it Resolved,* That the Baptists in the States of Kentucky, Tennessee, Ohio, Indiana, Mississippi, Georgia, Illinois, District of Columbia, Missouri, Alabama, North Carolina, South Carolina, Virginia, Texas, Florida, and others who may wish to attend, will send delegates to the meeting in the city of _____, State of _____, Thursday before the third Lord's day in February, 1874, for the purpose of organizing a Baptist convention.
> 2. *Be it Resolved,* That all Churches who will join the organization, will correspond immediately with Elder G. W. Dupee, Paducah, Ky., Box 463, or Elder N. G. Merry, Nashville, Tenn.[36]

The Southern brethren apparently succeeded, but their first session was not held until 1875. In the meantime the Northeastern leaders were also displeased with the ineffectiveness of the CABMC and used its announced reorganization as an excuse to form their own organization, the New England Baptist Missionary Convention, in August 1874. Its first president

---

[36]Missionary State Baptist Convention . . . *Minutes,* 1873, 8. Later this Convention changed its name to the General State Convention of Tennessee, North Alabama and South Kentucky. It always held its meetings in Nashville, Tennessee, at the Spruce Street Baptist Church, whose name was later changed to the First Baptist Church of Capitol Hill.

was Theodore Doughty Miller of Philadelphia. Rufus Perry even volunteered his services as its corresponding secretary, and the New England group welcomed him. But this did not change the fact that they had formed a group that really drained off some of the potential support for the Consolidated Convention. By the spring of 1875 the Southern brethren had finally gotten themselves organized into a group called the Southwestern and Southern Missionary Baptist Convention. It held its first meeting on 20 May 1875 in Montgomery, Alabama.[37]

D. W. Phillips, the white principal of the Nashville Institute, a ABHMS school for the freed people eventually known as Roger Williams University,[38] exerted a powerful influence on Nelson Merry and George W. Dupee, the major leaders of the Southern schism. In fact the agents of the white ABHMS encouraged rather than discouraged the split. Shortly after organizing, the Southwestern group appointed a committee "to whom was referred the subject of co-operating with the American Baptist Home Mission Society." This committee offered the following resolution, which was adopted.

> *Resolved.* That we will heartily respond and co-operate with the Home Mission Society, and do all we can to aid in building up their various institutes for the education of the colored people, and in promoting Christian education among us. We further recommend that the Convention take hold of some department of the work connected with the Nashville Institute, and do it as our work.[39]

For these Southern black Baptists, cooperating with the Northern white ABHMS meant maintaining their own independence, not betraying black sovereignty.

The Fall of the Consolidated Convention

The CABMC did not die a quick death. Even without the gradual erosion of support and the often intentional undermining by the white ABHMS,

---

[37]See *American Baptist Year Book,* 1876.

[38]Eugene TeSelle, "The Nashville Institute and Roger Williams University: Benevolence, Paternalism, and Black Consciousness, 1867-1910," *Tennessee Historical Quarterly* (Winter 1982): 360-79.

[39]Ibid.

the Convention itself was an implausible enterprise for poor blacks to maintain amidst the postwar economic problems of the United States. The expense of traveling to the annual meeting of the Convention alone was one of the major problems that led to the necessity for regional and local affiliates. This was one of the reasons why the Convention voted during its 1872 meeting to meet on a triennial basis beginning with its 1874 meeting. Although the minutes for the 1873 and 1874 meetings are not extant, surely much gloom hung over these meetings as a result of the disaffection of many supporters in practically every part of the country. Who was to blame for this situation? The part of the Executive Board's 1874 report that is extant complains about the lack of support and cooperation from the ABHMS and the Brooklyn-based American Bible Union. While relations were "as amicable as could be expected, yet," the board lamented, "there ought to be a more efficient cooperation" with the CABMC.[40] The brunt of the blame for the CABMC's problems fell on the shoulders of Corresponding Secretary Rufus Lewis Perry.

The one thing that kept the Convention from total collapse was its impeccable reputation for honesty, if not for efficiency. But all this ended during 1877 when a feud between the Executive Board and Corresponding Secretary Rufus Perry developed. The relationship between the Board and Perry had been strained ever since Justin D. Fulton, now the white pastor of the Centenary Baptist Church of Brooklyn, was asked to join the Board in 1876. Fulton was quite influential within the ABHMS and was a popular preacher. But he was rigidly opposed to Catholicism and to any Baptist agency that was unwilling to submit to the wise leadership of the American Baptist Home Mission Society. Apparently the black brethren had either forgotten or had forgiven Fulton for his instrumental role in disrupting Edward Turney's National Theological Institute and University.[41] Nevertheless, Fulton wasted little time in challenging the integrity and leadership of Rufus Lewis Perry. Perry's enemies on the Board saw their opportunity to oust him.

Soon after the preliminary business of the 1877 Convention was settled, Amos Johnson of Missouri, the president of the Convention, ap-

---

[40]*American Baptist Year Book,* 1875, 23.

[41]See chapter 4. Also see Robert S. MacArthur's biographical sketch of Fulton in Justin D. Fulton, *Rome in America* (New York: Funk & Wagnalls, 1884) ix-xxxix.

pointed a Committee of Investigation to examine the Executive Board's charges against Perry. The Board consisted of Charles Graham, Armstead Marble, Samuel Harris, George W. Talbutt, George B. Smith, Henry Williams, and Justin D. Fulton. Most of these men were following Fulton's leadership. The Committee of Investigation consisted of William Troy, E. G. Corprew, Henry N. Jeter, William Gray, Armstead Marble, A. M. Newman, Anthony Binga, Jr., R. M. Duling, J. E. Farrar, Wallace Shelton, Richard Wells, Richard Spiller, Richard DeBaptiste, and William Thomas Dixon. All these men were Perry's longstanding friends. Some of them had known him since their antislavery days in Canada. They were not about to allow a white man to railroad Perry out of office. They unanimously returned a verdict of acquittal to the Convention. The Convention accepted their report and reelected Perry to another term in office. The Committee report was quite explicit about who was to blame for bringing the charges against Perry.

> It is clearly shown [from the evidence] that the said charges would not have been made against the said Rufus L. Perry, Corresponding Secretary of this Convention, had it not been for the disagreement as to the management of the *National Monitor,* between the said Corresponding Secretary and the Rev. Justin D. Fulton, D.D.

The committee added,

> We believe that the alleging [of] said charges against the Corresponding Secretary was a conspiracy to injure the usefulness of said Corresponding Secretary, and to the disparagement of the ability of colored men in managing the work of evangelization.[42]

This was the last time in the history of black Baptists in the nineteenth century that they invited a white person to be in a position of power in their national denominational work.

Fulton's charges against Perry were not entirely unfounded, however. He just made too much out of them. It is unclear what the full range of the charges was, but it is clear what the basic issue was. In the perpetual financial crises that beset the CABMC, the Executive Board usually shifted funds from well-endowed budget items to cover lean spots in the budget.

---

[42]CABMC *Report,* 1877, 12.

Perry probably did this as a matter of course without consulting the Executive Board beforehand. But Fulton, an able administrator in his own right, was unaccustomed to this relaxed method of managing Baptist affairs. Moreover, the budgetary maneuvers were undertaken for the sake of saving the *National Monitor,* which took controversial positions regarding religion and politics and gave constant support to radical Republican issues. Fulton was both theologically and politically conservative. He apparently did not see how saving this newspaper could be more important to black Baptists than support of evangelization. Many black religious leaders, however, felt that they could not afford to make an artificial distinction between religion and politics.

Black religious newspapers like *The Christian Recorder* and the *National Monitor* provided a major means for sharing information and sounding the alarm against racial injustice. Thus it is not difficult to see why black Baptists would support Perry's decision. The CABMC did not allow Perry to escape without a minor reprimand, however. Apparently Perry used the pittance in the oldest, most neglected, and yet most cherished fund belonging to the CABMC's treasury, its Widow's Fund. The executors of the Fund stated, and the Convention concurred,

> that we do not find fault with the Convention, nor *Monitor,* for borrowing the money belonging to the Widow's Fund, when in distress, but we require the moneys to be paid back with interest, at the earliest possible period.[43]

The Convention voted to send a telegram from Richmond, Virginia, where it was meeting, to Charlotte H. Perry, Rufus Perry's spouse, announcing his acquittal and extending its apologies. It also directed that its findings be announced in the Baptist newspapers of the country. But it was too late. The damage had been done. At its 1878 meeting in Lexington, Kentucky and its 1879 meeting in Cincinnati, Ohio, the CABMC struggled to stay alive. It had fewer and fewer troops to fight its battle, a depleted treasury, and a reputation for mismanagement and misappropriation of funds. It was dissolved by the membership at the Cincinnati meeting.

Rufus Perry never again enjoyed national prominence as a denominational leader, yet he never gave up his struggle. He continued both the Free

---

[43]Ibid., 22.

Mission Society and the Consolidated Convention as paper organizations. He retained the title of Corresponding Secretary for both organizations apparently until his death in 1895. This title legally gave him executive power over the legacies bequeathed to the two organizations. Much of this money went for the support of a Haitian mission. Some of it was designated for "freedmen education." He also became the pastor of the small mission church in Brooklyn, a forerunner of the present-day Bethany Baptist Church. Perry continued to pursue a lifelong interest in ancient African history, partly because of his Masonic ties, but also because of his fine intellectual ability. He was a student of James Boise, onetime professor of classics at the University of Michigan and Brown University. As a result of his studies of the classics and ethnology, Perry produced a black cultural nationalist defense of peoplehood.[44]

Despite these unfortunate developments in the career of the Consolidated Convention and in Rufus Perry's life, the dream of creating a national union of black Baptists survived what might have otherwise been a fatal nightmare. The struggle that lay ahead for the seers of this vision proved to be an arduous one.

---

[44]Rufus L. Perry, *The Cushites, or the Descendants of Ham as Found in the Sacred Scriptures, and in Writings of Ancient Historians and Poets from Noah to the Christian Era* (Springfield MA: Wiley, 1893). Perry obviously deserves a fuller biographical sketch than I am able to give here. He was very active, for example, in black Brooklyn's struggles for civil rights such as education. Several studies provide helpful clues to his activities in this area, including Seth M. Scheiner, *Negro Mecca: A History of the Negro in New York City, 1865-1920* (New York: New York University Press, 1965) 176; Harold X. Connolly, *A Ghetto Grows in Brooklyn* (New York: New York University Press, 1977) 25, 28, 31; and Carleton Mabee, *Black Education in New York State: From Colonial to Modern Times* (Syracuse: Syracuse University Press, 1979) 101, 152. The Masonic ties between Justin D. Fulton and the CABMC leadership should not be underestimated. Fulton's anti-Catholicism and Perry's Ethiopianism represent different accents between black and white Masons. They also reflect different ideological emphases. Perry's *The Cushites* shows signs of his Masonic influences. These differences persisted between black and white Masons in this period. See Lynn Dumenil, *Freemasonry and American Culture, 1880-1930* (Princeton NJ: Princeton University Press, 1984) 123.

Part III

*The Rise
of Black Baptist
Nationalism*

6

The Making of a Church
with the Soul of a Nation,
1880-1889

It took sixteen years for the black Baptists to form a national denomination to replace the CABMC. In the meantime two major national bodies[1]
were organized in order to deal with certain persistent problems that eventually would be addressed by one body.

Predecessors of the 1895 Convention

The first of those two bodies, the Baptist Foreign Mission Convention
of the United States (BFMC), was organized in Montgomery, Alabama,
during December 1880, one year after the collapse of the CABMC. The
American National Baptist Convention (ANBC) convened for the first time
in St. Louis on 25-29 August 1886 for the purpose of devising means for
the creation of a national black Baptist denomination. Formation of these
two organizations amounted to an admission that the three regional conventions discussed in the preceding chapter were inadequate substitutes for
a national denomination. Moreover, many black Baptist leaders were determined to dispute the prevalent belief that they did not have the ability
to form and manage a national body.

---

[1]A black national Baptist Education Convention was organized 20-21 September 1892
in Savannah, Georgia. But its influence in the events that led in the creation of the National
Baptist Convention was minimal.

The Foreign Mission Movement. Although the creation of the BFMC in 1880 reflected a longstanding commitment of black Baptists to foreign missions, the story of the foreign mission movement is not germane to the story of the formation of a black national denomination.[2] Nonetheless, a closer look at the ideology of this convention illustrates its major contribution to the unification movement.

The BFMC operated on the assumption that it would conduct foreign mission work, mostly in West Africa, while local associations and state conventions, with the assistance of the ABHMS, would meet the evangelistic and educational needs of their local communities. Although there were several state conventions that supported African missions, this division of labor generally worked quite well so long as the brethren limited themselves to traditional forms of evangelism. But increasing discrimination against blacks in areas such as education, public accommodations, and jobs mandated a broadening of the preachers' understanding of evangelism. Some leaders began to accept the idea that dependence on traditional views of evangelism in the face of the enormous problems of their constituents was social irresponsibility. Most of them wanted to change the nation, not to escape from it.

These Baptist leaders believed that black problems were national in scope and needed a national solution. Although political reconstruction had come to an end, there were vestiges of the innovative social legislation of the national and state Reconstruction governments that offered legal deterrents to discrimination—at least on paper. Nevertheless, Jim Crow re-

---

[2]The 1880 date for the origin of the National Baptist Convention resulted from continuing the custom of claiming the date of origin to be the date of the founding of the oldest constituent body of the merging organizations. The founders of the CABMC did this in 1866. Another reason why twentieth-century black National Baptists have given a central role to the foreign mission movement is largely because its first historian, Lewis Garnett Jordan, longtime executive secretary of the Foreign Mission Board of the incorporated National Baptist Convention, simply listed the founding of the BFMC in 1880 as the date for the origin of the National Baptist Convention. There is no evidence that the organizers of the 1895 Convention held this view. Without being uncharitable it should be noted that Jordan left much evidence to support the claim that he was obsessed with the desire of the aged to be remembered. See *Atlanta Constitution,* 26 September 1895; and *Seventh Annual Report of Historian and General Missionary . . . . of the National Baptist Convention, U.S. [Inc.],* 1932, 28. The history of the black Baptist foreign mission movement still remains largely unrecorded. But important explorations into this immense enterprise have been made by Sandy Dwayne Martin, "Growth of Christian Missionary Interest in West Africa Among Southeastern Baptists, 1880-1915" (Ph.D. dissertation, Columbia University, 1981).

ceived a new lease on life when the United States Supreme Court nullified the civil rights gains of the 1870s in 1883. This decision, made in the twilight of black Reconstruction political gains, signaled that the federal government was willing to leave the resolution of black problems to state government. This proved to be disastrous for black people because most of the state governments by the mid-1880s had been ''Redeemed'' (or returned to the control of the legatees of slavocracy, the conservative Southern Democrats).

As John Hope Franklin has written, ''Reconstruction'' itself ''was essentially a national, not a sectional or racial problem.''[3] But the federal government experienced a failure of nerve. The termination of the Reconstruction experiment attendant on the famous 1877 Hayes-Tilden Compromise did not diminish the proportions of the black problem. Seemingly perpetual economic hardship, political instability, and the rise of an increasingly complex industrial society exacerbated the struggle to help freedmen overcome the deprivations engendered by slavery.

While one may not minimize the religious and social importance of a faith closely adhering to the teachings of the Bible, it is apparent that the black Baptist foreign mission movement nourished those biblicistic tendencies that helped black Baptist preachers to mollify the hardships of their parishioners. These preachers refused to believe that a God of justice placed blacks in America for no reason at all. Their theological justification for engaging in African missions was closely tied to their need to explain why blacks were enslaved. Emanuel Love, president of the BFMC in 1889, stated this belief more clearly than any of his predecessors.

> We have met to *think, talk, pray,* and *give* in order that the gospel may be given to Africa, the land of our fathers. There is no doubt in my mind that Africa is our field of operation, and that Moses was sent to deliver his brethren, and as the prophets were members of the race to whom they were sent, so I am convinced that God's purpose is to redeem Africa through us. The evils of slavery were turned to gracious account, conferring upon us the blessings of civilization, and in return placing the negro [*sic*] Christians of this great country under lasting obligation to the work of African

---

[3]Franklin, *From Slavery to Freedom* (New York: Alfred A. Knopf, 1967) 301.

evangelization. This work is ours by appointment, by inheritance, and by choice.[4]

Sentiments such as these enhanced black solidarity by nourishing a sense of self-confidence and purpose. Unlike some of the Yankee-minded leaders of the CABMC, the BFMC, consisting mainly of Southerners, was unprepared to relinquish its racial identity. It continuously rejected invitations to merge with the Northern white American Baptist Missionary Union (ABMU). It was quite explicit about why it rejected the ABMU's offer in 1886.

> We believe . . . that to continue our work as an organization will develop qualities and powers in us as a people that will not be developed if we go into another [white] organization.

It then accused the white Baptists of not really being seriously interested in evangelizing Africa.

> Now to give up our organization will be to throw a check upon our efforts, and to a large degree hinder the work of evangelizing Africa. There is no reason, to our mind, why we should cooperate, but many why we should not—we need experience, we need self-reliance, we need those blessings that come to those who discharge their duty to God and man.[5]

Despite these separatist sentiments the BFMC ran into the same difficulties that had also plagued the CABMC.[6] It repeatedly tried to district the country in order to raise more money for African missions. Moreover by 1886 a new black national organization arose, taking from and sharing many of its members with the BFMC.

The Unifying Role of the American Convention. The American National Baptist Convention (ANBC) was actually the most ambitious attempt to found a black Baptist national denomination since the demise of the CABMC. It mediated between the various factions of the black Baptist family and the powerful Northern white societies. The second article of its Constitution specified the ANBC's major objective.

---

[4]BFMC *Minutes,* 1889, 7-8.

[5]BFMC *Minutes,* 1886, 32.

[6]Ibid., 30-31.

The object of this Convention shall be to consider the moral, intellectual and religious growth of the denomination, and to deliberate upon those great questions which characterize the Baptist churches. And further, to devise and consider the best methods possible for bringing us more closely together as a church and as a race.[7]

This deliberative body provided a much needed intellectual outlet for many of the younger and more progressive brothers and sisters[8] who were graduating in large numbers from Northern-sponsored Southern black schools, such as Shaw University (Raleigh, North Carolina) and Wayland Theological Seminary (Richmond, Virginia). The annual minutes for this Convention overflow with papers that grappled with problems of Baptist polity and with social and ethical questions.

Perhaps the most important new factor in this convention was the rise of a new generation of leaders who were able to take control of this renewal of the movement toward unity. Between 1886 and 1890 the presidency of the ANBC was graced and energized by the dynamic leadership of William James Simmons, a 37-year-old minister from Kentucky who gratified conventioneers with his wit and clarity of mind. In fact Simmons was almost single-handedly responsible for calling the brethren together in the first place. As president of the black State University of Kentucky, editor of the popular newspaper, the *American Baptist* (Louisville, Ken-

---

[7]ANBC *Minutes,* 1886, 13.

[8]Women played a prominent role in these deliberations. Although they were not permitted to preach, they gave lectures on such topics as "Woman's Place in the Work of the Denomination." One woman, Miss Lucy Wilmot Smith of Louisville, Kentucky, was even elected Historian of the Convention. See ANBC *Journal and Lectures,* 1887, 45-58, 65-67. The new role of women constitutes more evidence for the broad spirit of William Simmons. Ida B. Wells, the first famous black female journalist, said of Simmons, "In every way he could, Dr. Simmons encouraged me to be a newspaper woman, and whatever fame I achieved in the line I owe in large measure to his influence and encouragement" (Alfreda M. Duster, ed., *Crusade for Justice: The Autobiography of Ida B. Wells,* John Hope Franklin, series ed., *Negro American Biographies and Autobiographies* [Chicago: The University of Chicago Press, 1970] 32). The work of Evelyn Brooks on the history of the women's rights movement within the black Baptist family adds much to our understanding of these dynamics. See her two published articles: "Nannie Burroughs and the Education of Black Women" in Sharon Harley and Rosalyn Terborg-Penn, eds., *The Afro-American Woman: Struggles and Images* (Port (Port Washington NY: Kennikate Press, 1978) 97-108, 131-33; and "The Feminist Theology of the Black Baptist Church, 1880-1900" in Amy Swerdlow and Hanna Lessinger, eds., *Class, Race, and Sex: The Dynamics of Control* (Boston: G. K. Hall, 1983) 31-59.

tucky),[9] and president and organizer of the National Negro Press Association, Simmons was in a strategic position to encourage the unification of the Baptists. According to Bishop Henry McNeal Turner of the African Methodist Episcopal Church, Simmons's biographer,[10] Simmons suggested a national convention of black Baptists in the 5 April issue of his newspaper. The meeting took place in August 1886. Simmons gave the denominational sermon, and was unanimously elected president of the Convention and chairman of its executive committee. Simmons's militant denominationalism contributed greatly to his rise to power among the black Baptists. Turner described him as a man whose motto was "God, my race and denomination." His contemporaries seemed to be dazed by the man's charm, energy, and administrative acumen. Ida B. Wells characterized him as "a big man, figuratively and physically."[11] Nevertheless, older leaders who had earned fame in the CABMC also contributed to the success of the new enterprise.

Fifty-five-year-old Richard DeBaptiste, former president of the CABMC, was elected statistician of the new group. He offered the first statistical analysis of the growth of black Baptists. It is difficult now to recapture the jubilation and surprise that greeted DeBaptiste's claim that there were 1,066,131 Afro-American Baptists who belonged to 9,061 congregations whose property was valued at nearly 1.5 million dollars. Moreover DeBaptiste claimed that there were more than 4,572 converts.[12] These sta-

---

[9]I have not been able to locate copies of this newspaper.

[10]Turner shared a deep interest in politics with Simmons. Both had earned national reputations as a result of their involvement in Reconstruction politics. Turner was a Georgia legislator and postmaster while Simmons worked on the county level in Florida before migrating to Kentucky. Both men were "race men" par excellence. See Turner's biographical sketch in Simmons, ed., *Men of Mark, Eminent, Progressive, and Rising* (Cleveland: George M. Rewell, 1887; reprint, New York: Arno Press, 1968) 5-19.

[11]Ibid., 15; Duster, *Crusade for Justice*, 31.

[12]It is impossible to establish the accuracy of DeBaptiste's figures since black Baptist data were gathered in haphazard fashion. The figures do seem to be plausible, however. DeBaptiste's rather crude but sensible method was simply to compare the statistics in his own compilation of association and convention minutes with those of the widely respected *American Baptist Year Book*. He was able to gather minutes that the editors of the *Year Book* never dreamed existed or were unable to secure. There were literally several hundreds

tistics gave DeBaptiste a solid basis for raising the central issue that confronted the 1886 ANBC as well as most of its subsequent meetings: the problem of the adequacy of Baptist polity for the enormous social needs of Afro-Americans.

> While it is evident that our church polity is favorable to the most wonderful expansion in growth of numbers, and the maintenance of entire uniformity in all essential points of doctrinal belief, it remains for us to demonstrate that it is equally adapted to obtaining the largest results in efficiency of service in proportion to numbers, and of liberality of contributions in proportions to means. [13]

DeBaptiste's latter query provided the backdrop in the 1886 meeting for black Baptists leaders to grapple with the tendency to use Baptist polity to sanction localism. Two papers presented at the 1886 meeting addressed this problem. Solomon T. Clanton, an 1883 black graduate of Baptist Union Theological Seminary,[14] delivered a paper entitled "Co-operative Union or Separation." After arguing that "race confidence" in black leadership would be enhanced through the union of black Baptist forces, Clanton, a fervent integrationist, argued that black Baptist unification would lead to greater cooperation among Baptist missionary endeavors, regardless of race. Furthermore he was convinced that more cooperation and unity on the part of black Baptists would stand as a testimony against the "foul" charge that blacks could not be amalgamated into American society. Clanton declared that it was the will of God that black Baptist unity should

> ring from the Atlantic to the Pacific, from the Lakes to the Gulf. In this way, prejudice, which is the child of ignorance, will be removed, the color-line, which is an invention of Satan, will be wiped out and race recognition

---

of them. DeBaptiste counted 311. The *American Baptist Year Book* people often confused black Southern associations with white ones because the adjectives African, Colored or Negro were often not used by black Baptist groups. DeBaptiste's figures doubled the standard figure of 500,000 which the *Year Book* usually listed as the total number of black Baptists in the United States.

[13]ANBC *Minutes*, 1886, 63, 67.

[14]This Seminary was located in Morgan Park, Illinois, and was the forerunner of the University of Chicago Divinity School. Other leaders of the ANBC also received their professional training at Baptist Union during the 1880s, including Charles Lewis Fisher, W. C. Jordan, and Robert J. Semple. See ANBC *Journal and Lectures*, 1887, 66.

on the ground of merit alone, without social amalgamation, will be secured on terms worthy of immortal men. [15]

James T. White of Arkansas, in another paper entitled "Need of Colored Baptists of the South," argued that black Baptists should unify in order to launch an attack against ignorant Southern preachers. He contended
that these men gave ammunition to the bishops of the African Methodist
Church who, White declared, spread "the impression abroad that the Baptists are an ignorant class at best." He added, "It is an advantage to the
Methodist church [sic] to appear wise, while, by blowing their own horn,
they make us appear to be ignorant." White confessed that this accusation,
which had some merit, was peculiarly applicable to the Southern brethren.
Although he himself was born in the North he felt compelled to come to
the defense of Southern black Baptists. White had the credentials for doing
this. He had served as a state senator from Helena, Arkansas, for a number
of years and for an even longer period served as pastor of the Centennial
Church. He argued that the major missionary concern of black Baptists
should still be in the South where a more intelligent pulpit and an affluent
pew were much needed. Since he did not see any possibility of black people leaving the South in great numbers, he believed that the most "profi-
cient means" of making Southern black people "more amiable and
attractive" would be "to maintain fraternal intercourse with each other.
How easy could that be done!" [16] Both of these papers revealed that a new
surge of black Baptist denominational loyalty was afoot.

While calling for unity, some leaders, unlike Richard DeBaptiste, entertained the possibility that disunity was the natural bedfellow of Baptist
polity. William Simmons dismissed this problem at the 1887 meeting as
an attempt to belittle Baptist efficiency and progress.

> If the Baptist churches had not been the churches of God, our enemies would
> have killed us long ago. It can stand apparently more worldly misman-
> agement and live than all the other bodies on earth. A Baptist split only
> produces another Baptist church. No one expects less, nor more. It can only
> increase the number of our churches.

---

[15]ANBC *Minutes*, 1886, 77.

[16]Ibid., 80.

While defending Baptist polity Simmons did not fail to prod uncooperative brethren. According to Simmons the black Baptist family

> is the largest religious denomination among our race in the United States, and is without doubt larger than all of them put together, but for want of organization has not wielded the power belonging even to its numerical strength.[17]

Yet Simmons realized that chastisement without subsequent action would do little to attack the problem of disunity. Between the August 1887 meeting of the ANBC and the April 1888 meeting of its executive board, Simmons, the chairman of the board, accepted an appointment from the ABHMS to be its District Secretary for the South. During this same period Simmons used his new office to rally black Baptists. According to Richard DeBaptiste he sought "to secure a unification of interests in the mission and educational work of the colored Baptists, and to promote a closer union of the general organization among us."[18] Simmons announced at the April Executive Board meeting that he had succeeded in getting the BFMC and the Baptist General Association of Western States and Territories to meet in conference with the officers of the ABHMS, who had already planned to meet with the ANBC. This "joint meeting" took place in Nashville, Tennessee, 18-26 September 1888.

The phrase "joint meeting" was a euphemism used to express the black Baptist desire for unification. Actually the brethren held separate business meetings, then later held a fellowship meeting where they harangued endlessly about the beauties of unification. The actual proposals for unification were drawn up by a committee consisting of the leaders of the several conventions. But the leaders at this 1888 Nashville meeting were unable to agree on a plan for forming a national black denomination. They were more concerned about forming alliances that would place them in a united position to solicit funds from the disunited Northern Baptist societies. They believed that those societies were unwilling to accept solicitations from a united black Baptist denomination, but were willing to assist united black Baptist societies with agendas and organizations similar to their own. In

---

[17]ANBC *Journal and Lectures,* 1887, 12.

[18]ANBC *Journal, Sermons and Lectures,* 1888, 64.

1888 the ABMU was more prepared to do this than the ABHMS, which was still determined to monopolize domestic mission work.[19]

R. J. Adams and E. F. Merriam represented the white ABMU at the Nashville meeting. They consulted with a joint committee consisting of the leaders of the BFMC and the Baptist General Association of Western States and Territories (BGA) to devise a "plan for the unification of all colored Baptists in foreign missions work, including a method of co-operation with the American Baptist Missionary Union." Actually the executive boards of the BFMC and the BGA "had met and recommended the report of the Joint Committee for adoption by their respective bodies."[20] The Joint Committee's Report called for the organization of a new body to be called the American Baptist Foreign Mission Convention. All black Baptist foreign mission societies were to merge with this new convention, which would be the only liaison between the white ABMU and black Baptists.

The internal organization of this proposed convention was quite similar to the CABMC's 1872 districting plan. This was partly the result of the influence of Rufus Lewis Perry. Still corresponding secretary of the CABMC (which existed only on paper), Perry was elected president of a joint session of the two foreign mission bodies. No doubt Perry's link with past efforts to achieve unity encouraged the separatist sentiments held by most of the brethren. Despite the prior approval of the boards the majority of the BFMC voted to table the plan so that the new foreign mission convention, which never came into existence, could consider the merits of affiliating with the white ABMU.

---

[19]The white Southern Baptist Convention was not resting on its tradition of discrimination toward black Baptists in the South. According to one historian, it "had some type of ministry to the Negroes during 1882 and 1884 in at least eleven states." See John Edward Hughes, "A History of the Southern Baptist Convention's Ministry to the Negro: 1845-1904" (Th.D. dissertation, Southern Baptist Theological Seminary, 1971) 155. By the 1880s both the Northern and Southern white Baptists had reached an undeclared agreement that black missionaries were better at evangelizing their own than were white missionaries. Although they did retain some white missionaries the majority of their labor force consisted of local or itinerant black preachers and a few laypersons. They also appointed state missionaries to coordinate and develop the work on this level. These missionaries usually worked with the cooperation of all the black Southern state conventions and a few of the white ones. The major outline of the Southern Baptist work in this regard is told in Hughes's dissertation at 46 n1. The Northern ABHMS's side of the story is told in several places. The black Baptist side of this story has yet to be told.

[20]*National Baptist* (Philadelphia), 4 October 1888.

Although the joint assembly expressed its appreciation for the presence of the ABMU's representatives, it distrusted the ABMU's motives. This longstanding distrust was aggravated by another event. Many of the delegates were angry because some of their colleagues had been locked out of first-class coaches of the Nashville, Chattanooga and St. Louis Railway even though they had paid for first-class tickets. A year later at another meeting this issue would gain greater prominence in the official proceedings of the conventions. But the 1888 delegates merely settled for passing a resolution that condemned discrimination on this occasion.[21] Despite this distraction, the foreign mission bodies still had to meet with the American National Baptist Convention.

The ANBC held its meeting 22-24 September 1888. The meeting with the representatives of the ABHMS took place on 25 September. It was originally scheduled to last two days, but was shortened because of the spread of yellow fever throughout the South. Despite this unforeseen event the ANBC's plan to unify the black Baptists in 1888 was temporarily subverted by the foreign mission bodies' attempt to unite. The localist leaders of the foreign mission groups were unprepared to merge with the nationalists in the ANBC.

Nonetheless the localists were exposed to the powerful nationalistic denominationalists in the ANBC, who were deeply committed to forging a truly national black Baptist denomination. Only one speech spoke directly to the challenge that faced the Baptists. The luminous oratory of D. W. Wisher, pastor of New York City's Olivet Baptist Church, posed the central questions, attacked segregation, and then depicted how the "glories" of unity would elevate a downtrodden race.

> The power of unity will raise us high above the level of the common. It will enable us to destroy all narrow-mindedness among ourselves, and like a stream rushing from a mountain, sweeping down all obstacles, it will sweep from our midst, among the other nations of the country, and break down all prejudice and race pride of them who acknowledge us not as their equals. It will lift up our denomination higher and higher, and show the world that our church, indeed, is the church of which it is said that the days of her widowhood are over, and she is coming forth, out of her chamber,

----

[21]ANBC, *Journal, Sermons and Lectures,* 1888, 27, 47.

as a bride, gloriously adorned in her wedding garments, prepared to meet
her groom.[22]

Wisher then lifted up a powerful and unforgettable[23] series of images.

Unity we need, and unity we want, but let it not be a unity of errors, but
a unity of truth. Let it not be like the waters of a stagnant pool, over which
the purifying breath of heaven sweeps in vain. Let it not be the unity of
darkness, like the cloud-covered midnight sky, where neither moon nor
star appears, neither the unity of a forced conformity, such as is found in
polar seas, where eternal winter has locked up the waves in fetters, but pray
that our unity, as Evangelical Protestants, as Baptists, may be like a fountain flowing ever fresh and free from the rock, like the rainbow that com-
bines the seven prismatic colors into one glorious arch of promise, spanning
the heavens, like old ocean's unfettered flow, as its waves rush in all their
majesty and might, "distinct as the billows, but one as the sea."[24]

Wisher pointed to racial needs as the primary reason for the unity of black
Baptists. Most of the delegates apparently shared his views. They too
yearned for greater cooperation and fellowship among the Baptists. But
questions of the distribution of power were not allowed to be dismissed
lightly. The only thing the 1888 union meeting could achieve was to agree
to hold joint anniversaries in 1889. Given this political reality many had
resigned themselves to dreaming and hoping for the fruition of that which
could not be seen. More was required than talking and dreaming, however, if the ANBC was to achieve its goal of unifying the Afro-American
Baptists. Many believed that a greater sense of racial solidarity was a prerequisite to forming a strong racial ecclesiastical bond. But they really did
not know how to create a greater sense of race loyalty in a society that

---

[22]Ibid., 99.

[23]This address was so well received that part of it was reprinted later at a crucial period
in the history of the movement to unify. See *National Baptist Magazine* 1 (January 1894):
27-29. By 1900 Wisher had fallen out with his New York Baptist brethren and joined the
African Methodist Episcopal Church. Ironically, he blamed his troubles on Baptist polity.
Black Baptist leaders dismissed this. See *National Baptist Magazine* 7 (March 1901): 243.
Wilson Jeremiah Moses's studies of black cultural nationalism during this period provide
helpful insights about the context of these sentiments. See Wilson Jeremiah Moses, *The
Golden Age of Black Nationalism, 1850-1925* (Hamden CT: Archon Books, 1978); and his
Black Messiahs and Uncle Toms: Social and Literary Manipulations of a Religious Myth
(University Park: Pennsylvania State University Press, 1982).

[24]ANBC *Journal, Sermons and Lectures,* 1888, 99-100.

frowned on black solidarity, and among white denominational brethren who had a history of working against such unions.

Preludes to the 1895 Convention

The romantic attraction of racial solidarity among these peculiar Baptists was strengthened as a result of an assault in 1889 on Emanuel King Love, the president of the BFMC. Then when the American Baptist Publication Society, responding to white pressure, reneged in 1890 on an agreement it had made with the major leaders of both the BFMC and the ANBC, black separatists found their cause célèbre.

The "Southern Outrage." On the surface the assault on Emanuel King Love and his entourage, who were headed for Indianapolis to attend the 1889 meeting of the black BFMC, was not an unusual event. It had become an infamous custom among some white Southerners to attack "niggers" whenever they were in the mood. The causes of these senseless assaults were many and varied. Racism was the major, but by no means the only, factor. Nevertheless, more and more white vigilante groups sought to enforce the unwritten laws of custom in the late 1880s. By 1890 the state legislatures of Georgia and Louisiana were able to reinstitute the apartheid "Black Codes" that had controlled the activities of antebellum free blacks, and, for a time, postwar emancipated blacks. Assaults against blacks were only one of the several infringements upon their human rights. Some blacks were quick to protest. Led by Harvey Johnson, pastor of the Union Baptist Church, black Baltimoreans organized the Brotherhood of Liberty to defend themselves against the tidal wave of discrimination, lynchings, and brutalities that plagued blacks in Maryland. August Meier reports that more than 350 leading black Georgians, including E. K. Love, met in 1888 to show solidarity in their support of pending education legislation and temperance, as well as their opposition to chain gangs, discrimination by common carriers, lynch law, disenfranchisement, and "inequities" in the jury system.[25]

---

[25]August Meier, *Negro Thought in America, 1880-1915: Racial Ideologies in the Age of Booker T. Washington* (Ann Arbor: University of Michigan Press, 1963) 70. Howard N. Rabinowitz (*Race Relations in the Urban South, 1865-1890* [New York: Oxford University Press, 1978]) provides an excellent general analysis of the impact of Southern urbanization upon race relations in the New South. Joel Williamson (*The Crucible of Race: Black-White Relations in the American South* [New York: Oxford University Press, 1984]) offers the most prodigious study of race relations during this era.

Despite these protests the ideology of White Supremacy gained a new lease on life, and suborned white Americans to engage in greater infringements on First Amendment rights of blacks. Not even black ministers of the Gospel were exempt from the consequences of ignoring unwritten segregationist customs. Love was not the first black minister to be deprived of his right to ride anywhere he wanted on a common carrier. The Reverend Mr. William H. Heard of the A.M.E. Church, who became a bishop after 1908, also received such treatment. When an A.M.E. bishop was ejected from his first-class seat, T. Thomas Fortune, editor of the *New York Age,* denounced the Southern railroads for relegating upstanding black leaders to the smoking cars ''where the vilest of impudent white scum resort to swear, to exhale rotten smoke and to expectorate pools of stinking excrementation of tobacco.''[26]

The response from white authorities proved to be token rather than decisive. The Interstate Commerce Commission, established in 1887, was responsible for regulating the activities of railroads, including charting regulations regarding seating. In 1887, 1888, and 1889 the Commission responded to suits brought against the railroads by black men such as William Heard, W. H. Councill, a black school principal, and E. K. Love. In each instance the Commission upheld an 1882 federal court ruling that blacks who purchased first-class tickets had a right to first-class accommodations, even though it also upheld the doctrine of ''separate but equal'' facilities. The Commission's rulings were never enforced, however. In fact most of the Northern white newspapers ignored it.[27] Since the legal system failed them black leaders turned to the political process. The reaction to the assault on the Love entourage illustrates how the largest group of black Christians responded to this new racial challenge.

The Baxley Incident. Emanuel Love, pastor of the First African Baptist Church of Savannah and editor of the *Weekly Sentinel,* was approached by an agent of the East Tennessee, Virginia and Georgia Rail Road[28] to per-

---

[26]Quoted in Meier, *Negro Thought in America,* 71.

[27]See Rayford W. Logan, *The Betrayal of the Negro* (London: Collier-Macmillan, 1965) 191.

[28]This railroad line was having troubles of its own that had resulted from the expansion and consolidation of various smaller lines. See C. Vann Woodward, *Origins of the New South, 1877-1913* (Baton Rouge: Louisiana State University Press, 1971) 121-23.

suade his delegates to travel over this road. According to Love the agent assured him that his delegates could get first-class accommodations through to Indianapolis. Love subsequently published an article to this effect in the *Georgia Baptist,* and urged all of the Georgia delegates to the black Foreign Mission Convention to patronize this line. By prior arrangement the delegates from Brunswick, Georgia, agreed to meet Love in Jesup on Monday, 9 September 1889. Love, G. M. Spratling and John Williams, Deacon J. H. Brown, Mrs. Janie Garnet, and others purchased tickets for seating in the first-class car. The delegates assumed that the ticket agent had enough blacks to fill a first-class car so that segregated seating could be arranged as custom demanded. But the train only had one first-class car and one smoking car. Since Love and most of his entourage had first-class tickets and were avid opponents of smoking and drinking, sitting in the smoking car was unthinkable.

As soon as the train was underway, Pastor Love went through the two cars saluting his comrades, including a black Methodist presiding elder. He then noticed that the white conductors and passengers began to whisper among themselves. A black workman warned him that trouble was ahead. Love immediately retraced his steps in order to warn his friends that danger was imminent. But he was too late.

Someone telegraphed ahead that Love, a well-known black preacher, and his group had taken seats among the white people. When they reached Baxley, Georgia, fifty or more men, armed with clubs, pieces of iron, and pistols, rushed into the car and brutally assaulted the "well-dressed" black delegates. Some of the delegates defended themselves. But most of them, including Love, had to flee for their lives. Mrs. Janie Garnet, a graduate of Atlanta University and a Brunswick school teacher, screamed from fright. One of the ruffians "put a cocked pistol to her breast and said, "You G-d D——d heffer, if you don't hush your mouth and get out of here, I will blow your G-d D——d brains out."[29] She fainted. After being treated for bruises and broken bones, most of the delegates, including Love, proceeded to Indianapolis to attend the national meetings.

This assault on influential black religious leaders was viewed by the denominational press and the black newspapers as an unusual instance of white Southern brutality and lawlessness. Most of the secular white-owned

---

[29]*National Baptist* (Philadelphia), 10 October 1889.

newspapers either ignored the incident or played down its significance. The incident angered most of the middle-class-minded national leaders of the black Baptists. It reminded them that no black person, regardless of social status, was immune from becoming the victim of white "ruffians." Furthermore it tested the effectiveness of their ties to the Republican Party. Love and his comrades, in a letter to the editor of the Philadelphia *National Baptist,* raised the salient questions in this regard.

> We look to God and ask what are we to do? What is the use of appealing to the Government? Our sufferings and inhuman outrages are known. The crimes are not committed in a corner—the men were not masked. The Government [has] known our condition. The Government protects its citizens abroad[.] It does seem that the glory of American citizenship means no glory for us. What are we to do?[30]

This last question was the primary one confronting the other delegates when their colleagues from Georgia arrived in Indianapolis.

The 1889 Indianapolis Meetings. Since the Northern white ABMU and its domestic counterpart, the ABHMS, had met with the black Convention the previous year, it was the American Baptist Publication Society's turn in 1889. The BFMC held its meeting, 12-14 September, while the ANBC met 15-18 September. Thus the meetings lasted one week, beginning and ending on a Thursday. The delegates then met in special session with the officers of the Publication Society on 18-19 September. These meetings, according to prior planning, were supposed to focus on celebrating the twenty-fifth anniversary of the Publication Society's work with freedmen. But the Love assault hovered over the proceedings like a cloud. One eyewitness expressed the regnant mood of the delegates.

> When our brethren saw with their own eyes these unmistakable evidences of oppression, knowing these delegates from the State of Georgia as distinguished far and near as peaceable, honest, well educated, temperate gentlemen, and realizing that things were coming to a terrible pass when our ministers of the gospel find it unsafe for their lives and persons to visit

---

[30]Ibid. Also see *Baptist Home Mission Monthly* 11 (November 1889): 295-96, and the *Indianapolis Journal,* 12-14 September 1889.

our annual gatherings to assist in their humble way in solving the problems of America, strong men were moved to copious tears.[31]

Despite the assault Love was in the chair to gavel the meeting of the Foreign Mission Convention to order on Thursday 12 September, just three days after he and his companions were attacked. The minutes of this gathering are unrevealing about the tension that filled the sanctuary of the Second Colored Church as bruised President Love chaired the opening exercises. With typical but obvious indifference to his own physical wounds, Love greeted the delegates; and with deep pathos declared,

> Though you may have met Apolyon on many battlefields since we were together last, and though you may have received severe wounds and have been greatly discouraged at times, let me earnestly hope that the Holy Spirit has revived your souls and that you are greatly encouraged on your pilgrim journey.[32]

The implied reference to the troubles of his delegation is graphic but still concealed. His strange silence throughout the remainder of the proceedings is unbelievable. Surely he said something in his own behalf. Again, the minutes are unrevealing. Nonetheless, even if he failed to speak up in his own behalf[33] the more aggressive members of the Convention were not to be silenced. George Boling of Kentucky early in the proceedings interrupted routine business to ask whether or not the Committee on Resolutions would bring his resolution concerning the Love assault to the attention of the members of the Convention. President Love would have none of this, however. His Convention would be run according to its stated agenda. He did not allow Boling's resolution to come before the Convention until Sunday 15 September, as previously agreed. Given the delegates' anger it might have seemed wise not to consider the matter until later in the proceedings lest this issue eclipse the unification plan. The chair had little reason, how-

---

[31]*Washington Bee* (District of Columbia), 9 November 1889.

[32]BFMC *Minutes,* 1889, 7.

[33]Love was usually an outspoken defender of the race. His earnest desire to emphathize with his Southern white neighbors, while bolstered by the ethics of Christian pacifism, appeared to placate racism when chastisement seemed more in order. See his *A Sermon on Lynch Law and Raping: Preached by Rev. E. K. Love, D. D., at 1st African Baptist Church, Savannah, Ga. . . . November 5th, 1893* (Augusta GA: Georgia Baptist Print, 1894) 3.

ever, to fear that this would have happened since Boling's resolution joined the issue of black Baptist unification with the need for black political solidarity.

Boling's resolution went beyond mere protest. He called for black Baptist solidarity on all fronts. He spoke the mind of many of the delegates as he declared that the attacks on the Love entourage had convinced them that "the time has come for us as heralds of the cross of Christ to teach our people the necessity of joining common cause." He proposed that solidarity could be shown by sending out a circular letter that would call on all Afro-Americans to contribute money to assist the victims of the assault in a suit against the railroad.[34] He also implied that black Baptist unity was a prerequisite to racial unity.

The Convention discussed Boling's resolution but did not act. After all it was meeting on the Lord's Day. Business of such a distasteful nature would not be allowed to dampen the movement of the Spirit. Nevertheless Harvey Johnson (whose separatist ideology will figure in later discussions) preached the 11 a.m. sermon. It was not his custom to dodge an opportunity to defend the race and call for race unity.

Johnson was the chief spokesman for the aggressive members of the Foreign Mission Convention who would not allow the Love Assault matter to fade away. Johnson insisted on the Monday following the Sunday debate over the Boling resolution that the clerk of the Convention read a communication from the prestigious First African Baptist Church of Savannah. The telegram stated that Love's congregation would voluntarily defray all expenses needed to prosecute the assailants. Johnson then urged the members of the Convention who endorsed the telegram to stand and sing the doxology. According to Solomon T. Clanton, the recording secretary, "This was enthusiastically sung by the great Convention."[35] The Convention also voted to ask the President of the United States to set aside a day of fasting and prayer in behalf of oppressed black Southerners. It then held a very brief meeting on Monday 16 September before it adjourned in order for its members to attend the ANBC. This convention then opened its deliberations once the BFMC adjourned.

---

[34]Ibid., 17.

[35]Ibid., 28.

The purpose of these sequential meetings, as has already been noted, was to formulate plans for the eventual unification of all national black Baptist forces. But the serious political divisions within the BFMC once again forestalled unification. These divisions are evident in the different positions that each convention took regarding the Love Assault.

The ANBC delegates were seemingly more inclined to make the Love Assault a cause célèbre than the more cautious, conservative, and older Foreign Missioners. Mostly Southern in origin and in numbers, the black BFMC apparently had more to lose than to gain in making a national issue of the affair; most of its members had to live in the deep South.[36] The ANBC was caught in the same dilemma, but its leadership came primarily from the border states and from the Southeastern seaboard states, Virginia and Maryland in particular, where racial pressures were less intense.

The ANBC responded to the Love Assault by passing a series of resolutions that had a stronger political bent than the one resolution passed by the BFMC. The ANBC's resolutions in effect condemned the assault and called upon President Benjamin Harrison to take appropriate action against the lawlessness of white Southerners. These resolutions were passed on the last day of the meetings after the ANBC delegates had waited in vain for the BFMC brethren to take action.

James A. Taylor of Virginia moved that a committee of five be appointed "to frame a memorial to present to the President of the United States, and Dr. [William James] Simmons [president of the ANBC] be chairman."[37] The motion passed, and Simmons appointed Walter Henderson Brooks of Washington, D.C., Harrison N. Boney of Alabama, Emanuel M. Brawley of Tennessee, and James A. Taylor of Virginia, to the committee. All of these men were known to be outspoken black separatists. Their separatist sentiments were reflected in the tone and recommendations contained in their important resolutions.

---

[36]One black reporter described the sentiments of the Southern brethren vis-à-vis the more militant ones. Some believed that "the only way the colored man can save himself from being kicked to death is to kick back." Others were more conservative, and feared that measures of a nature too aggressive would aggravate the present difficulties and endanger the lives of the delegates when they returned home. See *Washington Bee* (District of Columbia), 21 September 1889.

[37]ANBC *Journal,* 1889, 19.

Walter Henderson Brooks, pastor of the old Nineteenth Street Baptist Church, still smarting from confrontations with the ABHMS over its control of Wayland Theological Seminary in Richmond,[38] presented the committee's proposed resolutions to be submitted to the President of the United States. Brooks reported that the committee felt that the major blame for the Love Assault should be placed on the managers of the railroad because the railroad had the responsibility of protecting its passengers. They believed that the railroad was especially at fault if, as it had been rumored, its employees took part in the "Baxley ambush." The committee pointed out that something should be done to curb railroads that advertised as if they did not discriminate against blacks, but still catered to local segregationists' customs and laws that ignored the rights of black people. They suggested that any railroad that did not abide by federal civil rights should be prosecuted by the Interstate Commerce Commission.[39]

These resolutions reflected the belief of the ANBC delegates that black Baptists should go beyond the pious recommendation of the BFMC that the President of the United States should call for the nation to set aside the third Sunday in October as a day of prayer and fasting in behalf of the colored people of the United States. Although they concurred with the Foreign Mission brethren, the committee felt that this new display of racial hatred demanded a political solution. Therefore they asked the ANBC to endorse a resolution calling on President Benjamin Harrison "to recommend to the United States Congress an appropriation of $100,000,000 to aid the colored people in leaving the South." The amount was changed to $50 million by the time the committee gathered later in the year in the offices of the *Washington Bee* (District of Columbia) to explain its recent action to the black press. But the basic proposal remained intact. The committee had reached the conclusion, and the Convention concurred, that the South was hostile territory for black people, especially if "decent" and

---

[38]James M. McPherson, *The Abolitionist Legacy: From Reconstruction to the NAACP* (Princeton: Princeton University Press, 1975) 285-86; and Adolph H. Grundman, "Northern Baptists and the Founding of Virginia Union University: The Perils of Paternalism," *Journal of Negro History* 63 (January 1978): 26-41.

[39]Apparently the black Baptist brethren misunderstood the self-imposed limitation of the Interstate Commerce Commission's powers. Citing *U.S. vs. Buntin* (1882), the Commission refused to undermine racial segregation on railroad coaches. See Meier, *Negro Thought in America*, 72.

law abiding black folk were not protected by the very law they sought to obey. The resolutions also called on white ministers to show leadership by counseling their people against brutality aimed at blacks. But given the history of indifference on the part of most white ministers, the black elders declared that this was a needful but vain hope.

As if grasping desperately for a long-range solution to the problem of racial hatred, they also advised young black men to take their families or themselves West where they could, in the words of Horace Greeley, "obtain lands and recognition and grow up with the country." They employed an Old Testament analogy to give biblical credentials to this prophetic advice to black young people. They declared, "The exodus of the Israelites from Egypt will be a small sized excursion compared to the move there will be [from] the South."[40] Before offering resolutions dealing with other denominational concerns of less importance, Brooks felt obliged to explain why a national black religious body should take the leadership in giving much needed political advice.

> Our political leaders are few, and even those we have cannot reach the people; therefore, it becomes our duty to speak out upon all questions that affect our people socially, economically, as well as religiously.

"God has always, in all ages," he added, "instructed and ruled the people through his own chosen and called men."[41] The Convention adopted all of the Committee's resolutions.

Although the minutes of the BGA are not extant, we know that this group, which met in Indianapolis along with the other black Baptist groups, also took action. It sent a telegram to President Harrison denouncing the Love Assault, and called on the president to take appropriate action. O. L. Pruden, assistant presidential secretary, telegraphed a reply informing the delegates that the president had referred the matter "to the Attorney-General for attention."[42] How the government finally dealt with this event is unclear.

---

[40]*Washington Bee* (District of Columbia), 9 November 1889.

[41]ANBC *Journal,* 1889, 19.

[42]BFMC Minutes, 1889, 29.

Furthermore it was unclear whether or not this incident would deepen the racial chasm between black and white Baptists.[43] Several months passed before Baptists knew where they stood with Northern white Baptist leaders in regard to the resurgence of Jim Crow. They already knew where they stood with the Southern Baptists. Black bitterness about the complicity of white Southern Baptists still lingered. Robert A. McGuinn, black general missionary in Maryland, reflected the views of most black leaders when he stated that white Southern Baptists during slavery had "taught one-half the Gospel; they practiced one-fourth. Twenty-five years cannot remove it."[44]

The ABHMS, on the other hand, had not improved its popularity largely because its executive secretary, Henry Lyman Morehouse, responded angrily to the movement among black Southerners to gain control of its schools in the South. Morehouse attacked the separatist ideology that, he felt, encouraged black leaders to follow this path. While speaking before the 1888 black delegates in Nashville, he decried the dominance of the race spirit. He declared that his society had engaged in a "vast expenditure of energy" and money in behalf of "the black man in America" because it wanted blacks to "arise to the full stature of American and Christian manhood." He believed that after twenty-five years since emancipation the black man "should be a man with sympathies as broad as those of any other human being." He charged that "we hear much about the Negro in America. I want to hear more about America in the Negro—the American spirit of lively interest in all mankind. Let the American spirit be dominant over the race spirit."[45] These words fell on deaf ears, however. Blacks ignored hypocritical white leaders who preached that black people should practice Christian charity while they themselves resisted the call to share denominational wealth and power.

-----

[43]Nevertheless the prestigious white Philadelphia Baptist Ministers' Conference did send a telegram to the BFMC denouncing the incident. See ibid., 29-30.

[44]Robert A. McGuinn, *The Race Problem in the Churches* (Baltimore: J. F. Weishampel, 1890) 53.

[45]Quoted in Edward M. Brawley, ed., *The Negro Baptist Pulpit: A Collection of Sermons and Papers on Baptist Doctrine and Missionary and Educational Work by Colored Baptist Ministers* (Philadelphia: American Baptist Publication Society, 1890; reprint Freeport NY: Books for Libraries Press, 1971) 299.

Black Baptist leaders also did not know where they stood with the American Baptist Publication Society. We have already seen how the black brethren rebuffed the ecumenical advances of the ABMU and the ABHMS in 1888. But how would they relate to the Publication Society? The separatist mood of the 1888 delegates convinced their leaders that organic union with white Baptists was untenable.

Having learned this lesson, black Baptist leaders proceeded to negotiate cooperative ventures with the Publication Society. But separatist rhetoric, widely publicized in black minutes and newspapers, created more problems than black Baptist leaders had expected. They discovered that some of the leaders of the Publication Society could not summon enough moral courage to challenge white supremacy. Indeed, the Society's own precarious economic structure made it just as determined in the 1880s to maintain a monopoly over publishing Baptist evangelistic literature as the ABHMS was determined in the 1860s and 1870s to control the evangelization of the freedmen. Conflict came swiftly as the surge of independence among a new generation of smart and aggressive young black leaders encountered the tough and determined hegemony of the Publication Society.

7

The Seeming End
of a Painful Quest,
1889–1895

The renewal of corporate self-confidence encouraged African-American Baptists to place more demands on their white friends. But their demands were usually carefully considered and quite moderate. In the age of Jim Crow, however, any request for a greater share of social power struck most white power brokers as unreasonable, if not absurd. There were few white Baptist leaders who were open enough to listen to black views, and moderate enough to share social power wherever possible. One such white moderate was Benjamin Griffith, head of the American Baptist Publication Society (ABPS). That is why William James Simmons was sure he could get him to support some of the demands of the black Baptist nationalists.

Confrontation with the Publication Society

A special meeting with the ABPS was arranged for 1889 during Benjamin Griffith's visit to the 1888 Nashville meetings. William James Simmons was the chief negotiator who set up this meeting as well as all of the other special meetings with the Northern societies. His success in making these arrangements relates directly to developments in his career.

Since 1880 Simmons had been president of the Normal and Theological Institute in Louisville, Kentucky. From this strategic position he awarded numerous Doctor of Divinity degrees, ministered to a local church, trained leading clergy, organized political events, edited a newspaper, and presided over the ANBC. In short, Simmons was an ecclesiastical politician with a powerful patronage system. His influence had grown so large by 1887, the year that he published *Men of Mark,* his classic collection of black biographies, that the ABHMS placed him in charge of its Southern Department.

With the aggressive support of other members of the ANBC's executive board, which included two women, Lucy Wilmot Smith and Mary V. Cook,[1] Simmons advanced a proposal in 1887 to form an alliance with the Publication Society that would mutually benefit the Society and the ANBC. The Executive Committee of the ABPS, burdened with the problems of inflation, responded enthusiastically to Simmons's proposal, which it hoped would yield greater revenue.

Founded in 1824, the ABPS had never been greatly interested in black evangelism since it ministered to the literate, not the illiterate.[2] Nevertheless its executive committee responded by dispatching the popular Benjamin H. Griffith to represent the Society at the ANBC's 1888 Nashville meeting.

Griffith, who had led the ABPS for more than thirty years, was its general secretary. Since he was the Society's chief envoy, Griffith's words carried much authority at the Nashville meeting when he endorsed Simmons's bid for greater black involvement in the work of the Society. He declared before this highly race-conscious assembly that his society tried

---

[1]Both women taught at Simmons's Institute. In fact one-third of the fifteen-member executive board came from Kentucky. Two other women held office in the Convention but did not serve on its board. Mrs. A. V. Nelson of Kentucky was a state vice-president; and Miss M. F. Jones of Kansas served as the Convention's corresponding secretary for that state. The role of women in Simmons's administration of the American Convention largely explains the Convention's initial success. Simmons was very supportive of women's rights. He was editor of *Our Women and Children,* the first important black religious women's monthly in the United States. One advertisement for it declared that "as an educator it has no superior. It is useful to the wife, mother, children and sisters, while the male sex can be guided and helped. We shall defend *Women from Wrongs and demand for her Justice.* The ablest writers male and female have been secured, and this publication shall be an encyclopedia of the times." See ANBC *Journal and Lectures,* 1887, 2:67.

[2]According to Henry Allen Bullock, "less than half the South's Negro population ten years of age and over could read and write in 1890" (*A History of Negro Education in the South* [New York: Praeger, 1967] 171).

to provide for every want of the people North, South, East, and West. We provide some things especially for your race. If there is anything you really want and ought to have, there is nothing we would rather do for you.[3]

Griffith was quick to affirm the new demand for recognition of black educational achievements. "You will think," he said, "that you prepare them better than anybody else. All right, do it, and then we will print them." He appeared to be unconcerned about who would author the books, tracts, and Sunday School periodicals, but was quick to presume that only his society had the right and ability to publish all Baptist literature. Yet he was also careful to encourage black self-help and to offer evidence of the Society's new respect for black ability and judgment.

We want the help you in this [your] Sunday School work. We want to help you help yourselves. Hitherto we have been selecting the Sunday school missionaries, we [have] been wonderfully fortunate. Some of your best men have been our missionaries. We see that it is not the best plan, and we want these organizations [that is, black state conventions] in the South to select these men themselves, at least co-operate in doing it. They knew them better than we do. We want their recommendation and instruction.[4]

The last sentence would later return to haunt Griffith. But then it was received with open arms.

Despite Griffith's charm, most of the black delegates were in no mood to cooperate with the ABPS even though some of their leaders, such as Walter Henderson Brooks, Emanuel K. Love, W. A. Burch, M. W. Gilbert, Elias Camp Morris, and Solomon T. Clanton, were its paid agents.[5] Given the apparent conflict of interest, there seemed to be little rancor about this. As practical ecclesiastical politicians these black leaders were adept at using their connections with white denominational executives to further both their careers and their nationalist aims. We shall see later that there were hazards in having one's feet in different racial camps.

Despite their own conflict of interest and the separatist mood of the delegates, these men pressed for greater cooperation with the Publication Society. They were certainly in a position to do this. With the exception

---

[3]ANBC, *Journal, Sermons and Lectures,* 1888, 56.

[4]Ibid., 58.

[5]Ibid., 28.

of the ubiquitous Walter Brooks, each of these men, besides being the authorized agents of the ABPS, also constituted the majority of the nine-member executive board of the ANBC. This board initiated the proposal for the 1889 special meeting with the ABPS. Moreover, it made plans for another proposal, to be presented at that upcoming gathering, which seemed to benefit the entire denomination, the ABPS, the black race, and themselves, especially Brothers Simmons, Brooks, and Love.[6] The contents of this proposal were not revealed until the time of the 1889 special meeting.

As soon as the ANBC finished its own business on 17 September 1889, it joined the other two black conventions in hosting a special meeting in honor of the silver anniversary of the Publication Society's labors among Afro-Americans. Several lectures, sermons, and addresses were delivered with the intent of showing the nature and extent of the Society's past work.

The executive officers of the Society and the black conventions agreed before the meeting that the Reverend C. C. Bitting, the ABPS's Bible and missionary secretary, would preside over this gathering. His position on the program answered a symbolic and political problem that confronted the planners of the special meeting: How were they to conduct themselves so that they would not offend the racial angularity of the Southern Baptists? They decided to ask Dr. Bitting to chair the meeting.

Most SBC leaders viewed Bitting as a trustworthy friend and moderate on the issue of racial reform. Bitting, a Pennsylvanian by birth, had served Baptist churches in Virginia for more than a decade before he assumed his office in the ABPS in 1883. A man like Bitting was needed in this sensitive position because the Southern Baptists were threatening to withdraw support from the Society.

The danger of losing SBC support was real enough. Spurred by the leadership of the Reverend James M. Frost of Nashville, the Southern Baptists made no secret that they were trying to rejuvenate the dead bones of the old Southern Baptist Publication Society.[7] Ironically, C. C. Bitting

---

[6]These men presided over the major black Baptist national programs. Brooks was the chairman of the ANBC's Bureau of Education. As secretary of the ABHMS's Southern Department, Simmons had power over the appointment of home missionaries. He was also the president of a small publishing concern called the National Publishing Company. Love was the president of the BFMC.

[7]ABPS *Minutes,* 1889, 64-70; Robert A. Baker. *The Southern Baptist Convention and Its People, 1607-1972* (Nashville: Broadman Press, 1974) 269-76.

had served as the first executive secretary of this then defunct enterprise in 1868 and 1869.

Several years had passed since Bitting had resided in the South, but he was aware that the Southern white brethren still longed to establish their own publishing concern. In fact they were already publishing a series for their young people entitled "Kind Words." Moreover, five months before the September meeting with the black Baptists, a committee appointed by the SBC met in Boston at the annual meeting of the ABPS. The Society reluctantly agreed, as a result of this meeting, to desist from discouraging the Southern brethren in their modest publishing venture. The final and predictable split between Northern and Southern white Baptists was de-layed at least for awhile.

Given this delicate state of affairs, the special meeting with the black Baptists had to be handled with the utmost care. But the Society's black constituency was not sympathetic. In addition to applauding the Society's work, blacks insisted that the Society should make some public recogni-tion of the amazing progress made by black Baptists in just twenty-five years since emancipation.

The black leaders offered a plan that would give wider recognition to themselves, as noteworthy black achievers, as well as recognition to the ABPS. They told Secretary Bitting that they would lead an effort to drum up greater support for the Society within the black fold if the Society's board would invite competent black Baptists to be agents and writers. S. A. Neal, a black minister from Augusta, Georgia, even went so far as to suggest that the Society should appoint (or ask) black leaders in each state of the Union to oversee its work without cost to the Society. He declared, "The time has come when the freedmen want a voice in things that they are called upon to support, so our suggestion, we think will go far to meet the desire of many anxious minds."[8] Neal's advice is quite representative of the sentiments behind most of the addresses. The delegates wanted black folk to have a greater share influence in the ABPS. They passed a reso-lution that sought to test the Society's willingness to recognize publicly the existence of its black patrons. This resolution urged the Society's execu-tive committee to publish the proceedings of this special meeting in the form

---

[8]Solomon T. Clanton, comp., *A Special Meeting in Behalf of the American Baptist Publication Society, Held at Indianapolis, Indiana, September 18-19, 1889* (Philadelphia: American Baptist Publication Society, 1889[?]) 50.

of a book or pamphlet. They even suggested a title: "The First Fruits of
the Twenty-five Years of Work Among the Colored People in This Country by the Society." In exchange for meeting this demand, they promised
to "energetically aid the Society in the sale and distribution of the work."[9]

But there was attached to this proposal a price tag that the black delegates dared not express in a formal vote. If the ABPS wanted greater black
support, it would have to disregard race and include talented black people
in all levels of its operation. Matthew William Gilbert of Tennessee, later
to become president of the ANBC, spoke to this point. He urged that
"Baptists should so concentrate their efforts, without regard to race or color,
as to make our periodicals always the purest and best in the whole earth."
Although he mentioned several periodicals in his speech, he singled out
the *Baptist Teacher* twice and boasted that it "is unsurpassed by any similar monthly in the world."[10] He then advised the Society to initiate major
racial reform by hiring black contributors for the *Teacher*. No doubt the
other black delegates privately urged Secretary Bitting to encourage the
Society's executive committee not only to adopt their proposal to publish
the proceedings, but also to hire black writers. At any rate, they left the
September special meeting expecting the ABPS's executive committee to
act favorably on their resolutions and suggestions.

That committee did indeed approve most of these proposals at its October meeting. It also decided to add the names of Simmons, Love, and
Brooks to the list of contributors to the *Baptist Teacher*.[11] The committee
gave public notice of its new posture by immediately putting these men to
work. The last quarterly issue of 1889 announced that articles by these black
leaders would be published in the first 1890 quarterly issue—on "The
Doctrine of God" (Brooks), "Regeneration" (Love), and the "Lord's
Supper" (Simmons).

---

[9]Ibid., 46.

[10]Ibid., 52, 54, 55.

[11]Since it was first issued in 1871 in response to the Baptist National Sunday School
Convention movement, which began in St. Louis in 1869, this periodical "immediately
commanded wide approval" throughout the denomination and in other denominations as
well. Baptists were the prime movers in developing a uniform plan for Sunday School les-
sons that led to the establishment of an International Lesson Committee. See Lemuel Call
Barnes, *Pioneers of Light: The First Century of the American Baptist Publication Society,
1824-1924* (Philadelphia: The American Baptist Publication Society, 1925[?]) 138-40.

Given the theological importance of these subjects and the denominational prestige of the *Teacher,* this was no small victory for these black leaders. They interpreted their success as a victory for the race as well. So did their constituents. Five months later this optimism had been washed away by what appeared to be a tidal wave of denominational racism. The ABPS's executive committee had underestimated the depth of the Southern resistance to racial reform.

When this news reached the ears of the Southern white brethren, a major furor ensued. It is unclear how this word reached the large Southern constituency, but it probably came abruptly since there were no officials of the SBC on the ABPS's executive committee.[12] The Society did, however, employ several excellent Southern writers, such as John A. Broadus of Kentucky, who was president of Southern Baptist Theological Seminary, and Amzi C. Dixon of Maryland, who later became the editor of the famous tracts called *The Fundamentals.* These Southern Baptists had little control over the Society's editorial policies, but they had much influence below the Mason-Dixon line. The ABPS's unprecedented action predictably riled many white Southerners and pleased few.

They were especially displeased with the ''Negro'' writers who were selected. While these black men wrote in black newspapers with the intention of giving counsel and comfort to the black masses, many white Southerners were offended by their candor. According to one major SBC leader, they ''outraged the people of the South in language that should be condemned in any court of common decency.''[13] Most SBC leaders led the protest against this movement toward racial reform on the pretext that ''Southern people refuse to have [ignorant] negroes [sic] set up as their instructors.''[14] The ideology of white supremacy even cloaked the fact that these men were among the most intelligent and well-educated leaders of

---

[12]Two prominent Southern Baptists had served on the Society's board of managers—H. H. Tucker of Georgia, who was editor of the *Christian Index,* an influential newspaper with a large circulation, and Joshua Levering of Maryland. In fact both men were vice-presidents of the Society. But Tucker had died earlier that year, and Levering was from a border state, not from the deep South.

[13]James M. Frost, ''Mr. Johnson-Dr. Griffith Correspondence,'' *Western Recorder* (Louisville KY), 16 October 1890.

[14]Robert A. McGuinn, *The Race Problem in the Churches* (Baltimore: J. F. Weishampel, 1890) 57.

Afro-America. White Southern Baptists threatened to withdraw support from the Society if it followed through with its plan to publish the writings of the three black ministers. Indeed, this was a move they had been contemplating anyway. The race issue only served to deepen a chasm that already existed between Northern and Southern white Baptists.

But the financially insecure ABPS was in no mood to test the patience of the South any further. It "erased" the names of Brooks, Love, and Simmons from the list. In an effort to strike a compromise, however, it did invite these men to permit the Society to publish their articles as tracts. Apparently the three ministers bristled at this suggestion.

The response from the black Baptist community was swift. The black Baptist Minister's Conference of the District of Columbia, where Walter Brooks pastored, passed a resolution condemning the Publication Society "for ignoring the rights of the colored race in matters of religious co-operation."[15] This conference, which included ministers from Maryland and Virginia, held Walter Brooks in high esteem. Its members received news of the erasure of his name as an affront to one of the best writers the race had to offer. But the most effective response came from black Baptists in the Old Dominion.

The black Virginia Baptist State Convention met in Bedford City between 14 and 18 May 1890, less than one month before the ABPS's annual meeting that was to be held in Chicago in concert with the anniversaries of the other Northern societies. This was indeed a conspicuous setting for black Baptists to use whatever moral leverage they had left. The Virginia Convention sent the Reverend Anthony J. Binga, Jr., the son of the old Canadian abolitionist, to deliver resolutions that it passed during the Bedford meeting. The resolutions, full of pathos, denounced the ABPS for its cowardice.

> WHEREAS, we believe the religion of the Lord Jesus Christ knows no color of his skin, nor texture of hair, but recognizes all alike, whether found in hut or palace. And,
>
> WHEREAS, we believe discrimination because of color incompatible with Christianity, and at war with the principles of that kingdom which is distinguished from others by the equality of its members, as shown by the

---

[15]*Washington Bee* (District of Columbia), 15 February 1890.

intercessory prayer of its King, who prayed that its subjects might be "one." And,

WHEREAS, the American Baptist Publication Society has offered (inadvertently, we trust) an indignity to the colored Baptists of the United States by dropping the names of the Rev. E. K. Love, D. D., Rev. W. J. Simmons, D. D., LL.D., and Rev. Walter H. Brooks from the list of contributors to the *Baptist Teacher*, without any discovery of incompetency or proof of general unfitness, which fact leads us to believe that it was actuated by a wrong spirit. Therefore,

Resolved, That while we feel a profound sense of appreciation for all the kindnesses shown us in the past by the Society, yet we can but condemn the act of sacrificing the colored brethren for the sake of gain or hope of gratifying blind justice.

Resolved, That these resolutions are not intended to express an unkind or ungrateful feeling, but that of self-respect and a sense of violated justice.[16]

The ABPS politely received this communication and referred "the whole matter" to its board "for further consideration and action."[17] Two other factors had a bearing upon the way the Board of Managers dispensed with this issue.

It became apparent during the course of the other societies' meetings, especially during that of the ABHMS, that the Southern white delegates were using racial slurs more profusely and glibly than they had since the 1870s. The Reverend J. W. Ford, a white minister from St. Louis, caused an uproar when he opined that among black Christians "there is a race animosity so bitter and strong that converted Christians wonder with a bewilderment of wonder whether the end may not come with the ending of the weaker party [that is, black people]." His deep reactionary racism became patently obvious as he concluded his speech.

Then comes the question of moral mastery—whether brawn or brain shall master all that fair Southland. This is our question, not only the South's. The alternative is to elevate or exterminate, to use the Bible or bullet. There

---

[16]ABPS *Report*, 1890, 67.

[17]Ibid., 68.

is either one or the other of these alternatives for the black man of the South. A great national peril calls for a great national movement.[18]

The Reverend W. A. Burch, a black minister from Chicago, immediately arose to denounce this racism. But he was asked to wait until later to deliver his views. During the course of the meeting not only Burch but several other ministers, white and black, attacked Ford's remarks. Ironically, the greatest furor from the white delegates came in response to a remark accredited to William James Simmons. Someone started a rumor accusing Simmons of saying, in response to Ford's speech, that black people should resort to "arson and assassination." Simmons was particularly vulnerable to slander since he was the ABHMS's secretary for the Southern District. Nonetheless he "strongly denied the charge," and was later reappointed.

In the midst of this commotion, a more conciliatory word came from another quarter of the black constituency. Edward Brawley of South Carolina, then editor of the *Baptist Pioneer*,[19] tried to cajole the ABPS by delivering an address that reviewed what it had accomplished for black people without dealing with the crisis at hand. He argued that the ABPS "is encouraging colored authors of ability to write by publishing their productions."[20] He then held up a copy of the first book by a black person ever published by the ABPS. The book was part of the Society's Sunday School Library series, and was a Victorian novelette entitled *Clarence and Corinne: or, God's Way.* It was written by Mrs. A. E. Johnson, the wife of the outspoken Baltimorean.[21] But Brawley's views were not shared by Harvey Johnson and most certainly not by most other black Baptists. This was evident after the ABPS's board deliberated on the Virginia Convention's resolution during June.

In a published letter, dated 6 June, Secretary Griffith addressed a missive containing a resolution in behalf of his board to the Virginia State Convention.

---

[18]*National Baptist* (Philadelphia), 5 June 1890.

[19]Albert W. Pegues, *Our Baptist Ministers and Schools* (Springfield MA: Wiley, 1892) 82.

[20]ABPS *Report,* 1890, 44.

[21]The ABPS later published two other novelettes by Mrs. Johnson entitled *The Hazeley Family* (1894) and *Martina Merden, or, What is My Motive?* (1901).

Neither the Society, its Board of officers have at any time or in any way intended to cast an ''indignity'' upon any of your race, much less upon the brethren named. We believed at the time, and believe still, that in inviting Drs. E. K. Love, W. J. Simmons and Walter H. Brooks to write each a permanent tract instead of a transient article for the *Teacher* we honored them in asking them to confer a more difficult and useful service than that to which they were first invited.[22]

Secretary Griffith then recounted what the Society had done for the ''colored'' people, asked that his board's resolution be published in the minutes of the Virginia Convention and be sent to black newspapers.

The Virginia Convention formally received this communication and described the ABPS's action as ''an amicable settlement of the whole matter.'' This was indeed an adequate political settlement for some, but it failed to heal the wound felt by many others. The Reverend J. Maurice Armistead, president-elect of the Virginia Convention, aimed a verbal sally at the conscience of the ABPS in behalf of this disgruntled group.

Our loyalty to this organization [ABPS] can't be called into question. And its innumberable benefits to us cannot be disputed; and yet, this organization should not judge us incapable of keenly feeling the gross injustice done us at the command of certain gentlemen, whose misfortune it was to be actuated by the wrong spirit.

The society cannot reasonably expect our continued patronage, unless it believes us void of manhood, when with one stroke of the pen such men of God as Drs. W. J. Simmons, E. K. Love, and W. H. Brooks, are stricken from the list of contributors to the *Baptist Teacher*. And should we fail to present our earnest protest against this injustice, the society would rightly consider us not worthy of common respect.[23]

Given this feeling of betrayal, the ABPS felt obliged to assuage its disaffected black friends by making two political concessions. First, its executive committee finally acknowledged that the best way to rally greater black support was to invite black leaders to take charge of this work. The committee therefore invited Edward Brawley and Solomon Clanton to serve, respectively, as the district secretaries for the Atlantic Coast and

---

[22]Quoted in Virginia Baptist State Convention *Minutes,* 1890, 40.

[23]Ibid., 56.

Southwestern regions.[24] The second concession made by the ABPS originated in its Publication Committee. This committee approved the publication of the first collection of theological and denominational articles ever written and edited by black Baptists. The collection was entitled *The Negro Baptist Pulpit* (1890), and was edited by Edward Brawley. This was apparently the only reciprocal concession Brawley made to the Publication Society because, rather than accept the secretariat of the Atlantic Coast District, he accepted the call to pastor the Harrison Street Baptist Church of Petersburg, Virginia.[25] Clanton did accept the ABPS's invitation.

Despite these appeasements, most black leaders felt that they had little, if any, influence over the policies of the ABPS. In their minds these concessions merely confirmed the reality of the injustice, and did not go far enough in ameliorating it. Three years later a movement to establish a black Baptist publishing house became the major cause célèbre of the separatists. In the meantime the entire episode with the ABPS quickened the separatist impulse, and set the stage for a new style of national leadership that neither desired nor sought cooperation with white Baptists of either region. That some leaders would become alienated in the course of this new development was unavoidable.

The Joys and Perils of Solidarity

Almost as soon as black Baptist nationalists achieved more recognition from the Publication Society, some rather sudden events catapulted them into another maelstrom. But this time the turbulence was internal. On 30 October 1890 they were stunned by news that William James Simmons, the founding president of the ANBC, had died at the age of forty-two, barely a month after the closing gavel of the ANBC's annual meeting. Simmons's death set off a power struggle that lasted four years. Of course this internal strife further delayed the movement toward unity. The ANBC continues to deserve center stage here because it was indeed the harbinger of both the dream of unity and the maelstrom that delayed its embodiment.

The American Convention's Identity Crisis. This new crisis exacerbated a far quieter, and yet more profound dilemma that really surfaced during the 1889 meeting. It was evident even then that this convention was

---

[24]ANBC *Journal,* 1890, 33.

[25]Pegues, *Our Baptist Ministers and Schools,* 82.

losing support largely because its reason for existence was unclear. Its bid for unity was a frustrating and slow process because its dream of denominational unity based on race paled when contrasted with the romantic appeal of African missions. This made it difficult to solicit mass support for an organization that was overshadowed by the dramatic work of the BFMC, especially in a period when "the wide, wide world was called to . . . attention mainly as a mission field."[26] Visions of redeeming the African homeland had traditionally provided the rationale for forming black Baptist organizations above the congregational level. The ANBC, however, represented a new departure in the movement toward national unity because, unlike any of its siblings or its predecessor, the CABMC, it was only concerned with the American scene. No leader had advocated this philosophy as strongly as Simmons, who was primarily concerned with national problems that afflicted Afro-Americans. Moreover, Simmons was convinced that black Baptists must lead the way. He left this ideological impress upon his convention.

This was evident in the last report of the executive board issued under his administration. That report defended the ANBC against the charge, reminiscent of the same indictment against the CABMC, that its existence served little purpose other than to encourage talking about political and social matters that seemed beyond the competence of a religious organization. This was an accurate charge insofar as the leaders of the Convention felt the Convention itself was a black version of the Baptist Congress.[27] The executive board was not embarrassed by this charge. It freely admitted that "we regard our Convention more after the model and work of a Baptist Congress, doing work among the Colored Baptists of America, untouched by any one of our existing missionary institutions."[28] The more

---

[26]Harry Emerson Fosdick, *The Living of These Days: An Autobiography* (New York: Harper and Brothers, 1956) 24. Two studies are fine general introductions to the black foreign mission movement: Sylvia M. Jacobs, *The African Nexus: Black American Perspectives on the European Partitioning of Africa, 1880-1920* (Westport CT: Greenwood Press, 1981) and Walter L. Williams, *Black Americans and the Evangelization of Africa, 1877-1900* (Madison: University of Wisconsin Press, 1982).

[27]The Baptist Congresses were a series of annual denominational meetings between 1882 and 1912 devoted exclusively to discussing theological and ecclesiastical issues of importance to Baptists.

[28]ANBC *Journal*, 1889, 22.

serious charge was that the Convention served no serious religious purpose. The Board adamantly offered the counter argument that the reality
of the national race problem mandated a national black Baptist convention
that would be concerned with addressing racism in both the nation and the
denomination.

> Many have sincerely and seriously inquired into the province and specific
> work of this Convention. They say, we know why the Foreign Mission Or-
> ganizations . . . are to be maintained, but why maintain the American Na-
> tional Baptist Convention?
>
> In regard to this natural question the Board desires to say, that this
> Convention does not propose to antagonize, in any way, any of our nec-
> essary and divinely useful missionary societies in their great work, but that
> this Convention has a place and a share in Christian work, all its own, in
> the present condition of our people, which will develop our latent talent
> and resources in a way consistent with a proper regard, and an honorable
> recognition of what has been done for us by our true and tried [white]
> friends.[29]

We have already seen how the Convention worked to achieve its purpose in terms of addressing national and denominational racial issues. But
the Convention was also concerned about the "self-elevation" of black
Baptists through social and educational renovation. This internal agenda
proved to the be the most difficult one to realize both because of competing
programs within Afro-America[30] and because there was no consensus regarding whether the advocacy of political action or of educational programs should take precedence. The Convention tried to do both with its
sparse resources and its fragile base of support. Simmons held these problems at bay by glossing over differences, and insisting that a greater emphasis on God's agenda for black Baptists would subordinate ideological
differences. An aggressive denominationalist was needed to replace Simmons as mediator between these forces. Some believed Edward Brawley,

---

[29]Ibid., 21.

[30]More independent-minded black Baptists such as Benjamin Gaston of Georgia were
convinced emigrationists. They initiated emigrationist schemes of their own, responded to
the calls of venerable American Colonization Society, or joined the efforts of other black
leaders such as Bishop Henry McNeal Turner of the African Methodist Episcopal Church.
See Edwin S. Redkey, *Black Exodus: Black Nationalist Movements, 1890-1910* (New Haven: Yale University Press, 1969) 73-194.

vice-president of the ANBC, might fulfill this need when he assumed the presidency on the death of Simmons. But in the eyes of the separatists, who competed for the same position, Brawley's commitment to integration disqualified him even though he was a staunch denominationalist. Brawley fervently believed that black Baptists "should merge race feeling in the broader spirit of an American Christianity. This is the proper aim; for it is Christlike." This belief clashed with those who feared white dominance.[31]

Other black leaders who had a broader base of mass support eschewed Brawley's theology by paying lip service to it while acting differently. This was especially true when issues arose in the convention that demanded greater cooperation with white Baptists.

The first important issue to arise in the ANBC after Simmons's death illustrates their strategy. It concerned the establishment of a national black Baptist university. Simmons had worked hard to realize this vision before his death, and hoped that the ANBC would eventually charter one of his own schools for that purpose. Hailing Simmons as "one of the greatest Negro leaders of the Nineteenth Century, and one of the foremost Baptists in the world," a special committee, appointed by Brawley at the 1891 meeting of the ANBC, sought to memorialize Simmons by supporting the creation of a national university. Even Malcolm McVicar, the ABHMS's superintendent of education, had come all the way from Atlanta to this meeting in Dallas, Texas, to announce that his society concurred with the trustees of the Eckstein Norton Industrial University of Cane Spring, Kentucky, who had just voted to transfer ownership of that property to the ANBC. Since Simmons formed that school, and was a staunch champion of industrial education,[32] many felt the ANBC should accept this offer. But when a resolution to this effect was presented to the 1891 Convention, it

---

[31]Brawley, ed., *The Negro Baptist Pulpit* (Philadelphia: American Baptist Publication Society, 1890; reprint, Freeport NY: Books for Libraries Press, 1971) 298. Brawley argued elsewhere that the ABHMS seeks to make "the Negro a *Christian* citizen" while the Publication Society seeks "to make him a broad man." He even wailed against those "colored people" who "in their missionary operations" believe that their work should be confined to Africa. See ABPS *Report*, 1890, 42; Pegues, *Our Baptist Ministers and Schools*, 78-82. See also William J. Simmons, *Men of Mark: Eminent, Progressive, and Rising* (Cleveland: George M. Rewell, 1887; reprint, New York: Arno Press, 1968) 644-47. Brawley, born free in 1851, was proud of his mulatto background. He saw himself as an American and a Christian, not simply as a Negro.

[32]Simmons wrote a widely circulated pamphlet, *Industrial Education* (1886).

"provoked an animated discussion."[33] When it was clear that there was a "decided opposition . . . to the adoption of the report," the Convention tabled the resolution and referred it to the Executive Board, which was ordered to report on the matter the following year.

Although the resolution concerned the Eckstein University per se, far more was at stake than this. The ABHMS, because of the national inflationary spiral, was trying to bring more efficiency to the operation of its holdings in the South. In fact Malcolm McVicar came to the Dallas meeting with a special proposal to achieve the ABHMS's desire for greater efficiency and economic solvency. He outlined a plan "for uniting, as colleges and academies of one University, all of the Baptist institutions for the higher education of the colored people."[34] Despite strong pressure from the ABHMS, the ANBC's board received the Society's "proposition by a majority vote," and submitted it "without any comments or qualifications" for the "disposal" of the Convention.

The ANBC's board was more divided on this issue than it admitted. Consolidation of black Southern schools under the control of the Society either meant that many schools would have to go out of business or that the Society would have to concede greater power to the divided national black leadership. The ABHMS was more prone to do the latter than the former, but black delegates from the South were unwilling to give up local black control or influence over the boards of trustees of those schools.[35] Although they had long desired a national black Baptist university and seminary,[36] they were unwilling to give this much power either to their own executive board or to the ABHMS. This was an opportune time for some leader to advocate a point of view that would solve this dilemma. That leader turned out to be Elias Camp Morris.

---

[33]ANBC Journal, 1891, 54.

[34]ABHMS *Report,* 1892, 84. The Society actually wanted to create a black version of the University of Chicago, which was founded in 1890 with an initial endowment of $35,000,000 from John D. Rockefeller, a Baptist layman.

[35]The struggle for black control of predominantly black educational institutions, owned by the Home Mission Society had been underway since the 1880s. See James M. McPherson, *The The Abolitionist Legacy: From Reconstruction to the NAACP* (Princeton: Princeton University Press, 1975) 284-91.

[36]See chapter 3.

In what proved to be a successful effort to defeat the move to create a national university that would undermine the general movement toward local black control, Morris, who later became president of the American Convention, proposed that a Committee on the National University be formed instead of simply referring the matter to the executive board, which had already expressed its lukewarm approval of McVicar's proposal. Morris, president of the Arkansas Baptist College, suggested that the committee consist of himself, Joseph Endom Jones of Virginia Union University, Albert W. Pegues of Shaw University in North Carolina, Solomon T. Clanton, and G. M. Ward. This group of professional educators was hurriedly approved by President Brawley. They then met and brought in a proposal to expand the committee to include Brawley, Brooks, and Love. According to their report this reconstituted committee would be charged with the responsibility of negotiating with the ABHMS in behalf of the ANBC. This report was adopted. Instead of resulting in the creation of a national university, however, the deliberations of the committee led to the formation of the National Baptist Educational Convention in 1892. In short, when the ANBC refused to respond enthusiastically to this new opportunity, the educated elite of the Convention formed this body in response. Even though some of these same members had chastised Booker T. Washington in 1890 for his criticism of "ignorant" black clergy,[37] they still believed that an educated ministry was the hope of the black race. As one report asserted, they believed that education is a "necessity in the proper development of true Christ-like lives."[38]

In May 1892 the Committee on the National University called together other interested parties to meet with the Virginia Baptist State Convention, scheduled to meet 20-21 September. The Committee wanted to assure "a grand representation of the brainiest men and women of the denomination."[39] The Committee's lobbying efforts were in vain, however. When the Convention finally met in September, it also had trouble settling the

---

[37]ANBC *Journal*, 1890, 33-34; *Washington Bee* (District of Columbia) 29 November 1890. See Louis Harlan, *Booker T. Washington: The Making of a Black Leader, 1856-1901* (New York: Oxford University Press, 1972) 194-97, for a fuller discussion of the impact of Washington's criticism.

[38]ANBC *Journal*, 1891, 56.

[39]NBEC *Journal* 1892, 11.

controversy over the national university. It did approve a resolution to accept the property of Eckstein Norton University.[40] But it decided nothing about the national university idea.

Although the black records indicate the national university idea evoked a tremendous controversy among black Baptists, we have a sharply different account in the ABHMS's reporting of black views on the subject. Malcolm McVicar claimed that the ANBC had "strongly endorsed" this plan. He also later asserted that an "equally strong endorsement" was given by the black state conventions of Texas, Virginia and Florida as well as by "every gathering of colored ministers at which the subject has been presented."[41] I do not know whether or not McVicar was prompted by the need to present a calm front for the purpose of raising capital or for other reasons. But I do know that his recollection contradicts the black records.[42] The black state conventions of Texas, Georgia, and Tennessee, for example, were beset by fierce disagreements over whether or not blacks should push ahead in the effort to control black schools. Of course McVicar only mentioned the state of Texas. But even here he cloaked the fierce battle over whether or not the black state convention should control Bishop College. That convention eventually split over this issue in 1893. The largest faction, led by two young preachers, Richard Boyd and David Abner, Jr.,[43] later played a significant role in the formation of the National Baptist Convention in 1895.

Whatever his reasons McVicar misread the black situation. There was indeed "a decided opposition" to the national university idea. Although the substantive details of the debate are unknown to me, I do know that two distinct ideological parties became visible after Simmons died. Professor James M. McPherson correctly and handily identifies these two groups as "separatists" and "cooperationists." The separatists, who really

---

[40]Ibid., 14.

[41]ABHMS *Report,* 1892, 84.

[42]Another student of this controversy conjectures that perhaps the ABHMS simply regarded black controversies as "a passing fancy." See McManus, "The American Baptist Home Mission Society . . ." 445.

[43]Abner's father was the well-known black Texas state legislator. See Pegues, *Our Baptist Ministers and Schools,* 29.

dubbed themselves, sometimes called themselves "progressives."[44] They were advocates of black power. On the other hand the cooperationists simply felt that, given the economic and social plight of Afro-Americans, the money and wisdom of white guardians were needed. There was much more fusion and fission between these two groups, depending on the issue, than Professor McPherson's labels reflect, but the cleavage was indeed as deep as these epithets suggest. The one notable conflict that is germane to this study occurred in 1892.

The two parties clashed at the 1892 ANBC meeting over whether or not the Convention should endorse the ABHMS's attempt to sell the property of Roger Williams University. This "Tennessee Fuss," which was really centered in Nashville, lasted until the 1893 meeting. Although the minutes of the 1892-1894 meetings of the ANBC are not extant, we do know who the leaders of that controversy were: Michael Vann, president-elect of the Convention, and Jesse E. Purdy, M.D., pastor of the Spruce Street Baptist Church, a splinter from the venerable First Colored Baptist Church, brought their Nashville battle over whether or not the property of Roger Williams University should be sold to the Convention. Unfortunately the energetic thirty-three year old Michael Vann found himself on the wrong side of this controversy. As the president of the *Nashville Tribune* newspaper company and the ABHMS's general missionary for the state of Tennessee, he had the vehicles to launch his quite vocal support of the Roger Williams trustees' proposal to sell the property. Nevertheless, his position as the ABHMS's agent in Tennessee was viewed by many observers as a serious conflict of interest.[45]

Purdy, on the other hand, apparently led the opposition against the Roger Williams trustees both in Nashville and later at the 1892 and 1893 meetings of the ANBC in Savannah and Washington, D.C. The pressure exerted on the administrators of Roger Williams was so great that the

---

[44]McPherson, *The Abolitionist Legacy,* 284.

[45]This was the plight of most of the leaders of the Convention. Despite the fact that some of them were brazen separatists, they were great believers in independent action. Moreover many of them did not see the societies as enemies but as obstacles to black opportunities for self-help. The perceptive Professor McPherson correctly captures their mood in regard to the Home Mission Society's schools: "Though the separatists talked of supporting their own schools, what they really seemed to want was control of the society's schools *and* of the northern money they hoped would continue to flow south to finance them." Ibid., 289.

school's white president had to retract an earlier description of black sentiment about the matter.

> I think it proper to say notwithstanding the advantages that might accrue in the matter of buildings and endowments, the sentiment of the colored people is strongly against the sale. They believe the location and associations outweigh any pecuniary advantage. How far they are right I cannot say. But I think I ought to correct any misapprehension in regard to the real feeling among those interested in the welfare of the school.[46]

The will of Purdy's group not only worked itself against the Roger Williams authorities but also in the ANBC itself when the controversial Michael Vann lost his ideological sway over the Convention. Vann quickly changed his posture in the face of defeat. Nonetheless, the separatist forces under the control of Elias C. Morris were able to weaken Vann considerably, mainly because he was identified with those whom Richard Boyd characterized as black people "who would try to sell" the "race to a white man's soulless corporation."[47] Vann retained the presidency until 1894, but he was an ineffectual office holder.

In his remarks Boyd not only had black cooperationists in mind; he also was condemning the Northern societies' paternal attitudes toward black Baptists. But as far as the separatists were concerned, this was also an apt description of the other societies, especially the Publication Society. There was a feeling among black Baptists that the Northern societies were increasingly becoming more and more businesslike, imitating their wealthy patrons such as John D. Rockefeller and the deceased John P. Crozer. When Baptist activities are compared to the affluent Congregationalist American Missionary Association, this view is seen to be exaggerated somewhat. Yet the black separatists summoned their latent feelings of moral superiority to deal anew with the Northern societies' heavy-handedness.

White Racism and the Publishing House Movement. With the powerful support of experienced separatists such as Harvey Johnson, William Bishop Johnson, Emanuel Love, Walter Brooks, John Frank, and numerous others, Morris led the fight to establish a black Baptist publishing house. This movement was partly a response to a similar development among other

---

[46]The *Baptist Home Mission Monthly* 13 (October 1891): 290.

[47]Quoted in McPherson, *The Abolitionist Legacy*, 288.

black denominations. But it was largely a response to denominational racism. The state of race relations within the denomination provides an important backdrop at this point for understanding the separatists' persistent interest in publishing.

In 1889 and 1890, Southern Baptists escalated their use of racist rhetoric in denominational circles. This racist crescendo continued in the 1890s. Northern Baptists, on the other hand, also continued to give concrete manifestation of the reality of racism because of their "manifest destiny" ideology. Nevertheless the problem of racism between Afro-American Baptists and white Southern Baptists was far more acute. They each hurled invective at one another regarding the nature and destiny of black personhood and Southern livelihood. One notable verbal assault came from the Home Mission Board of the SBC, which asserted in the midst of the awful lynchings and burnings of black Southerners during 1891 that the inability of black people to accept their inferior natures was the real cause of the race situation.

> Nothing is plainer to any one who knows this race than its perfect willingness to accept a subordinate place, provided there be confidence that in that position of subordination it will receive justice and kindness. That is the condition it prefers above all others, and this is the condition in which it attains the highest development of every attribute of manhood. Whenever it shall understandingly and cheerfully accept this condition, the race problem is settled forever.[48]

The major leaders of the American Convention, such as Walter Brooks, responded to this assertion. Brooks spoke out at the May 1892 meeting of the black Virginia State Convention, offering a resolution that called the Southern Baptist statement "simply absurd." The resolution also declared that the authors of the Southern Baptist statement were

> perfectly sincere, but blinded by their own prejudices and false education, deserve our pity, and render it the solemn duty of all well-wishers of our common humanity to pray God to remove their blindness of mind and hardness of heart, that the land may have rest.[49]

---

[48]Home Mission Board Report in the SBC *Proceedings*, 1891, Appendix B, 36.

[49]Virginia Baptist State Convention *Minutes*, 1892, 18.

The resolution added that it was the prayer of black Christians that God somehow ''grant enlightenment of mind, and forgive them for so grossly misrepresenting the facts of the Afro-American's history and the sentiments of his heart.''

Such statements did not penetrate the thick veneer of racism that separated the black and white world views. The following year the SBC's Home Mission Board offered further unabashed evidence of its willingness to use its view of Afro-American history to argue that it could best assist by educating black ministers. The board declared that when black folk were

> brought to this country and sold as slaves, they were placed in the only relation to the white people in which it was possible for them to exist. The miasma emanating from the vices and corruptions of our civilization is death to any inferior race with which we come in contact, unless that race be subordinated to our control.[50]

Against this background Morris and company fought to establish a black Baptist publishing house, in addition to their other campaigns against white Baptist control. It had become clearer to them that both the Northern Baptists and the Southern Baptists were unwilling to recognize black talent. They believed that the dignity of the race was at stake. John H. Frank of Kentucky began his long leadership of this branch of black Baptist work by chairing a committee of the 1893 ANBC meeting that argued for the creation of an American National Baptist Convention Publishing Company and Book Establishment. Why? The enabling resolution quite clearly stated that

> it is plainly evident that as a [black] denomination we shall never attain to the broad influence and elevated dignity worthy of so vast a body of Baptists, so long as our literary productions remain unpublished, our work unsystematized, and its success remains dependent upon the option of our friends for prosecution.[51]

These words from the Publishing House Committee were adopted by the Convention.

---

[50]SBC *Proceedings,* 1892, Appendix A, 4.

[51]Quoted in E. C. Morris, *Sermons, Addresses and Reminiscences,* 59.

The sentiments expressed by Elias Camp Morris, however, won the day, as he cogently delineated both the pathos and separatist reasoning behind this new attempt to found a publishing concern. In a speech entitled "The Demand for a Negro Publishing House," Morris argued that a black Baptist publishing house was necessary because it would provide more "race employment," "race development," "a bequest to posterity," and business experience. This address captured the mood of the delegates: They wanted unity and concrete actions to combat racism.

The seven-year-old ANBC was at last tired of the old divisions between separatists and cooperationists. Rejecting the cooperationist view, it openly affirmed its belief in the separatist view, and proceeded to organize accordingly. One Western commentator, P. D. Skinner, said after this meeting that black Baptists needed to form enterprises that would reflect their strength and their commitment to racial justice. The old battles between regions and the educated and uneducated clergy was called to a halt not only because of gross Southern outrages against black folk but also because of the 1893 nationwide depression. In light of these extraordinary circumstances, the same black Western commentator summed up the mood of the conventioneers.

> The Bible demands that there be a oneness among the Baptists. We are commanded to speak the same thing, and be perfectly joined together in the same mind, and in the same judgment, and that there be no division among us.
>
> We should have one general plan for work in regard to home and foreign missions; one plan in reference to the Church Edifice fund; one general plan for raising the revenue to carry on the work of our denomination, and all should be willing and ready to come under the one rule for the good of our zion.[52]

The mood for unity reflected in this statement encouraged someone at the 1893 Convention to suggest that Afro-American Baptists should at least make a toddler's step toward unification by consolidating their foreign mission work. The three major foreign mission bodies adopted this advice, and promised to meet in Montgomery, Alabama, along with the ANBC, as customary, in 1894. As Lewis Jordan, an eyewitness, recollected, "each of these organizations had live, long tendrils, feeling for something of value

---

[52]*Baptist Headlight* (Topeka, Kansas), 17 November 1893.

to which they might cling."[53] Although the New England and the Western Baptist foreign mission conventions failed to meet as promised in 1893, something more far-reaching occurred. This event even dwarfed the separatists' campaigns for black control of the Home Mission schools as well as their bid to issue their own publications. Many more blacks were subsequently to conclude that ecclesiastical racial equality was not on the white agenda.

The Plan of Cooperation. On 12 September 1894 representatives of the Northern Home Mission Society met with representatives of the Southern Baptist Convention at Fortress Monroe, Virginia, in order to reach some comity agreements. The basic items discussed involved the ABHMS's management of its Southern missionary and educational work among the black Baptists. By 14 September this group had formulated a new plan of cooperation between these regional white bodies. They adopted two resolutions and merely approved a third one.

The group, chaired by James L. Howard, voted to recommend that the ABHMS and the SBC would cooperate in establishing "local advisory committees" wherever the ABHMS's black schools were located. These committees were to have no legal clout, but would provide recommendations to the ABHMS. The second resolution called on both the SBC and the ABHMS to cooperate in evangelizing black Southerners. In order to effect this, they agreed to recommend to their parent bodies that they should endorse a move to have black and white state conventions jointly appoint general missionaries for their own states. This resolution also called upon the parent bodies to endorse elementary level theological workshops, to be called "New Era Institutes," for ministers and deacons, and to cooperate with the black Baptists in improving the efficiency of their missionary work. The third agreement called for Northern and Southern Baptists to respect the territorial boundaries established by tradition. This agreement meant in essence that the Home Mission Board of the SBC and the ABHMS should agree to cooperate without antagonism wherever the ABHMS controlled an enterprise in the South. More importantly, however, this third agreement discouraged the ABHMS from starting any new ventures in the South.[54]

---

[53]Historical and Research Department of the National Baptist Convention *Report*, 1929, 18.

[54]Robert A. Baker, *A Baptist Source Book, with Particular Reference to Southern Baptists* (Nashville: Broadman Press, 1966) 161-62.

Most black Baptist leaders appreciated the degree to which the financial depression burdened the ABHMS. But they were equally unappreciative of the racist implications of the two bodies making comity agreements about Southern Afro-American Baptists without including them in that discussion. Since the 1894 and 1895 minutes for the black national bodies have not been discovered, I do not have their official word on this matter. The agreement had ignored these bodies anyway. Nevertheless we do know that the black Georgia Baptists underwent a serious schism, lasting to this day, because the Plan of Cooperation brought to the surface deep disagreements between black separatists and cooperationists within that body.[55] The factions were led by Emanuel Love of Savannah and William Jefferson White of Augusta. White, a mulatto, proved himself more than equal to defending the cooperationist party line in the columns of his newspaper, *The Georgia Baptist*. Despite this advantage over Love, he seldom failed to publish Love's responses to the paper's searing editorials.

The national black Baptist response to the comity agreements was manifest more in action than in rhetoric. Black separatist leaders seized this opportunity. They declared that the need for Afro-American Baptist unity was never more apparent. The Fortress Monroe agreements had the unintended effect of solidifying the normally divided national black Baptist leadership.

The Other 1895 Atlanta Compromise. At the 1894 Montgomery, Alabama, meeting, the national black bodies laid the groundwork for their unification in the 1895 Atlanta meeting. Albert W. Pegues of North Carolina offered a motion to turn the Educational Convention, the Baptist Foreign Mission Convention, and the American National Baptist Convention into Boards of Education, Foreign Missions, and Home Missions.[56] In other words they would become, like the boards of the SBC, departments of one convention. There was no difference between this plan and the organizational structure of the SBC. The national bodies agreed to take Pegues's proposal under advisement by appointing a joint committee that was asked to report at the 1895 meeting. That committee consisted of Pegues, William H. McAlpine, Joseph Endom Jones, Andrew S. Jackson, John H.

---

[55]The details of this split are related in McManus, ''The American Baptist Home Society . . .'' 435-72.

[56]See Edward A. Freeman, *The Epoch of Negro Baptists and the Foreign Mission Board* (Kansas City, Kansas, 1953) 81-82.

Frank, A. Hobbs, Jacob Bennett, Wesley G. Parks, and Andrew J. Stokes. These men drafted a more detailed proposal to be presented at the 1895 meeting with the prior understanding that their report would not be binding on the three national bodies unless the 1895 joint assembly agreed to place all or part of the suggestions in the new convention's constitution.

The success of William Bishop Johnson's founding of *The National Baptist Magazine* in 1894 from his base as pastor of Second Baptist Church of Washington, D.C., greatly enhanced the execution of the 1894 Montgomery plan. This monthly journal between its first issue of July 1894 and its September 1895 issue broadcast the word among Afro-American Baptists that the great dream could only be realized if representative delegations attended from every state in the Union. Johnson urged the fellowship to make a concerted effort, despite economic hardship, to show up in Atlanta.

> It is a principle of natural Philosophy that large bodies move slowly. At this stage of Negro Baptist history, we should profit by the truthfulness of this saying. Three distinct boards properly managed would accomplish more, each in its line, than either or all of the general bodies has effected from their organization to the present. We need this consolidation. Circumstances connected with denominational effort in the past, all the conditions confronting us in the present, demand that we shall have unity of effort along denominational lines. Mere boasting of numerical strength beyond that of other denominations will not give us the place in the religious world we should have. Numbers unorganized is a sign of weakness and has been used effectively by other denominations against Negro Baptists in this country. We have intelligence in the pew, and executive ability coupled with intellectual force in the pulpit, to make a better showing than we do in the work of the great Baptist family. *We must either do something worthy of our numbers or be relegated to a back seat.* Our strong men owe it, not only to the denomination, but to themselves, to see to it that the Christian world is made to recognize Baptist organic union and its results in the creation and support of educational institutions, the successful conduct of missionary enterprises, and the perfect development of our literary force.[57]

---

[57]*The National Baptist Magazine* 2 (July 1895): 172.

The response was quite enthusiastic. More than five hundred delegates and observers attended the Atlanta meeting. The great publicity attendant on the opening exercises of the Cotton States and International Exposition in September, where Booker T. Washington gave his now famous address, certainly encouraged black Baptists to attend the historic 1895 Convention. Unfortunately the minutes for that Convention have been lost. But the *Atlanta Constitution* carried daily accounts of the sessions, which lasted for one week and were held at the old Friendship Baptist Church. The *Constitution* reported that there were several heated debates, undoubtedly between the separatists and cooperationists. But the separatists were dominant largely because of the huge Texas delegation, which numbered more than two hundred.[58] The splits in the Tennessee, Georgia and Mississippi state conventions over the Plan of Cooperation apparently had reduced their numbers considerably. But this was not the case with the Texas Convention because the Texans, accustomed to bold ventures largely independent of the ABHMS, were led by such firebrands as Richard Boyd, David Abner, Jr., and Isaac Tolliver. Representatives from most of the Midwestern and Western states, however, did not appear. Of course the South was represented, but not in proportion to its great number of black Baptists.

Despite the feuding and the sparse numbers from the South, most of the influential leaders were there and led in the formation of the most successful consolidation of Afro-American Baptist forces since the collapse of the CABMC in 1879. The Convention accepted many of the recommendations of the 1894 joint planning committee. The new constitution, however, left the black Baptists one major problem that would not be resolved until 1897—it did not provide for a separate department for publication, nor did it adequately address the problems besieging the floundering foreign mission program. Nevertheless, by 1897 these problems were addressed under the leadership of the first president of the National Baptist Convention, Elias Camp Morris.

---

[58]*Atlanta Constitution*, 1 October 1895.

The Enduring Legacy of Separatism

Webster's Ninth New Collegiate Dictionary defines an epilogue as "a concluding section that rounds out the design of a literary work." I interpret this to mean that an epilogue should be a confessional conclusion where the author enumerates motivations and discusses prospects for future study. Since I discuss motivations in the preface and prospects for future study in the bibliographical essay, the emphasis here is on concluding remarks.

Historians are midwives who help the present allow the past to be born anew. That means we are often required to pause in our narratives and explain events when the narrative itself either does not disclose enough up to that point or does not disclose it soon enough. I have benefited greatly from Peter Gay's sound observation that "historical narration without analysis is trivial, and analysis without narration is incomplete."[1] (Sydney Ahlstrom often called this an "analytical narrative.") Unless we have this bifocal vision, the reader often experiences a certain sense of suspended animation. That is why this section has two objectives: 1) to offer some indication of subsequent events; and 2) to restate the central theme in a summary fashion.

The Institutionalization of the Separatist Spirit. Miles Mark Fisher, the first professional black Baptist church historian, once argued that in order "to account for the progress of Negro Baptists" we have to understand why

---

[1] Peter Gay, *Style in History* (New York: McGraw-Hill, 1974) 189.

"racial consciousness" is so important to them. Fisher ventured his own conjecture that most black Baptist leaders, reflecting the beliefs of their constituency, believed that "cooperation [with white Baptists] meant subordination."[2] This view is still prevalent within the National Baptist Convention, U. S. A., Inc., the direct successor to the 1895 Convention. The Reverend Dr. Joseph Harrison Jackson, its president between 1953 and 1982, once admonished those who joined white Baptist organizations that white Baptists would not share power easily.

> If all Negro Baptists joined with white Baptists of America in forming one big Baptist organization, we would still have some Negroes forming units that they might well call a black caucus, and these caucuses would not be for the purpose of urging Negroes to refine the talents that they have and harness the same in making the new body politic more spiritual and more dedicated to the cause of freedom and redemption. But there would be the drawing up of a list of demands and then protesting to the white majority for certain things the black minority felt they should have and receive.[3]

As we know from the story told in this book, this is an old sentiment. Indeed, it is now a strong tradition that became even stronger after the formation of the National Baptist Convention in 1895. We need to review some of the events following the 1895 Convention that demonstrate how and why separatism rather than integration became dominant.

Resistance to Racial Subordination. The determined interest in foreign missions on the part of some clashed with a new breed of radical separatism matched only in an earlier period by Rufus Lewis Perry, who died just a few months before the 1895 consolidation. The presence of Henry McNeal Turner, a bishop of the African Methodist Episcopal Church who had been invited to address the 1895 Convention, was a clear sign of the successful resurgence of the separatist spirit not only within this reorganized denomination but also within African-American life and culture in general.

Turner warned the delegates not to subordinate themselves to white people and turn to God. He argued that the new fetish among white folk was to color God white. If God has pigmentation, Turner argued, then he

---

[2]Miles Mark Fisher, *A Short History of the Baptist Denomination* (Nashville: Sunday School Publishing Board, 1933) 111.

[3]National Baptist Convention, U. S. A., Inc. *Minutes,* 1970, 286.

would believe God is black rather than believe God is white. The outspoken Henry Lyman Morehouse, secretary of the American Baptist Home Mission Society, declared that "talk of this sort is the race spirit gone mad."[4] But neither Turner nor the Convention leaders were embracing insanity. The white majority itself seems to be a better candidate to receive this label. In 1895 alone more than 112 blacks were lynched. This was only one form of violence experienced by the black community. The psychic cost of being different had always exacted a high toll as well. Turner's black separatism may have been reactionary, but it most certainly was not unfounded.[5]

While Turner and current events certainly influenced this radical mood among black Baptists, they had a separatist tradition of their own that accounts for the same phenomenon. Two powerful black Baptist leaders amplified the logic of the separatist ideology that resulted in the formation of the National Baptist Convention in 1895. They insisted that the 1896 Convention be more forthright about its black nationalist ideology. The strong separatist voices of Harvey Johnson and Emanuel K. Love were heralds for this separatist ideology. Both preachers were separatists, but for different reasons.

Johnson, pastor of the Union Baptist Church of Baltimore, argued for African-American separatism on strict ecclesiological grounds, not on grounds of expediency. His "Fraternal Letter" to the Convention was uncompromising. He urged black Baptists to sever relations totally. He declared quite bluntly that "I believe in an entire separation, because of existing circumstances and conditions of things," and then confessed that "I have not always believed and felt that way, but I do now." He was careful to defend himself against any charge that he hated white people. For him separation was a matter of institutional and ethical integrity.

I also want you ever to bear this one thing in mind: that when I speak of a

---

[4]See *Atlanta Constitution*, 2 September through 1 October 1895; *Baptist Home Mission Monthly* 17 (November 1895): 413-14. For a fine discussion of Turner's black nationalist views, see Edwin S. Redkey, *Black Exodus: Black Nationalist and Back-to-Africa Movements, 1890-1910* (New Haven: Yale University Press, 1969).

[5]Joel Williamson (*The Crucible of Race* [New York: Oxford University Press, 1985] 180), characterizes "race relations in the South" during this period as "in violence veritas." Also see C. Vann Woodward's powerful review of this book in *The New Republic* (15 October 1984): 29-31.

total separation from the whites, I do not mean antagonism to them, nor do I mean hatred for them in any degree or respect, but simply an exhibition and exemplification of individuality and personality, necessary to all well-regulated institutions.[6]

Johnson then challenged the 1896 Convention to become a distinct Afro-American denomination. He challenged the fellowship to become a new, race-conscious, and exclusively Afro-American Baptist denomination. He listed five crucial reasons for becoming an organic body.

1st. Because we are organically a distinct, separate denomination—we are the Colored Baptist denomination, and they are the White Baptist denomination.

2nd. Because we, being a separate organization, have all the functions, duties, responsibilties and obligations attaching to the same, to fulfill.

3rd. Because it is a moral and physical impossibility for us, as a denomination, to fulfill with honor and credit to ourselves the obligations devolved upon us, so long as we serve simply as the means to an end for the white man's greater and stronger organizations.

4th. Because the white man's race-pride and race-prejudice so entirely and completely unfits him to accord to us in his organizations, those offices and positions that are so necessary to our development into the best leadership; and because the facts prove that we can get such opportunities nowhere else but in organizations of our own.

5th. Because so long as we retain any organic relationship with the white man in a cooperative sense, he is sure to take the honor to himself for whatever we do and are. So if we are to ever do and be anything to ourselves and among ourselves, the logic of the facts teaches that we must do it ourselves.[7]

Emanuel Love's radical separatism was not as pronounced as Johnson's. But he was just as forceful and determined. His radical turn came after the death of the gentle and generous Benjamin Griffith, secretary of the American Baptist Publication Society. With the death of Griffith in 1895, Love believed all hope of replacing him with a fair-minded person seemed vain. Love believed that under the leadership of the new general secretary, A. J. Rowland, the ABPS would be ''so scorched under the

---

[6]*National Baptist Magazine* 3 (January 1896): 16, 17.

[7]Ibid.

burning sun of Southern prejudice'' that it would wither and die. ''While Dr. Griffith lived,'' he told the delegates.

> I never gave my vote in favor of a National Publishing House, because my hopes for all we needed in the American Baptist Publication Society lived as long as Dr. Griffith lived. He is dead and my hopes are buried.

Love added,

> As closely connected, and as affectionately attached to the American Baptist Publication Society as I am, I could not be so disloyal to rebel against my race and denomination after the National Baptist Convention had decided by a vote to establish a National Baptist Publishing House. I am a loyal Baptist and a loyal Negro. I will stand or fall, live or die, with my race and denomination; where they die ''I will die, and there will be buried.''[8]

Love's move to embrace separatism signaled the new Convention's final break with the ABPS. After Love spoke, the Convention passed a resolution establishing a new Publication Committee under the charge of its Home Mission Board. President E. C. Morris designated Little Rock, Arkansas, as headquarters for the Home Mission Board for two obvious reasons. The board's chairman, the Reverend G. W. D. Gaines, was a local pastor there. And Morris himself lived in Pine Bluff, Arkansas. He began immediately to consolidate his power. This effort eventually led to a clash with the Reverend Richard H. Boyd, an astute entrepreneur and fine business manager who became the secretary of the National Baptist publishing concern.

The resolution authorizing this historic venture mandated that ''said committee be empowered and is hereby ordered to publish series of Sunday School quarterlies, ready for our Sunday schools for the first of January, 1897.''[9] This resolution evoked more resentment among the cooperationists in the states of Virginia, Maryland, and North Carolina than the 1896 delegates anticipated.

------

[8]*National Baptist Magazine* 4 (October 1896): 260-61.

[9]Quoted in Historical and Research Department of the National Baptist Convention *Report*, 1929, 19.

Lewis Garnett Jordan, who was elected to succeed the recently deceased Lucius M. Luke as corresponding secretary of the Foreign Mission
Board in the same St. Louis meeting, later recalled the response of the cooperationists. Most of them were not present at the St. Louis meeting.

> It was done, and I can never forget the feelings against those who helped
> to bring it about. The [black] agents of the Northern societies in our South-
> land being products of the Home Mission Schools, were in the main the
> most learned and influential men among us, so they make us quake. These
> two branches of opinion carried this contention to the Negro Baptist
> churches everywhere, and so intense was their controversy that it dis-
> turbed the white Baptists, North and South.[10]

Jordan had forgotten, however, that the Plan of Cooperation was a major
element in the dispute that followed the establishment of a black Baptist
publishing concern. But his memory did not fail him in regard to the mutual feeling of alienation between the separatists and the cooperationists
resulting from the new Convention's decision to sever ties with the Publication Society. The livelihood and social identity of most of those black
agents for the Northern societies, especially the Publication Society, were
at stake. The 1896 meeting set the stage for the overt manifestation of a
class cleavage from which black Baptist nationalists have never recovered.

Between the 1896 St. Louis meeting and the 1897 meeting in Boston,
a fierce debate occurred between the covers of the *National Baptist Magazine* and in the local denominational newspapers about the propriety of
splitting from the Publication Society. P. F. Morris of Virginia ignored the
more radical posture of Harvey Johnson and attacked Love's reasons for
becoming a radical separatist. He offered the faith claim that "God can
and will, if He has not already, raise up just as wise and conscientious a
leader as Dr. Griffith, who will respect the rights of the colored Baptists
and carry out His will in the management" of the Publication Society. He
warned those who supported the establishment of a black publishing concern in the St. Louis meeting that, if they voted for that move on the basis
of Love's reasoning, "it is clear that great and serious mistakes will and
must be made as a natural consequence."[11]

---

[10]Ibid.

[11]*National Baptist Magazine* 5 (April 1897): 329.

But P. F. Morris underestimated the powerful urge of A. J. Rowland, the new chief administrator of the ABPS, to bring "efficiency" to that operation. That required making a more concerted effort to recapture Southern Baptist support. Rowland failed to realize the latter agenda and only succeeded in alienating many patrons, especially black ones. William Bishop Johnson announced to the readers of the *National Baptist Magazine* that he was "shocked" at the new "business methods of the society." As a gesture of friendship toward black Baptists, Johnson had been asked to be the first black contributor to the *Baptist Teacher* since the fiasco of 1889. The editors asked him to write a small article on the "Life and Work of St. Paul." But they told him that it would not be published until eleven months later in the November 1897 issue. They then added financial injury to insult by refusing to pay him directly. They "credited" his honorarium to the account of his church and also deducted from a bill the *National Baptist Magazine* owed the Society. Johnson declared that "if the Society desires to retain our respect it must cease to take advantage of our churches by showing how little confidence they have in Negro organizations."[12]

When the National Baptist Convention met during the week of 14 September 1897, separatist leaders of the Convention insisted on a complete separation from the Northern societies, especially the ABPS. On the very first day of the session, President E. C. Morris called on Harvey Johnson to deliver the "Fraternal Address" he had published earlier in the *National Baptist*. Johnson reiterated his call for black Baptists to separate from all white Baptist societies. Johnson's speech was well received by most of the delegates. But the small number of delegates who were strict cooperationists looked on such racial harangues with utter disdain.

Ironically, the cooperationists did not try to counter the powerful oratory of the separatists. Instead, they attacked the feeble Convention's foreign mission program. This was weakest program because it inherited a moribund foreign mission program that had been practically devastated by the sudden death of its corresponding secretary and by the grave financial hardships resulting from the Depression of 1893. The cooperationists who disagreed with the majority's radical discontinuance of past policies toward the white Baptists included such ministers as Calvin S. Brown, Albert W. Pegues, and Samuel N. Vass of North Carolina; John M. Armistead

---

[12]Ibid., 371.

and Anthony Binga, Jr. of Virginia; and W. M. Alexander and W. J. How-ard of Maryland. They accused the separatists of being ungrateful for the generous support assistance that white Baptists had given to blacks. In fact they were so disgruntled that they met in Washington, D. C., a few weeks after the 1897 Boston meeting to form a new foreign mission convention.

Calvin S. Brown was actually the major leader of this schismatic group. Brown, a pastor in Raleigh, North Carolina, was also the ABHMS's mis-sionary for that state. Most of Brown's group were from the Eastern sea-board states—Maryland, Washington, D.C., Virginia, Florida, and especially North Carolina. Moreover, most of them did work for the Northern societies in order to supplement their incomes. And most of them were graduates of Shaw University and Richmond Theological Institute. For example, when the Reverend John A. Whitted, a black cooperationist pastor in North Carolina, reported on the results of the Plan of Cooperation in his state, he emphasized the critical educational work of Shaw Univer-sity, the ABHMS's major school in his state. "It has been said of North Carolina that no state among the colored Baptists had a better ministry, in-tellectually and spiritually, Whitted said."[13] Whitted himself was a grad-uate of Shaw University's theological department. The ABHMS considered Shaw and Richmond Institute of Virginia, later to become Virginia Union University, to be the two leading theological seminaries for blacks. In fact Colonel T. J. Morgan bragged that the future black church leaders were "pursuing a course of study similar to that pursued in the best theological seminaries in the North where white young men are fitting themselves to be pastors of churches."[14] As graduates of these schools, the cooperation-ists had an arrogant attitude toward lesser-trained clergy. They believed other leaders were too inept to run their own denominational enterprises.

White Baptists were in full agreement with this sentiment. They, too, could not understand why the National Baptist Convention wanted a pub-lishing house or any other independent enterprise. *The Examiner* (Boston) published an editorial praising "progressive" black Baptist leaders who stood against ignorant black "visionaries" who would lead the black race to social failure. "It is absurd to suppose," the editorial reasoned,

---

[13]*Baptist Home Mission Monthly* 20 (May 1898): 163.

[14]*Baptist Home Mission Monthly* 19 (December 1897): 398.

that there is needed a special Sunday-school literature for Negroes. We have not one Gospel for whites and another for blacks. The way of salvation is the same for one race as for another. The literature for white people is equally suitable for black people of the same grade of culture. There is no virtue in exposition of a Sunday-school lesson simply because it was prepared by a man with a black skin. We regard the efforts on the part of many of our Negro brethren who discriminate against the literature of the Publication Society, simply because it is not prepared and printed by Negroes, as most foolish and hurtful. In our view, the success of all those who are pushing this movement would hinder and not help the progress of the race.[15]

Many white Baptists believed that most black church people were not "of the same grade of culture." So did the Brown group. But neither the whites nor Brown's group seemed to recognize that genuine cultural preferences and differences demanded a literature that was not afraid of displaying black racial pride.

When the Brown cooperationists made their presence felt in the Boston meeting, they tried to intimidate the less educated clergy by belittling their commitment to black independence. According to Jordan, they invented the slogan, "Organize for Foreign Mission" in order "to throw us [separatists] in confusion and make us desert the idea of Negro literature."[16] They denounced the new Convention's nonexistent foreign mission program when they were unable to work their will. They left the Convention with much anger. They met again on 16 September, exactly three months after the closing gavel of the 1896 Convention, at the Shiloh Baptist Church in Washington, D.C., and formed the "Lott Carey Foreign Missionary Society." After 1903 they called themselves a convention rather than a society.

Despite opposition from the Lott Carey group and the new pressures fostered by the Plan of Cooperation, African-American Baptists had at last formed the national union that had escaped their grasp since the heyday of the Consolidated Convention. But other battles lay ahead, leading to the formation of the unincorporated National Baptist Convention of America in 1916 and the Progressive National Baptist Convention in 1961. The achievement of 1895 proved to be a seeming rather than a final end to this

---

[15]Quoted in *Baptist Home Mission Monthly* 19 (November 1897): 263.

[16]Historical and Research Department of the NBC *Report,* 19.

frustrated fellowship's yearning for unity. What appeared to be a rather simple desire to modernize the way African-American Baptists conducted their business caused the biggest split in the history of the black Baptist nationalist movement.[17] Although the development of this complex story cannot be told here, the ideological cleavages had their roots in the immediate aftermath of the formation of the National Baptist Convention in 1895. In a sequel to this book I will discuss this story more fully and analyze twentieth-century developments.

The Struggle for Incorporation. Those who remembered the difficult days of the CABMC knew the history of black Baptist nationalists up the reorganization in 1895 augured troubled days ahead. But most of the new leaders of the National Baptist Convention were born in the late 1850s or 1860s. The new denomination reflected the outlook of a fresh breed of black leaders who were mostly born in the South, trained in missionary schools, and were determined to take advantage of what Paul Gaston calls the "New South Creed."[18] This was a social and political doctrine that tried to minimize racial differences and accent the feisty capitalistic and Victorian pragmatism of the Gilded Age. They represented what some called a "new Negro."

This leadership class lamented and resisted Jim Crow's demeaning spirit, and hated the anarchism of white lynch mobs. They had all the optimism of youth, however, and cherished the day when justice in America would be "color blind." Some of them strained to see beyond the depressing terrorism aimed against the black community, especially in the South. But they believed that what was at stake was nothing less than "Christian civilization" itself. J. W. E. Bowen spoke eloquently for this reformed black Victorian outlook.

I am an optimist of the purest type, touching the Negro. I believe that God

---

[17]This movement to incorporate the NBC should be seen as part of a broader movement within American society toward incorporation. See Alan Trachtenberg, *The Incorporation of America: Culture and Society in the Gilded Age* (New York: Hill and Wang, 1982). Trachtenberg understands incorporation as a cultural as well as a legal phenomenon.

[18]Paul M. Gaston, *The New South Creed: A Study in Southern Mythmaking* (New York: Vintage Books, 1973); Frederick A. Bode, *Protestantism and the New South: North Carolina Baptists and Methodists in Political Crisis, 1894-1903* (Charlottesville VA: University Press of Virginia, 1975) is a fine case study of the effect of this idea in religious circles.

has hidden somewhere in the unrevealed future the solution of all these problems which so vex and disturb us to-day.[19]

Bowen was far more cautious about making positive declarations regarding improvements in race relations. But the Reverend John T. C. Newsom of Texas did not hesitate to embrace the New South doctrine as a new day for black entrepreneurs.

> Contemporaneously with the New South, the New Negro has appeared upon the scene, the Negro born of schools and colleges, and bent more on acquiring a home, amassing wealth, and the improvement of the social condition of his home, than the support of the grog shop, the gambling hall, and other institutions of idleness.
>
> Thus in speaking of the improved sentiment throughout the South, in respect to the Negro we must not consider this change as absolute, but that the Negro himself has made this condition possible by reason of his better conduct and improvement.
>
> The South, therefore, deserves credit for its prompt and just recognition of the meritorious side of the colored man's cause.[20]

Despite the different emphases in the views of Bowen and Newsom, they represent the outlook of many black leaders who sought to deal with the reality of being "an American, and a Negro." This was, however, a peculiar black bourgeois problem.[21] Indeed, if "class is defined by men as they live their own history,"[22] then we may discern some class differences

---

[19]J. W. E. Bowen, *What Shall the Harvest Be? A National Sermon: Or, a Series of Plain Talks to the Colored People of America, on Their Problems* (Washington, D. C.: Stafford Printing, 1892) 26.

[20]John T. C. Newsom, "The New South—The New Negro," *National Baptist Magazine* 3,2 (April 1896): 84.

[21]W. E. B. DuBois, *Souls of Black Folk: Essays and Sketches* (1903; reprint, Greenwich CT: Fawcett Publications, 1961) 17; and Charles H. Long's brilliant analysis of this motif in the thought of William James, Henry James, and W. E. B. DuBois in "The Oppressive Elements in Religion and the Religions of the Oppressed," *Harvard Theological Review* 69, 3-4 (1976): 397-412. Cf. also Joel Williamson's useful analysis of the same theme in *The Crucible of Race*, 399-413. Williamson's use of the term "Hegelianism" is overdrawn.

[22]E. P. Thompson, *The Making of the English Working Class* (New York: Vintage Books, 1966) 11.

among African-American Baptists. In fact I have already identified some of the competing social objectives.

Indeed, the great dispute between Booker T. Washington and W. E. B. DuBois that emerged in 1895 was largely a difference in cultural orientation. Washington announced at the opening session of the Atlanta Exposition that white philanthropists should give more support to black industrial education than to liberal arts education. He believed black Southerners should "drop their buckets" in the South and stop fantasizing about the promises of the industrial North. DuBois, on the other hand, believed that preparation for citizenship involved a thorough introduction to civic virtues that he believed could best be obtained through a liberal arts education. This continuing debate has been the source of much squabbling within the black intelligentsia. Alain Locke was bold enough to articulate this dilemma in the heyday of the Harlem Renaissance.

> Hitherto, it must be admitted that American Negroes have been a race more in name than in fact, or to be exact, more in sentiment than in experience. The chief bond between them has been that of a common condition rather than a common consciousness; a problem in common rather than a life in common.[23]

There is more truth to this generalization than many realize.

African-Americans in the Western Hemisphere represented the first sustained blending of African ethnic groups to occur in the history of African people. The magnitude of this development was enormous, especially when we recall that Africans speak more than 1,500 distinct languages, not dialects. Whatever aspect of the history of the African Diaspora one probes, it cannot be done without taking the intragroup and external political realities of their various situations into account. This is especially evident in the history of their religious institutions.

A Durkheimian appeal to religion as a form of collective group solidarity[24] can only help explain the powerful bonds in black congrega-

---

[23]Alain Locke, ed., *The New Negro* (New York: Atheneum, 1968) 7. Also see Nathan Irvin Huggins, *Harlem Renaissance* (London: Oxford University Press, 1971); and David Levering Lewis's more popular study, *When Harlem Was in Vogue* (New York: Vintage Books, 1982).

[24]Frederick Jameson has a very engaging critique of this notion in *The Political Unconscious: Narrative as a Socially Symbolic Act* (Ithaca NY: Cornell University Press, 1981) 292-96.

tions. But it will not explain the weak ties that exist between alliances of congregations among African-American Baptists. Even if we see them as participants in American religion's "quest for community,"[25] we still must account for the absence of effective bonding beyond congregational and regional boundaries.[26] This is especially urgent because they have the ability to direct enormous energies and resources to support the continuing struggle to defeat racism and the negative legacies of slavery.

We can identify at least three classes that had emerged in the history of the African-American religious community by 1895. Let us review these developments in order to understand the lines of class cleavage within the Black Baptist Movement up to and beyond 1895.

Sociological Profile. By 1895 the Baptist movement in the United States was actually a tricultural social phenomenon whose expressions are Northern, Southern, and African. But the African-American Baptists out of necessity became the most aggressive agents of progressive social and political change. While the Southern Baptists struggled with the ordeal of trying to maintain a fragile denominational confederation based on genteel values and populist evangelical fervor, blacks resisted this impulse because it was based on paternalistic, racist sentiments. The Northern Baptists, as the parent tradition, continued to struggle to realize the New England Puritan yearning to create the Kingdom of God in America, and meet the immense challenges presented by the tidal wave of new European immigrants.

Many black Baptists were suspicious about the excitement with which Northern white Baptists greeted these new white Americans as compared to their waning enthusiasm for black uplift. They believed supercilious and subtle forms of racial chauvinism often motivated Northern white Baptists to otherwise heroic efforts to reconstruct Southern culture and to introduce African-Americans to middle-class white culture. At the same time, most black leaders cherished white teachers, such as Joanna P. Moore, who was one of the hundreds of dedicated missionaries who went South during and after the Civil War. They taught the freed people, built churches, and of-

---

[25]Timothy L. Smith, "Congregation, State, and Denomination: The Forming of the American Religious Structure," *William and Mary Quarterly,* 3rd series 25 (1968): 176.

[26]I agree with the argument that weak ties are not necessarily a bad arrangement. Indeed, they can facilitate mobility and change to a greater degree than social bonds with strong ties. See Mark S. Granovetter, "The Strength of Weak Ties," *American Journal of Sociology* 78,6 (1973): 1360-80.

fered practical advice on how to deal with the pathologies of American racism in the labor market, politics, and in the commercial world. Those who have outlined this story forgot to tell, however, (or did not know) that blacks constituted a large proportion of that pious band.

As we observed in chapter 5, blacks who labored in the South during the antebellum period were somewhat resentful of the often insolent and chauvinistic behavior of many black and white "Yankee" missionaries. Yet they joined forces with the black missionaries to form political and religious organizations throughout the South. We have also discussed the role Baptists played during this democratic revolution called "Radical Reconstruction." Here is a chronological profile of the major organizations black Baptists formed before and after 1895.

1. Consolidated American Baptist Missionary Convention 1866
2. Baptist General Association of Western States and Territories 1873
3. New England Baptist Convention...1874
4. Baptist Foreign Mission Convention 1880
5. American National Baptist Convention 1886
6. National Baptist Convention, U.S.A., Inc. 1895
7. Lott Carey Foreign Mission Convention.................................1897
8. United American Free Will Baptist Church 1901
9. National Primitive Baptist Convention..................................1906
10. National Baptist Convention of America 1916
11. National Baptist Evangelical Life and Soul-Saving Assembly
    of the U.S.A. 1921
12. Progressive National Baptist Convention 1961

With more than fifty thousand congregations and nearly twelve million members, today the black Baptist movement is the largest social and religious movement in Afro-America. But it seems to lack the ability to focus all of that potential power. The largest of these bodies, the National Baptist Convention, USA, Inc., has yet to prove that it has the will and the ability to become a powerful social institution. Yet it remains a vigorous and enchanting religious movement.

The black Baptist traditions have distinctive ideological and, as in the case of the Primitive Baptists, liturgical differences. In fact four important historical currents shape this story.

The mainstream consists of those whom I call "bourgeois black Baptists." I do not use this notion in a pejorative sense. But I would be remiss not to mention the powerful influence of this middle-class ethos on black Baptist life and thought. The bourgeois commitment to a nuclear rather than an extended definition of family life and community[27] did much to define the social role of the black church movement in the twentieth century. The experience of their foreparents as chattel slaves threw them into the grips of what Orlando Patterson calls "natal alienation."[28]

Moreover, free blacks, many of whom were Baptists, became denizens—aliens grudgingly tolerated in their own native land. As Judge Colcock of South Carolina wrote in 1826, free black persons had "not, like the freed men of Rome, or Athens, become incorporated into the body politic."[29] They were certainly "subjects," but they were not partakers of the people's sovereignty. They were colonized and disfranchised because of their pigmentation. In the midst of the racist ethos of slavocracy as well as free black denizenship, the black church became "A Haven in a Heartless World."[30] Like the catacombs for early Roman Christians, black churches were refuges of hope. Their participation in the Abolitionist Movement and the Underground Railroad enabled them to be a clandestine mail service that kept black families in communication with each other. They sought the "inner security" and "inner freedom"[31] that was a distinctive of the bourgeois ethos, yet they used it in a far different way and for quite different purposes.

The tremendous impact of a distinctive urban spirituality that was nurtured among free blacks spread in the urban North and South. And as

---

[27]Three studies of the role of community as a major force in the history of Afro-America provide fascinating insights: John W. Blassingame, *The Slave Community* (New York: Oxford University Press, 1979); Herbert G. Gutman, *The Black Family in Slavery and Freedom, 1750-1925* (New York: Pantheon Books, 1976); and Thomas L. Webber, *Deep Like the Rivers: Education in the Slave Quarter Community, 1831-1865* (New York: W.W. Norton, 1978).

[28]Orlando Patterson, *Slavery and Social Death* (Cambridge: Harvard University Press, 1982).

[29]James H. Kettner, *The Development of American Citizenship, 1608-1870* (Chapel Hill: University of North Carolina Press, published for the Institute of Early American History and Culture, Williamsburg VA, 1978) 319.

[30]Christopher Lasch, *Haven in a Heartless World: The Family Besieged* (New York: Basic Books, 1977).

[31]John Lukacs, *The Passing of the Modern Age* (New York: Harper and Row, 1970) 201.

America itself became increasingly an urban nation, this spiritual praxis combined with a powerful progressive political current that I call "Prophetic Black Baptists."[32] This impulse received its primary impetus during the Abolitionist Movement between 1830 and 1863. "Black Baptist Folk Culture," however, became the most powerful liturgical tradition, the axis of a new American spirituality that has had an enduring effect on the black church movement in general. Through its sacred music, prayers, testimonies, and African rhythm, it wrestled mightily against white religious cultural imperialism. Furthermore, this folk culture gave birth to the Blues, Jazz, Soul, and, above all, Gospel Music.[33] The historical and anthropological relations between these currents that dominate the North American scene and the "Syncretistic African Baptists" of the Caribbean and South America merit further examination.[34] Their impact on urban life in such

---

[32]Cornel West (*Prophesy Deliverance!* [Philadelphia: Westminster Press, 1982] 16-24, 95-127) highlights and analyzes several major issues, persons, and events in the black prophetic stream. The writings of James H. Cone, the pioneer in this critical intellectual enterprise, provide a powerful and enduring critique of bourgeois American Christianity, both black and white. His *Black Theology and Black Power* (New York: Seabury Press, 1969) offers some suggestive profiles of prophetic black Christianity. Peter J. Paris, in a more specific way, analyzes the central currents in the black Baptist tradition in his study of *Black Leaders in Conflict: Joseph H. Jackson, Martin Luther King, Jr., Malcolm X, and Adam Clayton Powell, Jr.* (New York and Philadelphia: Pilgrim Press, 1978). Paris rightly examines these leaders in the context of the Civil Rights movement of the 1950s and 1960s, but overlooks their common links to the black Baptist tradition. Two recent studies use history to provide useful ethical social paradigms: Gayraud S. Wilmore, *Black Religion and Black Radicalism;* and Peter J. Paris, *The Social Teaching of the Black Churches* (Philadelphia: Fortress Press, 1985). Paris critically examines twentieth-century minutes of African-American Baptist denominations, and offers a rich profile of their social teachings.

[33]These three studies provide valuable and substantive introductions to this theme: Dena J. Epstein, *Sinful Tunes and Spirituals: Black Folk Music to the Civil War* (Urbana: University of Illinois Press, 1977); Lawrence W. Levine, *Black Culture and Black Consciousness: Afro-American Folk Thought from Slavery to Freedom* (New York: Oxford University Press, 1977); and Eileen Southern, *The Music of Black Americans: A History,* 2nd ed. (New York: W. W. Norton, 1983).

[34]Stephen D. Glazier, *Marchin' the Pilgrims Home: Leadership and Decision-Making in an Afro-Caribbean Faith* (Westport CT: Greenwood Press, 1983) is a fine case study of this phenomenon among the Spiritual Baptists in Trinidad. The Native Baptists of Jamaica are discussed by Monica Schuler, *"Alas, Alas, Kongo": A Social History of Indentured African Immigrants into Jamaica, 1841-1865* (Baltimore: John Hopkins University Press, 1980) 30-44; and Mary Turner, *Slaves and Missionaries,* 38-64. Sheila S. Walker, *Cere-*

cities as New York and Boston ought to make this a pressing social and intellectual concern. Furthermore, the links between this current and early black Baptist history in the ministries of George Liele, David George, Andrew Bryan, Moses Baker, and others are simply inseparable. There has also been continuous fellowship for more than 75 years between the National Baptist Convention, U.S.A., Inc. and the Jamaica Baptist Union.

Frustrated Fellowship. The fear of duplicating the racial dominance so prevalent in the society at large encouraged African-American Baptists to be fierce opponents of any form of ecclesiastical dominance. Even the caricature of the black pastor as an "authoritarian personality"[35] obscures the fact that "he" rules at the behest of the congregation only because "he" is committed to protecting the freedom and well-being of a people determined to be free. Thus black Baptist pastors tend to be exceptionally strong and independent leaders. And their churches tend to be more militantly congregational than those of other Baptists.

Some Conclusions. Black Baptist congregations are located in practically every state of the Union, and do not permit outside denominational agencies to oversee their work. Thus seemingly trivial, yet complex and important internal church politics, geography, and church polity, have often discouraged aspiring historians from tackling this highly significant religious group. In fact no professional historian has ever succeeded in completing a critical history of this religious movement. While this study makes a contribution to that critical history it cannot pretend to solve the problem. It is, however, an attempt to investigate the social significance of this movement by showing the relationship between the movement's internal developments and some of its leaders. The study itself focuses on the movement to unify black Baptists because this story best illustrates this relationship. But this story also illuminates the tremendous fragmentation and frustration resulting from the various ingredients of a power struggle involving *personality* and *property* as well as *internal and external politics.*

---

monial *Spirit Possession in Africa and Afro-America: Forms, Meanings, and Functional Significance for Individuals and Social Groups* (Leiden: E. J. Brill, 1972), and Hans A. Baer, *The Black Spiritual Movement: A Religious Response to Racism* (Knoxville: University of Tennessee Press, 1984) are excellent analyses of black spiritualism among African-Americans.

[35]E. Franklin Frazier and C. Eric Lincoln, *The Negro Church in America and The Black Church Since Frazier* (New York: Schocken Books, Inc., 1974) 47.

These factors are the central themes in a poignant drama reenacted annually by nationalistic black Baptists since 1840. These pilgrimages are not quests for spiritual power; black Baptists find that in abundance among their own local congregations. Rather, these are pilgrimages to an imaginary Mount Sinai. The leaders of the denomination search for what God has to say to their Israel. Representatives from the congregational tribes gather with a persistent hope that the impressive collective being of the black Baptists will at least receive recognition from among themselves, in the midst of a nation and a denominational family that encourages them to be what Victor Turner calls a "liminal" or a "threshold people." Black Baptists call it "waiting on the Lord." As in all bids for power, however, they find that each duly constituted plot often finds itself subverted by subplots and counterplots that have lost sight of the original revelation. But it has been the misfortune of black Baptists that they have not had enough faithful historians to recount where they have been and where they are. It will take time to rectify this neglect, but it must be done lest so noble a venture wither and die because it did not know its past. Although this enterprise cut many precious gems like Martin Luther King, Jr., it is now like a diamond cutter who has acute glaucoma and a palsied hand. Yet black Baptists have given the United States and the Christian community some of their greatest loyal dissenters. Their determined witness for conscience's sake reminded an amnesiac Republic and a Church captive to the worst consequences of a bourgeois culture of consumption that they have lost sight of their original moral vision.

I characterize this movement as a "frustrated fellowship" because it is an expression of *social identity* and a quest for *social power*. That social identity is ensconced in the powerful cultural revolution conceived and nurtured in the bosom of the local congregation. Black Baptists transformed the biological ecclesiology of "Puritan tribalism"[36] into a particularistic expression of the human yearning for freedom. This utopian project has often been maligned by the fierce investment of white Americans in a "pseudo-universalism"[37] of both overt and symbolic racial supremacy.

---

[36]Edmund S. Morgan uses this illuminating phrase to describe how New England managed by the late seventeenth century to convert a spiritual fellowship into a genealogical society. See chapter seven of *The Puritan Family* (New York: Harper and Row, 1966).

[37]Charles W. Amjad-Ali, "A Theory of Justice for an Ecumenical Praxis: A Critique of Eurocentric Pseudo-Universals" (Ph.D. dissertation, Princeton Theological Seminary, 1985) 93-119.

Black Baptist social power, however, is potential, not actual. Out of a determination to overcome the legacy of social invisibility fostered by white racism, they used the liturgical power of baptism by immersion to transform "a bastard people"[38] into a new social creation with its own "cosmology."[39] The Christian movement's ability to use its liturgies to forge distinctive theologies and spiritual praxes as vehicles for psychic and material deliverance is far more extensive than some have argued.[40]

Indeed, unsympathetic Victorian condemnations of spirituality were often knee-jerk accommodations to secularism.[41] The idea that good religion must always serve some utilitarian purpose callously assumed that "superior, intelligent" human beings ought to be strong enough to bear pain without the aid of spiritual anaesthesia. Perhaps this assumption is best preserved in Karl Marx's cynical remark that "religion is the opiate of the people." Of course this idea assumes that they might be able to fare better without religion. But our humanity demands that we somehow cope with the traumas of everyday life. Cultural enclaves have not succeeded in eradicating the burden of sudden change, catastrophes, and death. A kind of spiritual *technē* is still needed to defend our psychic well-being from the negative consequences of existential struggles.

This perennial human quest for an affective social womb became a central psychosocial rationale for the founding and spread of the black Baptist movement. Interspersed in seemingly trivial racial and institutional strife lies a modern expression of the ancient Christian commitment to what the early Christians called *koinonia,* but what we modern Christians often call "community." Sheldon Wolin argues that Christianity's

---

[38]James Baldwin, *Go Tell It On the Mountain* (New York: Dell Publishing, 1953) 137.

[39]Mechal Sobel, *Trabelin' On* (Westport CT: Greenwood Press, 1979) 3-75.

[40]There are many analyses of these phenomena in Christian history. Some studies have been most helpful to this work: Anscar J. Chupungco, *Cultural Adaptation of the Liturgy* (Ramsey NJ: Paulist Press, 1982); Peter Brown, *The Cult of the Saints: Its Rise and Function to Latin Christianity* (Chicago: University of Chicago Press, 1981) 44-48; Rosalind and Christopher Brooke, *Popular Religion in the Middle Ages: Western Europe, 1000-1300* (London: Thames and Hudson, 1984); George H. Williams, *The Radical Reformation* (Philadelphia: Westminster Press, 1962); Clarence C. Goen, *Revivalism and Separatism in New England* (New Haven: Yale University Press, 1962); and Rhys Isaac, *The Transformation of Virginia* (Chapel Hill: University of North Carolina Press, 1982) 161ff.

[41]See Paul A. Carter, *The Spiritual Crisis of the Gilded Age* (DeKalb IL: Northern Illinois University Press, 1971).

greatest contribution to social life and politics lies in its sociology, not its
theology. "Christianity succeeded where the Hellenistic and late classical
philosophies failed, because it put forward a new and powerful ideal of
community which recalled men to a life of meaningful participation."[42]

A more precise way of stating this insight would be to say that the significance of Christian praxis, apart from classical Judaism, lies in its understanding of the *regnum dei*, not in its *visio dei*. Thomas Bender offers
a definition of community that is very similar to the Christian understanding of the word *koinonia*. He argues that community is more than a sociological construct. It is something that happens. It is an event. Bender's
definition builds on Kai Erikson's marvelous study of the rebuilding of an
Appalachian town after a flood destroyed it. Erikson's *Everything in Its
Path* is a report of a sociologist's discovery that the soul of a community
has very little to do with physical location. It is an affective bond between
a group of people. Christians call this *koinonia*.[43]

What happens, however, when the social lineaments of that bond are
broken or, more probably, never really fused? In the case of the Black
Baptist Movement, fusion has never really taken place. The solidarity
needed to become an effective social and political force has been lacking
because the various sociological consequences of more than 250 years of
slavery have not been taken seriously by black Baptists themselves. After
emancipation in 1863 black Baptists, like most other black Christians, un-
questioningly accepted the ideology of American opportunism without
pressing more vigorously for reparations for unrequited labor. They bought
the Horatio Alger mythos without realizing that its "cash value" was virtually nil.

Black Baptists uncritically embraced this Americanist ideology of
works righteousness. Although this yearning for self-determination is evident throughout the course of black Baptist history, it achieved a consummate expression during Joseph Harrison Jackson's administration of the
National Baptist Convention. The price black Baptists paid, however, was
to be remembered as a reactionary institution that refused to take a pro-

---

[42]Sheldon Wolin, *Politics and Vision: Continuity and Innovation in Western Political
Thought* (Boston: Little, Brown and Company, 1960) 97.

[43]Thomas Bender, *Community and Social Change in America* (New Brunswick NJ:
Rutgers University Press, 1978).

phetic stance in support of Martin Luther King's historic Civil Rights movement. They could produce prophets, but they were still in bondage to a charismatic polity that depended on what Edward L. Wheeler correctly calls "one man rule."[44]

Many hoped the election of the Reverend Dr. Theodore Jemison in 1982 to the presidency of the National Baptist Convention, U. S. A., Inc., augured a new day, and rekindled once again an old desire for reunification. They yearned to be more than a threshold people. They believe God wants them to be one body. We all wait to see if their hopes will be realized.

---

[44]Edward L. Wheeler, "Beyond One Man: A General Survey of Black Baptist Church History," *Review and Expositor* 70 (1973): 309-19.

Bibliographical Essay

This essay presents an introduction to the places and texts that offer fruitful historical inroads into this complicated religious community. I shall examine methodological issues, outline where the major research material is located, and review the most useful resources.

Part I: Problems and Sources

Methodological Problems: Polity and Race

Professor Winthrop S. Hudson stated that the study of Afro-American Baptist history "is an almost completely untouched field for historical investigation and it is a field of greatest significance" in his "Themes for Research in Baptist History," *The Chronicle* 16 (January 1954): 23. Anyone who has tried to explore this history knows that Hudson's statement *seems* to be true more than thirty years later. I hope to dispel this illusion, however, in this introduction, and to provide some direction and tools for the further development of this exciting area of American church history.

Discussion of Baptist ecclesiology and polity centers on the problem of authority within the Free Church tradition. The theory of authority within this tradition includes not only problems of governance, but also problems of reconciling theological disagreements and discerning the credibility of the religious experience of probationary members as well as ministerial licentiates. Historically, approaches to these matters have drawn on three conflicting themes: radical individualism, strict congregationalism, and quasi-presbyterianism. Early samplings of these three latter impulses can be gleaned from William G. McLoughlin, *Isaac Backus and the American Pietistic Tradition* (1967), and Clarence C. Goen, *Revivalism and Separatism in New England, 1740-1800: Strict Congregationalists and Separate Baptists in the Great Awakening* (1962). The drift toward a more presbyterial form of governance among the American Baptist Churches, the parent denomination of the Baptists in the United States, is examined by Paul M. Harrison, *Authority and Power in the Free Church Tradition: A Case Study of the American Baptist Convention* (1959). Albert Henry Newman's *A History of the Baptist Churches in the United States* (1894) still remains the most comprehensive of the several general histories of Baptists in the United States. Newman interwove the theological and social factors that influenced the rise of personages, movements and ideas in the history of Baptists in this country. He argued persuasively in this classic study that the idea of ''regenerate membership,'' an inheritance from Puritanism, ''far more than the rejection of infant baptism, or insistence upon believer's baptism, or contention for the precise New Testament form of baptism, has always been fundamental with Baptists'' (3). With an uncritical sociological perspective, Robert G. Torbet agrees with Newman. Torbet's *A History of the Baptists* (3rd ed., 1963) is more useful, however. It is of recent vintage and contains a masterful bibliography and well-marshaled footnotes. But he employs Ernst Troeltsch's label of ''sect-type'' churches as the appropriate label for Baptist churches without being critical of its appropriateness. Troeltsch's development of his view of ''sect-type'' Christianity over against ''church-type'' Christianity depends heavily on his discussion of Baptist origins in the Radical Reformation. See his *The Social Teaching of the Christian Churches,* trans. from the German by Olive Wyon (1931; reprint 1960) 2:694-714. Troeltsch assumes a direct lineage between continental Anabaptists and British Baptists. This assumption has been questioned closely by several Baptist and Mennonite scholars. They concede, however, that there is a symbiotic rather than an organic relationship. See Ernest A. Payne, *The Fellowship of Believers: Baptist Thought and Practice Yesterday and Today* (1952) 16-17.

On the other hand, Torbet is correct in his belief that Baptist polity has itself been a divisive internal force within the fellowship. There have been three components to basic Baptist polity that explain its divisive nature. First of all, Baptists maintain the theological position that the Church consists of ''set apart'' or ''separate'' congregations. This is not a sociological necessity, as the Baptists view it; this is their conscious interpretative emulation of New Testament Christianity. Thus many Baptists believe that one should not speak of the Baptist denomination as one body. One should speak of the Baptist churches.

Baptists, however, do subscribe to the doctrine of the oneness or universality of the Church as constituting all who believe in the Lord Jesus Christ as their Savior and who accept ''antipedobaptism'' or ''adult baptism'' as the definitive rite of entry into Christian fellowship. There have been two notable attempts to unify the entire denomination since the great split over slavery in 1843 and 1845: In 1905 the Baptist General Convention was formed ''with a view to bringing the Baptists of all parts of America into closer fellowship and promoting an American Baptist *esprit de corps.*'' See Albert Henry Newman, *History of Antipedobaptism: from the Rise of Pedobaptism to A.D. 1609* (1897), his *A History of Baptist Churches in the United States* (1898), as well as his ''History of Baptist Organizations,'' *Review and Expositor* 8 (July 1911): 363-77. Black Baptists have participated in pan-Baptist international gatherings since the 1905 founding meeting of ''The Baptist World Alliance'' in London. This organization declared then that it seeks ''to manifest the essential oneness in the Lord Jesus Christ . . . of the churches of the Baptist order and faith throughout the world, and to promote the spirit of fellowship, service and cooperation among them, while recognizing the independence of each particular church and not assuming the functions of any existing organization" (quoted in Newman, 1911, 377). This statement reflects the ambivalence Baptists have toward their cautious belief in the Church Universal. They subscribe to this doctrine with certain pronounced modifications: they believe in a Universal Church if such only includes "churches of the Baptist order and faith," and if such an ephemeral society guarantees, recognizes, and refuses to usurp "the independence of each particular church," and "the functions of any existing organization." Despite this appeal to the universality of the church, Baptists, especially, in the nineteenth century, have maintained a persistent dislike for the ways of Catholicism. This position reflects their identification with the simplistic tenets of classical American evangelicalism.

Nonetheless, there is a wide disjunction between such theological postures and the sociological fact of American denominationalism. The presence of intradenominationalism is complicated by the additional presence of racial denominationalism. Consequently, there are five major Baptist denominations. The Southern Baptist Convention (founded in 1845) and the American Baptist Churches (consolidated in 1907) are the two major white Baptist denominations. The Afro-American Baptists have three large denominations, including the "National Baptist Convention, U.S.A., Inc.," which is the parent convention founded in 1895. The "National Baptist Convention, U.S.A., Uninc." was founded in 1916 as a result of a schism led by the Reverend Richard H. Boyd, one of several black leaders who formed the first black Baptist publishing concern; and more recently, the "Progressive National Baptist Convention of America," founded in 1961 under the leadership of L. Venchael Booth.

The persistence of racial denominationalism, as well as intraracial denominational schisms, are the most important factors that hamper those who seek to gather the fragmented story of what can only euphemistically be called the "Black Baptist Denomination." There are Baptist denominations, not a Baptist denomination. These denominations are divided along racial, denominational, and quasi-theological lines. The emphasis should be placed on sociological and ideological differences rather than theological differences—although there are some telling sub rosa theological distinctions among them.

Archival Resources

The most complete collection of nineteenth-century materials dealing with black Baptist history is at the American Baptist Historical Collection in Rochester, New York on the campus of the Colgate Rochester Divinity School. Dr. Edward Starr, its former curator, an informed student of Baptist resources, quietly completed the publication of his comprehensive bibliography, *A Baptist Bibliography*, before his retirement in 1976. This is an indispensable tool for research in this area. A fine guide to this collection has been compiled by Professor Lester B. Scherer and Ms. Susan M. Eltscher, director of this library: *Afro-American Baptists: A Guide to Records in the Library of the American Baptist Historical Society* (Rochester NY: American Baptist Historical Society, 1985).

The other major exclusively Baptist collections are at the Southern Baptist Theological Seminary in Louisville, Kentucky, and the repository at the Sunday School Publishing Board of the Southern Baptist Convention. The National Baptist Convention, U.S.A., Inc. recently opened its Joseph Harrison Jackson Library in Chicago. This library holds only material of recent importance, however. The Virginia Baptist Historical Society's collection in Richmond, Virginia, holds items of particular interest that illuminate the history of this important state in the nineteenth-century movement for black Baptist unity.

Nevertheless, these archives, with the exception of the American Baptist Historical Collection, do not approach the extensive but scattered and unidentified collections on black Baptists in the Schomburg Collection of the New York Public Library and the Moorland-Spingarn Collection of Howard University in Washington, D.C. Along with the Library of Congress, the Moorland-Spingarn Collection reflects a richer holding of material about and by black Baptists. For the important role of black Baptists in the civil rights movement, the most significant repository is the library of the Martin Luther King, Jr., Center for Nonviolent Social Change in Atlanta, Georgia.

Manuscript Sources

The newspaper "Scrapbook of the Reverend Edmund Kelly," which is in the possession of Mrs. George Haynes of Mt. Vernon, New York, is an invaluable source for getting first-hand accounts of a black denomination organizer and missionary about the Southern situation immediately after the war. Kelly was a correspondent for the *New Bedford Courier*. There are also letters from John Berry Meachum, William P. Newman, and William E. Walker in the Archives of Oberlin College.

Numerous other letters are located in innumerable historical collections throughout the country. The major correspondence between black Baptist leaders and the officials of the American Baptist Home Mission Society are in Home Mission Society's archives located at the headquarters of the American Baptist Churches, U.S.A., in Valley Forge, Pennsylvania. Some of the Society's archival material is also in Rochester, New York, in the collection of the American Baptist Historical Society.

Several letters between Richard Boyd and James Frost are preserved in the library of the Historical Commission of the Southern Baptist Convention in Nashville, Tennessee.

Periodicals

Numerous letters of black Baptist missionaries were printed in the *American Baptist* (New York). The discovery of these letters in this newspaper filled a major gap in the initial research for this study. Its use is indispensable for anyone doing either a study of abolitionism or racism among black and white Baptists. It throws new light on the crucial decade of the 1860s. Since it was the official organ of the abolitionist Free Mission Society, black missionaries were encouraged to make social and political comments. The letters of the Reverend Charles Satchell of New Orleans, Louisiana, are especially important because, as one-time chaplain of Louisiana's lower legislative house, he gave intimate and lucid depictions of political and social events. Similar weight should be given to the letters of Jesse Boulden of Mississippi.

The most complete collection of the *National Baptist Magazine,* a pioneer denominational periodical founded and edited by the Reverend William Bishop Johnson between 1894 and 1901, is located at the American Baptist Historical Society. This journal ranked with the *African Methodist Episcopal Review* and *African Methodist Episcopal Zion Quarterly*. It is unfortunate that it has rarely been used. The Historical Society also has the complete set of *The American Baptist Home Missionary Monthly*, from 1878 to 1909. This important journal contains most of the reports from the black state missionaries. From time to time, they also printed useful editorials and articles from prominent black pastors.

Denominational Minutes and Journals

The Historical Commission of the Southern Baptist Convention has completed its massive microfilming of all the black Baptist journals and minutes that it could locate and identify within its own collection and in the Historical Society's collection. The Historical Society has by far the largest collection. In fact it holds the largest single collection of the minutes and journals of black state conventions and local associations. These items were not microfilmed by the Historical Commission.

Part II: Studies

Good but uncritical histories of black Baptists have been done from biographical, state, national, interracial, and interdenominational perspectives. Biographical studies dominate this field, however.

Biographical Studies

There are seven major collective biographical sketchbooks, including Albert W. Pegues, *Our Baptist Ministers and Schools* (1892; reprint 1970); Edward Randolph Carter, *Biographical Sketches of Our Pulpit* (1888; reprinted in 1969); Theodore S. Boone, *From George Lisle to L. K. Williams* (1941): Samuel William Bacote, *Who's Who Among the Colored Baptists of the United States* (1913); William J. Simmons, *Men of Mark: Eminent, Progressive and Rising* (1887: reprint 1968); Ethel L. Williams, ed., *Biographical Director of Negro Ministers* (1965, 1970); L. Venchael Booth, *Who's Who in Baptist America* (1960). Important biographical vignettes of several ministers can be found in David M. Tucker's dissertation, *Black Pastors and Leaders: Memphis, 1819-1972* (1975). Included among these sketches are Morris Henderson, R. N. Countee, Taylor Nightingale, and especially good portraits of the Reverends Thomas Oscar Fuller, Charles H. Mason, and Sutton Earl Griggs. Mason was a Baptist minister before he and Charles Price Jones, another black Baptist, founded the Church of God in Christ (Holiness) after 1897.

Numerous biographies and autobiographies of individual black Baptist ministers are very useful. Several sources give precious sketches of pioneer black Baptist preachers, such as the occasional Baptist almanacs edited and published by John Rippon, the famous English Baptist divine. These almanacs were called *The Baptist Annual Register*. The 1790-1793 issue is of special importance to the historian of the early black Baptist period. They contain contemporary sketches of David George, George Liele, Thomas Swiggle, and Andrew Bryan—as well as a general picture of church life among Southern Baptist slaves. The *Registers* for 1798-1801 are of less importance; but they do give brief sketches of the development of the offspring of the

Silver Bluff Church, the parent black Baptist Church founded between 1773 and 1776 in Aiken County, South Carolina, on the Savannah River.

This chattel church marked a new period in the spread of the Separate Baptist movement throughout the South. It solidified the eighteenth-century idea that segregation in the House of the Lord is an expedient way to be neutral on the question of the Scriptural justification of slavery. The cultural origins of the black Baptists are to be found in the South rather than the North as was the case with the founding of the parent congregations of the African Methodist Church and the African Methodist Zion Churches in the mid-1970s. This basic difference still holds true for the black Baptists—even though they now dominate the urban scene. Regardless of this preponderance, these Churches are still characterized by a distinctly Southern religious milieu that stresses enthusiastic and demonstrative worship. The most useful and powerful study of antebellum African-American Baptist history to date is Mechal Sobel, *Trabelin' On: The Slave Journey to an Afro-Baptist Faith* (1979), which contains helpful information about local congregations and provides some but certainly not enough biographical data.

Other biographical sources are provided by J. B. Taylor, *Biography of Elder Lott Carey: Late Missionary to Africa* (1837) as well as Miles Mark Fisher's excellent account of this same pioneer black Baptist missionary to Africa ("Lott Carey, the Colonizing Missionary," *Journal of Negro History* 7 [October 1922]: 380-418). The slave narratives of the Reverends Edmund Kelly (1851), Noah Davis (1859), Israel S. Campbell (1861), John Sella Martin (1867), Elijah P. Marrs (1885), Elisha W. Green (1888), Thomas L. Johnson (1909), Miles Mark Fisher's biography of his father, *The Master's Slave: Elijah Fisher* (1922), and Lewis Garnett Jordan, *On Two Hemispheres: Being the Life of Lewis G. Jordan as Told by Himself* (n.d.) are useful. The life story of the famous black Baptist Virginian, "Uncle Jack," was written by one of his white contemporaries, the Reverend William S. White, and entitled *The African Preacher* (1859). One should also consult the works about the Reverend Nat Turner of Southampton County, Virginia, and his famous rebellion. Two books are especially important: Henrik Clarke, ed., *William Styron's Nat Turner: Ten Black Writers Respond* (1968) and Stephen B. Oates, *The Fires of Jubilee: Nat Turner's Fierce Rebellion* (1975). There is also a brief but highly informative sketch of some of the slavery experiences of the Reverend William Troy in Benjamin Drew's *A North-Side View of Slavery* (1855, reprint 1969) 249-52. Troy was a fugitive slave from Virginia; he was a Free Mission abolitionist and missionary in Amherstburg, Canada West, where he also served the First Baptist Church. He became an outstanding supporter of the Free Mission Society.

The story of the free black antebellum Baptist churches can be gleaned from the autobiography of Jeremiah Asher (1862) as well as a synoptic anticipation of the latter work that Asher wrote while in the British Isles where he was attempting to collect monies to pay off the mortgage of his Philadelphia church; the book was entitled *Incidents in the Life of the Rev. J. Asher* (1850, reprint 1971). Another pioneer preacher and founding pastor of the Abyssinian Baptist Church in New York City, and the Joy Street Baptist Church in Boston is noted in "The Reverend Thomas Paul and the Colored Baptist Churches," in *The Baptist Memorial and Monthly Chronicles* 8 (September 1849): 295-301. John W. Lewis, a noted black Free-will Baptist abolitionist in his own right, interpolated the journal of Elder Charles Bowles in his *The Life, Labor, and Travels of Elder Charles Bowles, of the Free-Will Baptist Denomination* (1852). A profile of Afro-American Baptist participation in the Underground Railroad in Ohio and Canada can be gleaned from the Reverend William M. Mitchell's *The Underground Railroad* (1860). Mitchell was a black missionary of the Free Mission Society. The autobiography of Israel Campbell also sheds much light on black church life in the antebellum Midwest and Canada. And some helpful insights can also be found in Leonard Black, one of the early pastors of the Concord Baptist Church of Christ (Brooklyn, New York), *The Life and Sufferings of Leonard Black: A Fugitive from Slavery* (1847).

St. Louis, Missouri, was the center of black Baptist activity west of the Mississippi. One can find accounts of its pioneer minister, John Berry Meachum, in Meachum's *An Address to All the Colored Citizens of the United States* (1846). John Richard Anderson, one of Meachum's numerous sons in the ministry, published a memorial sermon entitled, *A Sermon on the Life, Character, and Death of Rev. John B. Meachum: Late Pastor of the First African Baptist Church, Saint Louis, Mo.* (1854).

Biographical sketches of the Reverends Henry Adams (Kentucky), Jeremiah Asher, Gustavus Brown (Washington, D.C.), Moses Broyles (Indianapolis, Indiana), Andrew Bryan (Savannah, Georgia), Israel Campbell (Winchester and Franklin Counties in Tennessee; Ontario, Canada; Sandusky, Cleveland, and Toledo, Ohio; Baton Rouge, Gros Tete, Louisiana; Houston, Hearne, Columbus, and Galveston, Texas), Ralph Freeman, Caesar Johnson, John Jones, Nelson G. Merry (Nashville, Tennessee), Thomas Paul (Boston and New York City), Rufus L. Perry (Brooklyn, New York), W. A. Walton (Texas), and Joseph Willis (Louisiana) can be found in William Cathcart, ed., *A Baptist Encyclopedia* (1883). The most informative, and least available, biographical sketches in this work are those of Moses Broyles, Caesar Johnson, and W. A. Walton. There are also articles in this same work about J. Richard Anderson, John Berry Meachum, W. J. White of Georgia, and C. O. Boothe of Alabama. Howard Rabinowitz has written an excellent biographical study of Holland Thompson, an important Reconstruction civil rights activist in Montgomery, Alabama, and a lay preacher associated with the First Colored Baptist Church, later named the Dexter Avenue Baptist Church. Martin Luther King, Jr. later became the pastor of this church in the 1950s. It was from Dexter Avenue that he championed the Montgomery Bus Boycott. Rabinowitz's article is titled, "Holland Thompson and Black Political Participation in Montgomery, Alabama," in Howard Rabinowitz, ed., *Southern Black Leaders of the Reconstruction Era* (Urbana: University of Illinois Press, 1982) 249-80.

Particularly reliable biographical works about ministers of the post-Emancipation period include William Eldridge Hatcher, *John Jasper: Unmatched Negro Philosopher and Preacher* (1908); E. A. Randolph, *The Life of Rev. John Jasper, Pastor of Sixth Mt. Zion Baptist Church, Richmond, Virginia: From His Birth to the Present Time, With His Theory of the Rotation of the Sun* (1884); Miles Mark Fisher's biography of his father; Silas Xavier Floyd, *Life of Charles T.[homas] Walker, D.D.* (1902; reprint 1969); Charles S. Morris, *Pastor Henry N. Jeter's Twenty-five Years Experience with the Shiloh Baptist Church* (1901); Mansel P. Hall, *An Autobiography* (1905); and William Henry Johnson, *A Sketch of the Life of the Rev. William Henry Johnson, D.D.: Late Pastor of the Gilfield Baptist Church, Petersburg, Virginia . . .* (1901); T. O. Fuller, *Twenty Years in Public Life, 1890-1910, North Carolina—Tennessee* (1910); and Alfred William Nicholson, *Brief Sketch of the Life and Labors of Rev. Alexander Bettis: also an Account of the Founding and Development of the Bettis Academy* (1913).

Biographical works by and about Baptist leaders of more recent importance include the renowned biography of Booker T. Washington, the most noted black Baptist lay person of his times, by Louis R. Harlan, *Booker T. Washington: The Making of a Black Leader, 1856-1901* (New York: Oxford University Press, 1972) and the sequel to this volume, *Booker T. Washington: The Wizard of Tuskeegee, 1901-1915* (New York: Oxford University Press, 1983). See also Adam Clayton Powell, Sr., *Against the Tide: An Autobiography* (1938) and his famous son's works, as well as a controversial biography by Claude Lewis titled, *Adam Clayton Powell [Jr.]* (Greenwich CT: Fawcett Publications, 1963); Ridgely Torrence, *The Story of John Hope* (1948); Benjamin E. Mays, *Born to Rebel: An Autobiography* (New York: Charles Scribner's Sons, 1971); Martin Luther King, Jr., *Stride Toward Freedom: The Montgomery Story* (1958); David L. Lewis, *King: A Critical Biography* (1970); Elizabeth Yates, *Howard Thurman: Portrait of a Practical Dreamer* (1964); Howard Thurman, *With Head and Heart: The Autobiography of Howard Thurman* (New York: Harcourt Brace Jovanovich, 1979); E. Ray Tatum, *Conquest Or Failure?: Biography of J. Frank Norris* (1966); James W. English, *Handyman of the Lord: The Life and Ministry of the Rev. William Holmes Borders* (New York, 1967); Charley C. White (in collaboration with Ada Morehead Holland), *No Quittin' Sense* (1969); very brief spiritual autobiographical essays by Benjamin E. Mays, William Holmes Borders, Gardner C. Taylor, Walter C. Fauntroy, and Howard Thurman in Howard Thurman, ed., *Why I Believe There is a God: Sixteen Essays by Negro Clergymen* (Chicago: Johnson Publishing, 1965); Charles Emerson Boddie, *God's "Bad Boys"* (1972); and Andrew W. Tilly's *The Black Churchmen* (1973). L. Venchael Booth also recently edited Lillian B. Horace's important biography of L. K. Williams, the renowned Depression Era president of the incorporated National Baptist Convention, *"Crowned with Glory and Honor": The Life of Rev. Lacey Kirk Williams* (Hicksville NY: Exposition Press, 1978).

Raymond Gavins, "Gordon Blaine Hancock: Southern Black Leader in a Time of Crisis, 1920-1954" (Ph.D. dissertation, University of Virginia, 1970) and his "Gordon Blaine Hancock: A Profile from the New South," *Journal of Negro History,* 59 (July 1974): 207-27, are excellent studies. Nonetheless, Gavins fails to see Hancock's participation in the Social Gospel Movement. He was greatly influenced by Francis Greenwood Peabody while he was at Harvard. Hancock was also a serious hymnodist. Two of Hancock's hymns are in Dearing E. King, ed., *Progressive Baptist Hymnal,* 1st ed. (Washington, D.C.: Progressive National Baptist Convention,

1976) selections 77 and 431. Gavins's doctoral study has been published under the titled, *The Perils and Prospects of Southern Black Leadership, 1884-1970* (Durham NC: Duke University Press, 1977). Two anecdotal biographical studies also provide some insights into the complex lives of African American Baptist educators: Inez Bacoats, *Echoes from a Well-Spent Life: The Biography of Dr. John Alvin Bacoats* (Columbia SC: State Printing, 1970); and W. H. R. Powell, *Illustrations from a Supervised Life* (Philadelphia: Continental Press, 1968). Although he does not examine the religious views of his subject in his *George Washington Williams: A Biography* (Chicago, 1985), John Hope Franklin has written an outstanding portrait of this important nineteenth-century black Baptist minister. The three most significant introductions to the life and thought of Dr. Martin Luther King, Jr., are Stephen B. Oates, *Let the Trumpet Sound: The Life of Dr. Martin Luther King, Jr.* (New York: Harper and Row, 1983); James Melvin Washington, ed., *A Testament of Hope: The Essential Writings of Martin Luther King, Jr.* (San Francisco: Harper and Row, 1986); and David J. Garrow, *Bearing the Cross: Martin Luther King, Jr., and the Southern Christian Leadership Conference* (New York: William Morrow, 1986).

State Histories

The most notable state histories are written by Charles Octavius Boothe (Alabama, 1895), Azzie Briscoe Koger (Maryland, 1936), John Franklin Clark (Arkansas, n.d.), Thomas Oscar Fuller (Tennessee, 1936), William Hicks (Louisiana, 1914), Stevenson N. Reid (Alabama, 1949), Patrick H. Thompson (Mississippi, 1898), and John A. Whitted (North Carolina). Of this group, Thompson and Whitted wrote the most useful narratives. Two recent studies dealing with black Baptist support for education in the states of Tennessee and Virginia are rich with very useful information: Ruth Marie Powell, *Ventures in Education with Black Baptists* (New York: Carlton Press, 1979) and Lester F. Russell, *Black Baptist Secondary Schools in Virginia, 1887-1957* (Metuchen NJ: Scarecrow Press, 1981). Recent compilations of state records also provide much data about twentieth-century black state conventions: Alberta D. Shipley and David O. Shipley, ed., *History of Black Baptists in Missouri (National Baptist Convention, U. S. A., Inc.)* (1976) and Clarence M. Wagner, *Profiles of Black Georgia Baptists: Two Hundred and Six Years of Black Georgia Baptist History, One Hundred Years of National Baptist History* (Atlanta: Bennett Brothers Printing, 1980).

National Surveys

There have been four notable attempts to write denominational black Baptist history from a national perspective. Two of these studies deal with the denomination in isolation from the general Baptist movement in the United States. The other two try to show the relationships between the white and black Baptist movements. Owen D. Pelt and Ralph Lee Smith consciously wrote a well-written celebrationist history of the major black Baptist denomination, the National Baptist Convention, U.S.A., Inc., in their *The Story of the National Baptists* (1960). Moreover, Lewis Garnett Jordan's *Negro Baptist History, 1750-1930* is actually a precious compilation of denominational records. While weak on interpretation, Jordan did preserve several records that would otherwise be lost. Two fine but rather controversial surveys deal respectively with the Progressive National Baptist Convention and the National Baptist Convention, U. S. A., Inc.: William D. Booth, *The Progressive Story: New Baptist Roots* (1981), and Joseph H. Jackson, *A Story of Christian Activism: The History of the National Baptist Convention, U. S. A., Inc.* (Nashville: Townsend Press, 1980).

In addition to the above works, C. C. Adams's and Marshall A. Talley's *Negro Baptist and Foreign Missions* (1944), and Edward A. Freeman's *The Epoch of Negro Baptists and the Foreign Mission Board* (1953) are good treatises on the Foreign Mission Movement among black Baptists. They also contain useful information on the national history of the denomination. But they politely avoid a detailed account of the major national schisms. Freeman's books is the better of these two. His treatise was actually done at an earlier date as a Th.D. dissertation at Central Baptist Seminary in Kansas City, Kansas.

There have been three pronounced attempts to do a broad history. They were written by Miles Mark Fisher, a very able black religious historian, and Nathaniel H. Pius. Their monographs were respectively entitled *A Short History of the Baptist Denomination* (1933) and *An Outline of Baptist History* (1911). Both historians tried to integrate black Baptist history with the broader Baptist movement, but both underplayed the internal development of Afro-American Baptist church life.

Fisher might have corrected this oversight in his unpublished history of black Baptists. Earl Thorpe contends in *Black Historians* that he has seen an unpublished history of the movement by Fisher. I have yet to have that privilege. Dr. Fisher, who died in 1970, was a pioneer historian in this field who studied at the University of Chicago under Peter Mode and William Warren Sweet. Fisher's exuberance for the Baptist cause, however, often betrayed his critical training. He sometimes celebrated obscurantism, especially in his feverish romanticist effort to demonstrate that the black Spirituals expressed desires for expatriation in his published Ph.D. dissertation on *Negro Slave Songs in the United States*.

The third effort at broad history has been written from the perspective of the distinctive and creative pastoral praxis of this tradition by Leroy Fitts, *A History of Black Baptists* (Nashville: Broadman Press, 1985). This history fills a major gap, and is especially useful for catechetical and denominational purposes. But it does not satisfy the equally pressing need to introduce this community of faith to the general public from the standpoint of critical history.

Index

Aaron, S., 68
Abner, David, Jr., 176, 185
Abner, David, Sr., 176 n43
Abner, Sharon, xvi
Adam, Henry, 215
Adams, C. C., 218
Adams, R. J., 144
African Methodist Episcopal Church, 20, 188
Ahlstrom, Sydney Eckman, xvi, 12, 187
Alexander, W. M., 194
Allen, Richard, 20
Alston, Percel O., 52n
American Baptist (Brooklyn), 72, 76, 89, 94, 95, 96, 109
American Baptist (Louisville), 139
American Baptist Churches in the U.S.A., 83
American Baptist Free Mission Society (ABFMS), 43, 55-60, 62, 69-78, 81; financial controversy with ABHMS, 99, 101; demise of, 78, 130-31
American Baptist Home Mission Society (ABHMS), 54-55, 60, 63, 65-70, 74, 79, 80-81; racial discrimination against black Baptist conventions, 84-87; NTIU controversy, 87-95; financial controversy with CABMC, 95-105; appoints District Secretary for the South, 143; detractors of ANBC unification movement, 144, 156; financial crisis of 1890s and relation to ANBC, 174; McVicar Plan to create a national black Baptist university, 174-77; "Plan of Co-operation" (1894), 182-83
American Baptist Missionary Convention (ABMC), 38-43, 58, 61, 69, 72, 74, 76
American Baptist Missionary Union (ABMU), 80, 138, 144-45
American Baptist Publication Society (ABPS), 79, 150, 157; confrontation with ANBC leaders, 159-70
American National Baptist Convention (ANBC), 135, 138-47; black nationalist identity, 170-83; response to the "Plan of Cooperation" (1894), 182-83, 200

American National Baptist Convention Publishing Company and Book Establishment, 180
Amherstburg Baptist Association, 36-38, 71
Amjad-Ali, Charles W., 204n
Anderson, Duke William, 34, 34 n25, 64, 70, 74, 75, 87, 88, 92-93
Anderson, John Richard, 42n, 215
Anderson, Martin B., 63
Armistead, John Maurice, 169, 193
Armstrong, Alex, 59
Asher, Jeremiah, 215
Atlanta Constitution, 185

Backus, Isaac, 16
Backus, Jay S., 56, 60, 95-98, 100, 103
Bacoats, Inez, 217
Bacoats, John Alvin, 217
Bacote, Samuel William, 213
Baer, Hans A., 203n
Bailey, Kenneth K., xiiin, 11 n17
Bainton, Roland, H., xiin
Baker, Moses, 203
Baker, Robert A., 39n, 54n, 162n, 182n
Bank, William H., 117-18
Baptist Foreign Mission Convention (BFMC), 135-38, 144-56, 200
Baptist General Association of Western States and Territories (BGA), 125, 143, 155
Baptist Herald (Paducah KY), 121, 126
Baptist Pioneer, 168
Baptist Teacher controversy, 164-70
Barnes, Lemuel Call, 164n
Barnett, William John, 42
Barrow, David, 17, 27, 28
"Baxley Incident," 145-56
Bell, Howard Holman, 26
Bender, Thomas, 206
Benedict, David, 10, 31n
Benn, John, 14
Bercovitch, Sacvan, xin
Bettis, Alexander, 216
Binga, Anthony, Jr., 129, 166, 194